DATE DUE			

TIDE OF EMPIRES

PETER PADFIELD

TIDE OF EMPIRES

DECISIVE NAVAL CAMPAIGNS
IN THE RISE OF THE WEST

VOLUME ONE

1481–1654

ROUTLEDGE & KEGAN PAUL

LONDON AND HENLEY

First published in 1979
by Routledge & Kegan Paul Ltd
39 Store Street, London WC1E 7DD and
Broadway House, Newtown Road
Henley-on-Thames, Oxon RG9 1EN
Set in 10 on 12 Bell
and printed in Great Britain by
Ebenezer Baylis & Son Ltd, The Trinity Press,
Worcester, and London

British Library Cataloguing in Publication Data

Padfield, Peter

Tide of empires.
Vol. 1: 1481-1654
1. Naval History
I. Title
359.4'09'03   D215

ISBN 0 7100 0150 9

CONTENTS

TO ALISON AND JOHN STEVENS

ILLUSTRATIONS

PLATES BETWEEN PAGES 114 AND 115

MAPS

BATTLE DIAGRAMS

FOREWORD

Many people are reasonably familiar with the principal events in their national naval history such as the defeat of the Armada, Trafalgar, Hampton Roads, Midway; few are conversant with the whole range of the struggle for sea power which has for several centuries raged among European and finally among world powers. It is the story of this struggle which Peter Padfield tells in this book and in the subsequent volumes which he has planned, and he starts his tale in 1497 when Vasco da Gama sailed from Lisbon to open a sea route to the Indian Ocean. I have been asked to write this foreword to the work, and I am glad to do so because I believe that the history of the naval campaigns which have marked the rise to a dominant position in the world of what we call 'the West' is of continuing interest and importance, and will provide much food for thought for students of world affairs today. The tides within the general upsurge of wealth and strength are represented by the rise and fall of individual nations, the tides rising successively higher with the improvement of ships and armament. In this volume we see the Portuguese, the Spaniards and the Dutch, and then the beginning of the conflict between the Dutch and the English in the seventeenth century. The volume ends with the defeat of the Dutch in 1654, an interim stage in the rivalry between the two powers which continued into the beginning of the nineteenth century.

What I find particularly interesting in the author's treatment of the subject is his theory of the underlying forces that set the tides in motion. This is fully explained in his Introduction to the book. I do not propose to repeat here what he expounds so clearly, but I should like to touch on his theory because it is a most interesting setting for the story he then tells.

In effect, the author discards the glamorous motives which are usually thought to have actuated monarchs and their commanders who set forth as explorers, as navigators, and as pioneer adventurers. Religious zeal, personal ambition, and the pursuit of glory are merely the gloss on the history, and the great motive forces which he recognises are envy and wealth. A small nation seeking to improve its position starts with a large bank of envy of the wealth, usually represented by monopolistic trade, of its predecessor in the field. With the help as necessary of allies or partners it presses forward until its envy is dissipated and a bank of wealth is substituted. All methods are used, including piracy, privateering, and war, and plunder and destruction are the life and soul of the system. The whole process is marked throughout by a naked struggle for trade and markets, sea power being used for the capture and control of the largest possible markets for exclusive enjoyment.

Everyone may not accept this stark interpretation of maritime history. Some may be shocked at the thought of their many sea heroes being brought down to the level of men who simply sought to further the greedy ambitions of their masters who were seeking mercantile domination over rivals. Vasco da Gama is extolled in history as a great navigator and discoverer. In reality, as Padfield points out, he was sent forth to wrest from the Venetians their control of the lucrative spice trade which came to them from the Indian Ocean via the Middle East and the Arab caravans. This is an example of the nature of the struggles that succeeded each other through the years, and an objective view over the long sweep of history reached in the thorough manner that he adopts undoubtedly shows that his theory is hard to refute.

It should not be imagined that this book is designed merely to establish the truth of the author's hypothesis. It is a most thorough and stimulating account, in terms not difficult for the layman, of the wars that took place between the succession of nations seeking dominion at sea and rich markets in the East. I can most thoroughly commend it to all who have any interest in our history, in naval affairs, and in the events that marked the feats of exploration, grim though many of these are. The horrors perpetrated by the Portuguese in the lands bordering the Indian Ocean are peculiarly revolting to modern thought. It may be that the Portuguese were no more cruel than their successors, the Dutch, the French, and the English, but that being in the field earlier they were accustomed to a world in which abominable treatment was meted out to enemies and expected in reverse. As time went on it became realised that cruelty, dishonesty, and deception were not sensible companions of trade, and more humane methods prevailed.

Padfield draws clear distinction between sea powers, land powers, and hybrids. This is perhaps the most interesting aspect of his theory, because he seeks to demonstrate that it is the true sea power which dominates. The terrestrial power is constantly diverted from the task of pursuing worldwide influence and authority by the need to guard its land frontiers. He concludes that the values we have are the values of sea creatures and will survive only if the West survives as a successful sea creature.

It is tempting to draw conclusions and apply them to our present situation, though it would be better to await the development of the story in subsequent volumes before doing so. We have reached a stage when only two great super-powers have the wealth to keep large up-to-date sea, land and air forces. It will be interesting to see whether Padfield classes the Soviet Union and the USA as hybrids or as sea powers in his true meaning of the term. I shall look forward to reading his future volumes, and I am sure that many others will do the same.

General Sir Ian Jacob

ACKNOWLEDGMENTS

First I would like to thank Norman Franklin of Routledge & Kegan Paul for his encouragement in what still seems an ambitious project, undertaken as it is without grants or outside financial aid, and begun at a time when inflation and the foul death of the library lending rights bill threatened with extinction all authors in the middleground between a living in the ivory or red-brick-and-concrete towers and a stand at the airport bookstall. For similar reasons I am grateful to my bank manager, at the Woodbridge branch of the National Westminster.

Turning to naval history, there have been in recent years several independent revolts against what might be called the 'Mahan line,'* especially perhaps the idea that there are immutable 'principles' which can be discovered from a study of history to serve for all time. In the area of tactics the late John Cresswell's *British Admirals of the Eighteenth Century* brilliantly refuted the Mahan school's hatred of formal line of battle; independently and by an entirely different route, through a study of great gunnery and its influence on tactics, I had come to similar conclusions. Michael Howard has illuminated the difficulties of accepting unreservedly the Mahan 'Blue-Water' approach – or as Liddell Hart termed it, 'the British way in warfare' – for all problems in grand strategy. Now, in the wider field of naval strength as a continuing tool of national policy, has come Dr Paul Kennedy's *Rise and Fall of British Naval Mastery*, the first new, or post-Mahan school overview of British naval history, bringing to the forefront what is too often scarcely visible in the traditional naval historical approach, that is the intimate and direct connection between economic and naval strength, and the fine balance of choices between 'sea' and 'land' operations and expenditure; his treatment of these questions illuminated some of the central themes of this work. I should also like to thank him for permission to quote short passages from his book, published by Allen Lane.

I should like to thank the Navy Records Society for permission to quote

* Alfred Thayer Mahan, US Naval Captain and author of the seminal 'Influence of Sea Power' books in the 1890s.

extensively from *Letters and Papers relating to the First Dutch War*; the Hakluyt Society for permission to quote from *The Three Voyages of Vasco da Gama*, edited by H. E. J. Stanley; *A Journal of the First Voyage of Vasco da Gama*, edited by E. G. Ravenstein; *Cabral's Voyage to Brazil and India*, edited by W. B. Greenlee; *The Commentaries of the Great Affonso Dalboquerque*, edited by W. de Birch. I should like to thank the Editor of the *Mariner's Mirror*, the Journal of the Society for Nautical Research, for the numerous scholarly articles therein, and specifically for permission to quote from *Gorga's Seafight*, an important light on the 'Armada' campaign tactics contributed by T. Glasgow Jr.

And I should like to thank the following authors and publishers for permission to quote short extracts: Cambridge University Press, *The Journal of Maarten Harpertszoon Tromp*, edited by C. R. Boxer; Longmans Green, *Profit and Power*, by Charles Wilson; Hodder & Stoughton, *The Sultan's Admiral*, by Ernle Bradford; Methuen and Miss Dorothy Collins, *The Collected Poems of G. K. Chesterton*.

INTRODUCTION

This is an attempt to relate the fortunes of the West to the naval campaigns with which it encompassed and imposed its will on the world; that is the sense in which 'decisive' is intended – decisive for the decisive nations in the decisive phenomenon of the last four hundred years, the rise of the West. It is not an edifying story, nor is any story of naked conquest edifying. It is not a story of culture or values or the religions and dynasties with which written history is replete; these are surface phenomena derived from man's urge to think well of himself and explain his criminal past in acceptable terms. It is rather a tale of trade and wealth and the naval force used to divert the major share of world trade to the capitals of the West, for this was the decisive factor in Western expansion. It is possible now that the West is in retreat, threatened by far more hideous systems, to examine the nature of the rise, stripped of national sentiment, stripped of language that dignifies petty piracy and extortion as heroics, lust for prize money as duty, national envy as crusade, and attempt to construct a useful model into which real nations may fit.

If the theme of the following pages approximates to the truth, the model would have two central drives for each nation, 'wealth' and 'envy'. Wealth would be capital accumulated from and used in various wealth-producing activities. Envy would have no direct link to wealth; it would be linked to other nations' wealth accumulations – with allowance for temporary dis-engagement by means of an alliance mechanism. It would draw from the other national wealth non-exchangeable units of envy calculated by multi-plying the real wealth with credulity and need factors. The diagrams are somewhat complex and halt the narrative, hence they will be found later at p. 16; one illustrates a nation at the beginning of its rise with very little wealth casting covetous eyes at the more prosperous nations and drawing in huge stores of envy. The other shows the same nation near the end of its rise; its wealth has been puffed up to the size of its original envy, but as it is now the largest frog in the pool envy has become atrophied. The methods employed to bring this happy situation about are illustrated on the left;

they are either 'legal' and constructive, that is by industry, internal and external trade, neutral carrying trade and the development of colonies, or 'illegal' and constructive – smuggling – or 'illegal' and destructive, piracy, extortion and commercial war. The chief difference between nations at the beginning and the end of their rise is that in the beginning the methods usually labelled 'illegal' and aggressive, shown in the diagrams as 'Quick Profits', predominate; at the end the methods usually labelled 'legal' and constructive predominate and the wars in which the wealthy sea power takes part are usually defensive wars against envious nations trying in their turn to gain a larger share of the world's wealth.

There are no pretensions to scientific accuracy in the diagrams: there are no figures available and vital geographic and resource factors which might indicate whether nations could expect to gain or lose from all this mayhem – which when controlled by government regulation is known as the mercantilist system – have not been included. Directly they are included the complexity and lack of quantifiable evidence combine to make the exercise pointless. The diagrams are intended only to illustrate the chief features of the system.

A fundamental point that cannot be illustrated is that, like every other system in the universe, it is self-balancing; one tendency will always be for nations with comparatively small wealth, hence large envy to ally with others against those with the greatest wealth, and another tendency will be for any nation or group of nations which feels the balance swinging against it to seek out allies with the utmost energy wherever it can, even if this means cutting across what are usually labelled as 'sacred principles'; at the height of the Holy War against Islam in the Mediterranean, Catholic France allied with Muslim Turkey against Catholic Spain; at the height of the Counter-Reformation, the two principal Protestant powers, England and the Dutch United Provinces, were at each other's throats. From these and scores of other examples it is quite clear that the religious factors which have received so much attention in European history are subordinate to the principle of balance, and the same can be said of dynastic factors; so far as naval campaigns are concerned, neither have a place except in the area of national cohesion and morale. This is not to suggest that religious passion did not run high – it would be truer to say disgustingly low. It must be assumed that Charles V of Spain did not roast Protestants over slow fires for pleasure, and it is evident that Drake was a religious bigot of the first water. But it would be incredible to suppose that Spain launched four ruinously costly armadas and bankrupted herself several times in a vain attempt to return an undeveloped nest of pirates to the True Faith.

If the overriding principle of balance is accepted – and the evidence for it is conclusive in thousands of intelligence reports from all nations in the system detailing the size and building programmes of potential enemy fleets and proposals for action on the basis of the reports – it carries with it the principle of the margin. The results of maritime struggles will be marginal; the successful nations will build up their wealth – consequently their strength – by slow degrees in alliances, and as they grow the inexorable self-balancing nature of the system will be operating against them, drawing in more force to oppose them. A nation will prove ultimately successful when it has the whole world against it. And always the struggle will be fought at the margin of available resources of finance and manpower; taxation will be increased beyond tolerable limits for the mass of the people, loans will be raised at higher and higher rates of interest, the streets will be scoured – and the bedrooms and the church pews – and the gaols will be emptied to man the ships. When marginal resources become negative a nation will drop out of the struggle temporarily, making marginal adjustments in trade or colonies.

Obviously nations which can make the struggle pay, at least those who manage to put more into their own 'Quick Profits' and carrying trade than they lose to their opponents' 'Quick Profits' or to neutral carriers or smugglers, are adding to their own marginal resources while taking from their opponents'; this is relatively easier for newcomers to the game as they have far less to lose and far more to gain than their rich enemies, hence the comparative importance of piracy and aggressive war to the aspirant nations. This diminishes, however, during the course of each campaign as the enemies take more effective action to protect trade or transfer it to neutral bottoms. The astute players will gain much from the system by preserving neutrality; nevertheless, for those who cannot afford to await the harvest there is much to be gained by strikes at the most succulent enemy outposts before war is declared or before news of a declaration can reach the enemy overseas. In the early stages of a nation's growth there is no distinction between piracy and privateering and state warfare; in the latter stages the only distinction is that in formal war the trade of allied and neutral nations is excluded from legitimate plunder – despite which captains and admirals in the state service have better opportunities for amassing vast fortunes than pirates, and make good use of them. By the nature of the system plunder and smuggling are its life and soul.

The system was not unique to the Atlantic nations who spread Western civilisation around the globe; it came from the Mediterranean along with the capital which gave the first impetus to expansion – indeed the whole process of Western expansion can be viewed as a world-wide extension of Mediterranean techniques and capital.

At the core of the Mediterranean system, feeding wealth and envy was a belief in monopoly and staple rights. Each of the wealthy Mediterranean city states, in fact every large town throughout Europe sought exclusive rights to market the produce of its own region and of other regions for sale in its own region, taking a percentage of each exchange or import as a tax, and enabling its own merchants to make a profit four times – that is on purchase and on sale of imports and exports. Such a city was known as the Staple for the goods, and its privileged dealers as merchants of the Staple. Obviously the most successful cities were those who managed to enforce their staple rights furthest afield in the most lucrative trades, allowing their citizens profits on the carriage of goods in addition to their profits as middlemen, and there is little doubt that the most outstanding of these were seaports: Constantinople, Alexandria, Venice, Genoa heading the list. In the fifteenth century, as Western overseas expansion began, the most triumphant of these was Venice.

Situated at the head of the Adriatic, Venice was ideally placed between the eastern Mediterranean markets for the produce of the Orient and Black Sea area, and on the landward side the cities of the North Italian plain and the passes through the Alps into Germany, central and western Europe. In her use of this position and expansion from it, the features of subsequent Western global expansion are clear. Starting her career in the ninth and tenth centuries with mixed piracy and sea trade, chiefly in bulky and necessary goods, timber, salt for preserving food, fish, slaves from eastern Europe for the service and harems of Islam, she acquired a chain of colonies throughout the eastern Mediterranean; these started either as sites for warehouses to store goods between shipment and exchange (*entrepôts*), or as naval bases for gathering convoys and basing squadrons of warships against the enemies her success called into being, also for enforcing her navigation laws. These laws stipulated that any goods coming to Venice – interpreted as the whole Adriatic but only enforceable in the north – came either in Venetian ships or in ships of the country of origin of the goods. Her ideal was to force all suppliers and all customers in any given commodity to make their exchange through the Rialto at Venice after freighting in Venetian ships. The whole policy of the city was directed to this end, and the committee for foreign affairs was one and the same committee that organised merchant shipping and its protection.

Although no single city state could tie up the entire trade of the Mediterranean in this way, Venice was the most nearly successful in the most lucrative long-distance trades in spices and Oriental luxuries, and it is not surprising to find her the largest naval power in the Mediterranean at the time, with the most efficient merchant marine headed by great merchant galleys sailing on regular liner schedules, with a shipbuilding arsenal which was the largest industrial establishment in Europe, a mint employing more workers than any other, a wide range of industries from fine textiles and armour and armaments to printing and glass, in both of which she was a world leader, a powerhouse of commerce and industry and extravagant wealth, the envy of the civilised world.

She was also admired for her arts, her humanist thinkers and her constitution based on tortuous systems of checks on individual power. Comparisons with the Dutch in the seventeenth century or the British in the late eighteenth and nineteenth centuries are seductive, and become more so when it is realised that in each case the sun began to set with the growth of Continental neighbours whose resources, drawn from far greater extent of territory, outstripped their own and forced them into costly military alliances: in Venice's case the territorial enemies were Ottoman Turkey and France, in Holland's case France and the Empire, in Great Britain's case, Imperial Germany. But that is moving ahead of the story. The essence of Venice's rise, as it was of each of the European nations who carried the Western movement around the globe like successive waves of an ever-rising tide, was trade monopoly taken and held by naval force. Each nation sought to tie up both suppliers and consumers in vast, incredibly ambitious, oceanic cartels which would ensure them the middleman profits and full cargoes on each leg of the trading routes.

The key words are middleman and *entrepôt*. At the beginning of Western expansion – despite the brilliance of individual Italian city states – the dominant world civilisation was Islam. Islam held the commanding position at the centre of the board. From the Black Sea and the Balkans, down the eastern shore of the Mediterranean to Egypt, across the Arabian peninsula to northern India, and in the other direction across the Mediterranean coast of north Africa and some way down both eastern and western shores of that continent, there was no God but Allah, and Muhammed was his prophet. Islam held the middleman position on every route by land or sea between the increasingly prosperous Christian West, and the East, which provided spices, especially pepper, which in the days before refrigerators were vital ingredients of the salt-based food preserving industry; the East and the Middle East also provided luxuries, which in the manner of luxuries had become necessities to anyone who was anyone in the West. Besides holding every overland key to these trades which offered spectacular profits compared with the comparatively short-haul bulk trades of the Mediterranean world, Muslim merchants had an effective monopoly of the sea routes of the Indian Ocean, and their colonies in all the *entrepôt* ports of the west coast of India controlled the trade in spices and Chinese wares coming by sea, as well as more mundane products of India and Ceylon; similar colonies of Muslim merchants in the east African ports down to Mozambique controlled the gold, ivory, slave and bulk trades of that continent.

The movement of Western expansion around the southern tip of Africa into the Indian Ocean is consequently seen as an outflanking movement by the Christian West which eventually throttled the Muslim centre, and went on to encircle the Far East as well. Numerous studies have shown how the trick was accomplished. The West had better ships and guns, and this technical superiority, which increased as the Western nations fought one another at sea, allowed them to control oceanic trade, especially in spices, and divert it directly to their own ports.

Two things might perhaps have nipped the movement in the bud. The

Chinese, who had great, stoutly-constructed, multiple-masted, ocean-going ships long before the West, and had also developed guns and oceanic navigation much earlier, and whose route to the Indian Ocean on the monsoons was simpler than the Western route around Africa, could probably have thrown them back. However, Chinese oceanic expansion came to an abrupt end before the mid-fifteenth century when the Portuguese explorations down the west African coast had not even reached the Gulf of Guinea. Professor Needham's works on China make it clear that she was in the grip of a Confucian bureaucracy despising military affairs and looking towards the land as the proper field for investment; her inward-looking agriculturalist policy thereafter was so strong that in 1500, as the Portuguese campaign in the Indian Ocean began in earnest, it became a capital offence in China to build a ship with more than two masts. By this time her once-large navy had withered away; the Portuguese were opposed only by frail Indian and Arab craft which were no match for their own. Another way to view this is to see the great fleets which the Chinese sent to the Indian Ocean before the policy change as enormously costly and unprofitable – largely because there was nothing they wanted from the West; the flow of trade was the other way, with the West having to pay in precious metals for the Eastern goods they prized.

Failing the Chinese, who were not there at the vital time, the only way of turning back the Western tide would have been a determined and united effort by Islam. With interior lines from Aden to northern India and vastly greater resources it should have been possible for them, at the least, to have expelled the Christians from the bases essential for their oceanic command. This did not happen because Islam was no more united than Christendom. There were competing sea routes and competing land routes, thus competing ports and regions within the Islamic sphere, and Westerners from the Portuguese onwards naturally made it their business to ally with one or another against rivals, usually tilting the balance decisively to the side on which they came down. Thus the idea of a Western and Christian movement consciously outflanking Islam is as unhelpful as the idea of Catholics versus Protestants later; the True Faith was a banner under which the pioneer Portuguese sailed into the Indian Ocean, and which they stained with a system of extortion and terror as nauseatingly purposeful as that of the ancient Assyrians. From the exultant descriptions of wholesale and deliberate atrocities in Portuguese accounts – confirmed in Indian sources – it is clear that whatever was happening in the higher realms of theology or art, at the decisive point history was made by men who had not ascended in anything but material terms from the utmost depravity of the pre-Christian era, who regarded their opponents in the Indian Ocean as farmers might regard a plague of rats. It is true that they had nothing to teach Islam in the matter of cruelty and humiliation of enemies, they could even be said to have learnt it at Muslim hands, and they were of course a tiny handful of men surrounded by enemies, thousands of miles from home. Whatever balancing factors are adduced, Christ, whose red cross blazed on their sails, was mocked.

As for the results of their campaign, the system of terror was as senseless as it was evil. Their success rested on technical superiority and the alliance value this conferred in the area. Technical superiority was not simply stouter ships and more powerful guns but the fusion of these two into an altogether new system of naval warfare. For thousands of years warships in the Mediterranean system had been rather slim, light, oar-propelled craft known as galleys, which manœuvred in a similar way to lines of infantry and fought an essentially infantry battle on the water. However, what had evolved in the West in the half-century preceding the Portuguese entry into the Indian Ocean was nothing less than the floating castle defended by all-round batteries of quick-firing guns. Fleets of galleys were as powerless against these floating castles as armies were powerless against conventional stone castles, and the traditional way of reducing castles on land by siege operations could not be attempted because the floating castles were mobile and better able to keep the sea for longer periods than galleys. These mobile castles could be moved into position to command narrow straits, ports, capes around which sea trade flowed, thus commanding key areas as land castles commanded key passes, but with far greater economy because they were mobile – indeed the Portuguese proved that less than a dozen of them with a handful of men could control the entire trade of the Indian Ocean. The analogy with castles cannot be pushed too far since ships were not proof against gales and underwater damage, nor their crews against the diseases caused by lack of fresh food, hence they could only command the chosen area for a limited time, and were absolutely dependent on a secure land base where fresh provisions and naval stores and repair facilities could be found. The subsequent evolution of the Western warship was as much concerned with increasing its sea-keeping as its sailing and fighting powers, and although it was never able to manage without a secure base in the area of operations, advances in naval strategy were all tied to advances in the length of time a ship could keep the sea in the chosen area without being crippled by scurvy and the underwater ravages of worm and weed.

Put another way, the sailing warship which carried the West to global conquest had the prime military virtues of security, economy of force, mobility and facility of concentration, the last two giving it the priceless attribute of surprise; a force could be gathered and held, or sent out into the ocean, and the enemy might never know where or even who it would strike until they heard its guns. Its only weakness was dependence on a land base, yet even here it had advantages in an age when provisions could be brought more efficiently and cheaply by sea than overland; the base, once fortified with walls and bastions could be supplied with more ease than the besieging army. The base and the fleet were two complementary parts of the system, each dependent on and protecting the other.

With all the advantages of the new system of naval warfare, first demonstrated by the awesome advance of the Portuguese in the Indian Ocean, it was not surprising that whoever mastered it held the key to alliances with rivals of the main force in the area to be conquered. As it was the peoples on the Atlantic and North Sea fringe of Europe who mastered and developed the system, it was they who, despite their small population and comparatively minute share of the earth's surface, came to dominate the globe – not by sea power on its own but by ruthless use of a unique system of sea power to tip local balances decisively towards the masters of the system. The eventual winners of the game, in the sailing era Great Britain, and in the powered era the United States of America, were able to dominate the globe by a complex system of balances, the most important of which was the balance of western Europe itself. It was not surprising that territorial powers regarded the diplomacy of sea powers like Venice or Great Britain at their prime as extraordinarily supple, and on an altogether more cunning plane than their own.

It is not necessary to believe in the inherent superiority of sea power over territorial power in all circumstances and all epochs in the manner of A. T. Mahan, the high priest of naval history, to discern the sea power as an altogether different creature from the territorial or the hybrid territorial/sea power, and to recognise that in the decisive period of Western expansion from 1500 onwards sea power was superior, indeed decisive. It was a few small nations, Portugal, the fringes of Spain and France, Holland and Great Britain, aided by Denmark, Norway and Sweden, and given the first impetus by Genoese and Florentine capital derived from the highly successful use of sea power, which brought the West to global power while the great territorial states and inland groupings acted as little more than counterweights or scene changes behind the oceanic drama. Religions and dynasties and cultures collapsed or underwent sea changes as the great game was played over the oceans of the world and the system worked itself out, putting in place of religion, reason, in place of feudalism, industrial order, in place of absolutism, democracy. For these were the hallmarks of the successful sea creatures from Venice through Holland and Great Britain to the United States of America.

We are now in deep waters, for whether the United States can be described as a sea creature in the classic tradition of the first three is questionable; she rose to world power after the development of railways and improved road transport had given the advantage in extent of market, thus wealth accumulation, to territorial powers, and after sea power and communications had been further depreciated by air power. However, previous technological revolutions had benefited territorial powers in the same way as railways; gunpowder and artillery, for instance, had allowed the growth of the first nation states, Spain, Ottoman Turkey and France, which had swallowed up or eclipsed the city-based sea powers, of which the most successful were Venice and Genoa. But the territorial nation states had in their turn been overwhelmed, first by Dutch, then by British sea power, both of which were supported by far larger territorial bases than Venice, and both of which enjoyed excellent internal communications for their industries. Viewed in this light, the United States is simply the next step up the scale of territorial, population and inland communication base needed to support dominant sea power.

This conclusion is supported by pronounced features of the United States: diffused government and systematic checks on the growth of individual power, together with ethnic and religious toleration are key features of all the sea powers in the era under discussion. So too is strong industry. The growth of industry in Venice was so strong that the government passed law after law to try and prevent master craftsmen being swallowed up as wage-earners in a factory system controlled by concentrations of wealth. After them, the Dutch were the dominant industrialists of their age; their development of wind- and water-power, division of labour, and standardisation and prefabrication techniques formed an industrial revolution of the same kind as the British industrial revolution which followed in the next century when Great Britain was the dominant sea power. There is nothing surprising about this: the link between extent of market and division of labour is a basic principle of economics, and if the analysis in these pages is correct, sea power was concerned almost exclusively with control of the largest possible markets for its own exclusive use. Successful sea power, wide markets, industrialisation are, therefore, all parts of the same system, and mutually complementary. Industrialisation, thus cheaper unit costs, widens markets, creating the wealth necessary to expand sea power, which in turn widens the market again.

Another important feature of sea powers in the age of expansion was a relative freedom from Continental involvements; Venice, Holland, especially Great Britain all had water defences allowing them to concentrate on the sea affair; they employed armies for defence and paid mercenaries and mercenary states to engage their opponents' attention in the Continental territorial, religious and dynastic fandango, but in their successful periods this did not divert them from the sea, indeed sea trade paid for the Continental balances they employed; perhaps the most triumphant example is Great Britain in the Seven Years War and the Napoleonic Wars. Decline in all three classic examples was accompanied by large-scale Continental military involvements due to the growth of threateningly powerful territorial states.

It is reasonable to assume, then, that the true sea power is only successful when its territorial alliances are subordinate to its market-acquiring naval policies. This hypothesis seems to be supported by the relatively unsuccessful sea powers, Ottoman Turkey, Spain and France, who were hybrids, territorial powers with territorial ambitions and borders which had to be defended, who could never subordinate their armies to naval policy. Portugal was a successful sea power while she had no need to defend her only land border with Spain, but directly she became a part of the Spanish Empire she was dragged down in Continental involvements. Portugal, Spain and Ottoman Turkey, however, failed the other test of the true sea power in not developing strong industry, consequently they did not exhibit any of the outward signs of sea creatures, diffused government or religious and ethnic freedoms. This leaves France as the best test case of a relatively unsuccessful sea power.

France was at least two nations, a centralised territorial power controlled from Paris and a centrifugal fringe of sea ports, some like Le Havre, St Malo, La Rochelle facing the Atlantic, a vigorous part of the system of Western oceanic powers, others, notably Marseilles, cut off from these by the Iberian peninsula and facing the Mediterranean. Her eastern land border was immense, extending from the Spanish Netherlands and petty German princedoms and bishoprics to the Alps and the passes through to the Italian plain. Simply to state the geographical position is to state the problem. The long land border with so many tempting opportunities for attack and terri-torial aggrandisement, so many requirements for defence, inevitably drew resources from the sea. Time after time in peace France built up superb navies with a system and rigour of intellectual analysis superior to anything attempted by the sea creatures – with the exception perhaps of Venice – time after time at the crisis of each successive struggle with the sea powers she was forced by lack of money to abandon her navy.

The separation of her naval forces between the Mediterranean and the Atlantic, and the insolent British presence between them at Gibraltar, has been adduced as the major factor in her ultimate failure; it seems more likely to have been a symptom of the ultimate cause of her failure, a fatally split personality. Had she been a true sea creature, she would have taken Gibraltar, which was nearer to her than to England, and probably the Scilly Isles too, and with commanding concentrations from her Biscay ports to windward of the English Channel have caused such havoc to Dutch and English trade as to force them to concede the overseas empire she sought. As it was the smaller sea creatures – in the end Great Britain practically alone – always outbuilt her navy, forcing it on the defensive, stopping her sea trade, taking her colonies, acquiring her markets, crippling her industry, hence ensuring that what is recognised as the 'industrial revolution' took place in Great Britain.

The outward manifestations of a split personality in the Huguenot revolts centred on the centrifugal fringe, the frightful religious massacres and ex-pulsion of the Huguenots, the subsequent veering between extremes of centralised government under the 'Sun King', extremes of 'democracy' under the revolutionary mob, extremes of megalomaniac tyranny under the frightful Bonaparte, all support this interpretation, as does the fluctuating fortune of French industry, at one time far more impressive than British industry.

England, of course, had the same problems of split personality early in her rise, and it is noticeable that she did not take her place as a sea power of any consequence – despite all those Elizabethan sea dogs – until she had resolved the problem by civil war, which unlike the French example was eventually won by the centrifugal fringe, principally the City of London, not the territorial centre a few miles up the Thames. She had the added advantages of land borders with a small state even more undeveloped than herself, which she soon swallowed up.

These two prime examples, which spent more than a century fighting the issue out, support the interpretation of a true sea power as one which in crisis is allowed by geographical circumstances to concentrate a relatively greater part of its resources on market-acquiring maritime affairs than territorial or hybrid powers can. That this is a fundamental distinction between two different kinds of states and not just a convenient definition for the purpose of this work is suggested by basic differences in government and society. If the analysis is correct it is not the forms of society and government which help to determine whether a nation will become a successful sea power, but the reverse: those forms of society and government which may be summarised as common to the 'Free World' will only occur in true sea powers.

By all these tests the United States rose to world power, first under overt British protection and then during the Monroe Doctrine years under implicit British naval protection as a true sea creature – that is a market-acquiring, industrially-developing nation driven by wealth and envy. That sea power came to include air power makes little difference to the analysis since the same thing happened to land power – besides which the proportion of air to sea cargoes is minute so that it was and is ships and sea trade for which sea/air power existed – leaving aside for the moment the altogether novel dimension of nuclear power. By the same token Russia and China are territorial powers with immense land borders to defend – and tempt them – and enormous problems of internal control of the divers provinces and empires within their territorial empires. The present conflict between the super-powers is not a conflict between Capitalism and Communism any more than the earlier conflicts were between Christianity and Islam or Protestants and Catholics; it is the centuries-old struggle between sea power and territorial power. To call the Soviet Union a Communist state is as laughable as to dignify the Portuguese and Spanish conquistadores as Christians – or for that matter the slave-trading and slave-owning Dutch, English, Scots, French, Danes, Swedes, Norwegians and Americans – while all industrial societies are based on accumulated capital so that the term Capitalism has as many meanings as there are prejudices against its vices.

We have now caught up with history and reached the crux of the matter, which is nothing less than the final crisis for the age-old struggle between sea and territorial power, hence between the forms of government and society which go with one or the other – diffused or central control, toleration or inquisition, freedom or repression. The Western alliance, like all historic sea powers, is vitally dependent on sea trade, probably more than at any other period since both her industry and defence depend on one seaborne commodity, oil. The Soviet Union meanwhile has become a sea power of the first water – not if this analysis is correct a true sea power, but a hybrid like late-seventeenth- and eighteenth-century France which produced a superb appearance of naval force in peace but failed at every crisis. And although Western Europe entirely lacks one vital attribute of the successful true sea power, the moat that keeps territorial and hybrid armies out, it has in its place the threat of nuclear destruction. In the years since the Second World War this has proved as decisive as the English Channel in the seventeenth and eighteenth centuries. As then the great game is played out around the world in the unfortunate, less-developed countries. The weapons are perhaps a shade more complex, but the methods have not changed at all, nor has the decisive importance of sea power – as the Soviet Union has realised.

The situation is similar to the undeclared colonial warfare which went on throughout the earlier phases of Western expansion and was recognised in the doctrine of 'No Peace beyond the Line'. In the Victorian peace when the balances of the world were manipulated from London by skilful use of overwhelming industrial/sea power, the continuing struggle for colonies and markets or 'spheres of influence' was adjusted by bargaining backed or preceded by displays of armed force and alliance negotiations between the European powers. In the late-nineteenth century, two extra-European powers joined the game, the United States and Japan, both as oceanic, market-acquiring, industrial nations, true sea creatures, although Japan's modernisation was such a rapid, centrally-forced growth that she did not acquire the social and government manifestations. These two upset the European system, particularly Great Britain's naval control of the system. Meanwhile a territorial power of formidable strength had grown up in the centre of Europe and also set about acquiring sea power; this was Imperial Germany. She was a hybrid of the most marked colour. With extensive land borders to the east, south and west, and a potentially centrifugal collection of recently independent princedoms within her territorial empire, her army was an essential instrument of external and internal security. Yet her real strength was founded on wealth from trade and industry, whose chief outlets to the sea were on the short north-west coastline and, humiliatingly, through the great ports of the Netherlands. Envy of Great Britain and overseas market-acquiring compulsions made the building of a strong navy inevitable, and more clearly than ever we can watch the self-balancing nature of the system at work. Great Britain and France, deadly rivals since the seventeenth century, first increased their navies, then came together in an *entente* that became a military alliance in all but name and was associated with a Franco-Russian alliance; as the German navy continued to expand with inexorable purpose Great Britain, after making a naval alliance with Japan and coming to an understanding with the United States, withdrew her entire front-line strength from the colonial peripheries and the central commanding position in the Mediterranean to face the main enemy in the North Sea, meanwhile setting in hand unprecedented naval building programmes. However, her strategy in the two world wars which followed was primarily concerned with the military alliances in Europe; this was based on recognition of the fact that once a territorial power reached a size and controlled an extent of coastline enabling her to outbuild the dominant sea power, that territorial power had won the game. Consequently overwhelming British naval force was confined largely to holding the ring and protecting sea trade while her resources were poured into the European struggle and literally blown up, and instead of expanding her overseas markets and trade, both contracted and were entered by neutrals, particularly the United States. It is clear that she had lost control of the system, clear that technological factors, particularly railways and roads, had once again forced up the size of territorial and population base which could be controlled as an economic unit for dominant sea power.

By the end of the Second World War, Great Britain, although nominally on the winning side, had been forced out of the decisive area of the game. The United States, which had played strictly according to precedent, making gigantic gains as a neutral before entering the armed struggle, emerged as the dominant industrial/sea power and enjoyed a period of world hegemony similar to the Victorian period of British world power by manipulating the balances. The Soviet Union, however, had made equally huge strides in territorial power during the war period, and true to precedent, began to graft sea power on to her territorial system; by the early 1970s she had become a hybrid of truly formidable dimensions with a sufficient navy to challenge the United States' control of the world balances. In such a situation, without a single dominating power the world was back to 'No Peace beyond the Line'.

The 'Line' is not as clear as it was in the seventeenth century as it is defined, not by geography, but by subjective concepts of vital interest; these will be defended by strategic nuclear weapons, hence the modern 'Line' is drawn around what each side regards as its own 'vital interests'. The most vital of these for the United States is the preservation of the European border between the territorial East, and the maritime West, as if Russian and satellite armies were to overrun Western Europe, the Soviet empire would possess sufficient coastline and industrial resources to outbuild the United States as a sea power; the game would be lost. Hence the

European border is held by a barrier of nuclear terror, and the struggle continues 'beyond the Line'.

History cannot be used to forecast the future, and the danger of trying to tease principles or laws from its infinitely complex strands has been illustrated by too many famous names in the past – including Mahan in naval history. We may have gone too far already in simplifying the global history of some five hundred years into a struggle between sea creatures, territorial animals and hybrids. Nevertheless if there is any merit in the analysis, and if the assumption is made that the nuclear 'line' has been drawn with sufficient clarity on both sides to make it unthinkable that strategic nuclear weapons will be used by the major nuclear powers, the lesson of these pages is clear. It is that the sea creatures will prevail. This is not simply because international trade will continue to be carried in ships, but because the new forces to tilt the balance must come from the under-developed 'Third World' beyond the line in which the struggle is being fought. If history is any guide this 'New World' of today will inevitably fall to the market-acquiring sea creatures because they will be able to devote the major share of their resources to the struggle, and their system of wealth/market acquisition/industrial strength/greater wealth, and so on, is so formidable that it can only be stopped by a power several stages up the territorial scale. It is difficult to see how the Soviet Union or China can take this next step without overrunning Western Europe – which implies committing nuclear suicide.

It may be objected that it is not territorial but industrial bases that will be decisive, and that use of the term 'sea power' is misleading and should be changed to industrial power built up since the railway revolution through both internal and external markets. This would of course make nonsense of the preceding analysis and put in place of the assumed conflict between land and sea power, a simple conflict between different systems of society labelled 'free' and 'totalitarian'. The existence of such a totalitarian sea power as pre-war Japan or of freedom movements within inland states like Czechoslovakia could be used to show the fallacy of an hypothesis of sea versus land power. To these objections it might be said, obviously everyone prefers freedom, but the history of the last five hundred years suggests that only sea powers achieve a workable version of it; that the growth of internal markets has favoured the growth of freedom in exactly the same way as the growth of external markets, but a territorial power is one which has conquered and seeks to hold conquered peoples by armed force; it must therefore suppress freedom movements, which will be inevitably centrifugal, indeed the stronger the freedom movements in a territorial empire the greater repression will be used. A sea power is not subject to the same compulsions for a number of reasons, principally because its sources of strength are diffused and come *upwards* from commercial groups and corporations, not *downwards* by *Diktat*. Also the colonies of a sea power, whether overseas settlements in the historic sense or overseas corporations in the modern sense, are separated one from another and from the mother country, and there is not the same need for a powerful central control. Besides, the commercial drives of a sea power make profit all-important and directly the cost of holding a colony exceeds its return the tendency will be to discard it unless it is a vital strategic link in the imperial chain. At the height of British power in the nineteenth century the British government did its utmost not to acquire colonies despite urgent representations and often pre-emptive action by its own subjects overseas. When has a territorial power ever resisted aggrandisement within its grasp? Unless it is believed as it was in the nineteenth century that Anglo-Saxons have unique qualities not enjoyed by the lesser races the historic record is clear; there is a difference between a predominantly sea- and a predominantly land-power.

Once this difference is admitted, it disposes of the objection that the industrial and not the territorial base will be decisive for the great territorial powers of the future. For a territorial power cannot build its industrial base in the same way as a sea power without freeing its subject peoples to become market-acquiring commercial creatures themselves, thus increasing their centrifugal tendencies and increasing the need for central control – in short setting up intolerable tensions of the kind that distinguished the history of France and Imperial Germany. If these tensions result in the break-up of the territorial empire it loses its formidable strength; if they result in the victory of the market-acquiring peoples, the state changes its nature and becomes a sea power itself; if they result in a victory for central control, the market-acquiring tendencies are suppressed and neither industry nor commerce will be efficient. In other words, a territorial power cannot become an efficient industrial power unless it changes itself into a sea power. If it does so, its forms of government and society will also change.

There are equally serious constraints on dominant sea powers. One is that the freedom and lack of envy their societies enjoy tend towards a liberalisation of thought which seeks to interfere with the aggressive, market-acquiring drives vital for success. Here is the central paradox of the 'free' society; it can only exist by ruthless acquisition, ruthless exploitation of human and material resources and cynical manipulation of power balances, yet the more successful, hence the freer it becomes, the more delicate its intellectual conscience becomes. The other major constraint is in the finite nature of the globe. Market-acquisitive powers must deplete the earth's resources at an ever-increasing rate, and the alarm this has already caused in free societies may be more successful than the sensitive liberal conscience in stalling the whole machine. Once this happens the sea power, too, changes spots and becomes something else.

Because of these constraints and a multitude of imponderables, not least about the next stage of the technological revolution, to forecast inevitable victory for sea power – hence for toleration and freedom – in the present deadly game would be rash. The analysis is presented simply as an explanation of how we reached this position, and as an attempt to refute the idea that Western cultural values are 'inalienable'. Whatever values we have are the values of sea creatures, and will survive only if the West survives as a successful sea creature.

Now for the diagrams which illustrate the historical basis of the free orld system:

NATION A - near the start of her rise

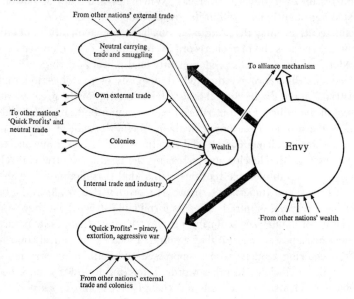

NATION B - near the end of her rise

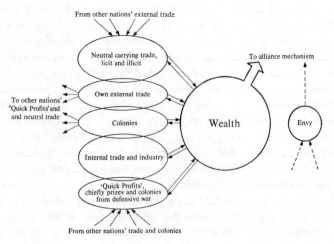

It will be noticed that, with minor modifications, the diagrams serve to illustrate the compulsions of each individual within a sea power and for each group, company or class as well as they illustrate the compulsions of the sea power as a whole. In short the system of sea power is homogeneous, working upwards and outwards from each individual within it, a dynamic whole in which the successful rise, the unsuccessful fall. A territorial power, by contrast, is based on central control, hence devolved rights and duties which are the reverse of dynamic. These internal differences derived from the nature of the beast account for the different forms of government and society, and it is noticeable that the differences are most marked when the power is on the upward slope of its cycle; thus developing successful sea powers are character- ised by very high social mobility and a slackening of constraints such as guild ties, while developing successful territorial powers are marked by a rigid social order in which the most impoverished hidalgo will retain his position above the wealthiest merchant. The decline of sea powers is accompanied by social ossification, the decline of land powers by tendencies towards greater social movement; if the decline is catastrophic the movement will be revolutionary and King Mob will rule for a while.

Both the fundamental human drives – for survival and succession or regeneration – and the higher intellectual and artistic drives have been omitted from the analysis, not because they are unimportant, but because in the former case they are basic to both systems, and in the latter case arise out of the system – chivalry a cover for brutal territorial aggrandise- ment, freedom for naked commercial aggression.

With freedom comes freedom of intellectual dissent, a luxury which is soon adopted as a necessity. Men with exceptional intellectual drive have always dissented whatever system they lived under, as the evil nature and results of both systems are contrary to man's intellectual aspirations. What they are dissenting from, however, is the nature of man himself, which is the driving core of both systems. Whether they do so before their society has attained freedom – as Thomas More and Alexander Solzhenitsyn – or whether they do so in a free society – as Karl Marx and Bertrand Russell – they can have no appreciable effect on the society, whose characteristics will be determined by the more fundamental drives described. To suggest that Marx, who on the face of it has had more success than most intellectuals, has changed any society anywhere is to suggest that states called Communist practice Communism, or for instance that Soviet Russia is basically different from Tsarist Russia; the evidence suggests otherwise. And Marxism can only make headway among the Western sea powers if those powers are already in decline and changing from their sea state; then it will provide a useful banner for central control to march under.

From all this it will be clear that the term sea power in these pages implies diffused commercial industrial power – otherwise naval strength is a more accurate term – and territorial power implies concentrated central power.

There was never, in the era under discussion, an absolute sea power or an absolute territorial power; all had some aspects of the opposite characteristic; what is termed a true sea power or true territorial power is one in which a single aspect predominates so decisively as to give that power its distinctive drives; the hybrid by contrast, is a power in which the two aspects are fairly evenly balanced and the drives wobble.

And everyman is the root of all evil, as the old religions knew very well; it is his nature and urgings which impel the leaders of the systems. Yet reason has placed him at the centre of the universe!

This is the story of the decisive sea powers and hybrids of the past five hundred years from the decline of Venice to the rise of the United States and Soviet Russia, told with as little technical and naval historical jargon as possible. It is intended for general readers who may know little or nothing of ships and naval weaponry or tactics and grand strategy, and these mysteries are explained from the beginning as they evolve without the naval historical dogma that by-passes analysis. Those nautical expressions which it would be unprofessional to paraphrase will be found in a glossary on p. 235.

CHAPTER 1

THE CAMPAIGN OF DISCOVERY

Vasco da Gama's departure from Lisbon in July 1497 glows through the centuries with a strange, delusive clarity. We can almost sense the high occasion as he and his company, with the King Manoel, soon to be known as 'The Fortunate', progress through city crowds towards the Cathedral to dedicate their voyage to God. We, knowing the outcome, can still feel awe at the magnitude and audacity of the enterprise on which they are embarked. Inside the building, we can recognise through incense rising like smoke on shafts of light from the great windows, men lifted by a common belief in the Divine presence amongst them, His blessing on their enterprise as the Bishop consecrates the Royal Standard and da Gama accepts it from the King's hands.

We can see da Gama's few ships leaving the mouth of the Tagus some days later, their sails ballooning and lifting, emblazoned with the red cross of Christ, mastheads dressed with bunting, the Royal Standard flying from the main of the flagship; we can smell the new paint, caulking tar, hemp, sun on fresh adzed timber, and distantly hear the cries of the crowds massed to see them off – to the Indies – to the unknown – a catch at the back of the throat. We know, as they knew, that few would return; they knew, as we know, they stood at a turning point in history.

It is all deceptively clear, the swell from the Atlantic with spindrift like moving caps of ice on blue, sparkling water, the sightly curves of the hulls lifting and settling as the small squadron moves at a walking pace in the direction of the Canary Isles. So brilliant in outline, the details of the scene are worn smooth by time. Who is da Gama? Why is King Manoel, who chose him, so confident of success in what appears a most desperate venture that he has marked the departure with ostentatious public ceremonies and has personally seen the expedition off from the mouth of the Tagus? What precisely are the orders he has given? Has da Gama's sailing plan to the Cape of Good Hope – which we know will be followed by all subsequent sailing vessels – been devised from positive evidence of the wind system of the South Atlantic gathered by navigators of whom no record remains,

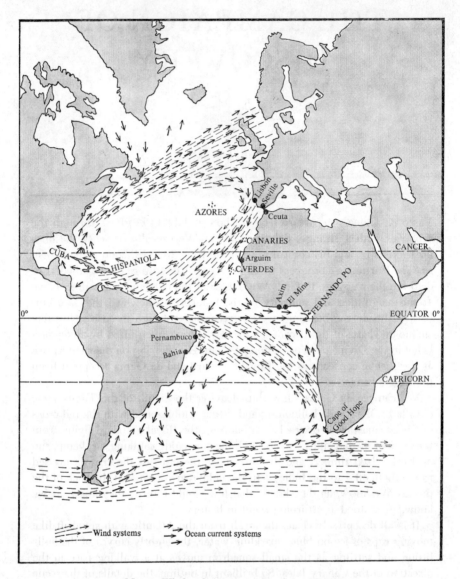

Map 1: Wind and current systems of the Atlantic

or are they a commonsense response to negative features of the routes sailed
by those expeditions we know of? Above all, perhaps, can we slough off
five hundred years to understand beneath the romantic aspect of the picture,
the fierce, haughty, naïve minds of these adventurers, so susceptible to
marvels and portents, so certain of the Faith, so stamped with notions of
personal reputation to be won in combat and hardened by race memory of
hatred and war with the Infidel?

Two things only are certain: da Gama's departure was the climax of a long campaign by the Portuguese to open a sea route to the Indian Ocean; King Manoel was so confident of success that he pulled aside the curtains of secrecy with which the campaign had been shrouded hitherto, and let the world see the grand design.

With hindsight and knowledge of the winds and currents of the Atlantic it seems evident that the Portuguese should have been the pioneers of the ocean routes; a glance at the wind system as it touches the western shores of the Iberian peninsula shows that seamen from this region had only to spread their sails and put their trust in God to be carried south-westerly towards the bulge of the west African coast and its off-lying island groups, the Madeiras, Canaries, Cape Verdes. On the way back they were bound to strike out into the Atlantic at right angles to the prevailing north-east trades – thus north-westerly for they could make northing no other way – until they found westerlies to take them back to Europe; they were thus bound at some time to discover the Azores. Once established in the island groups with planting colonies and trade between them and the mother country it would have been astonishing if they had not built up a sound working knowledge of the wind belts and currents and sea and air signs of this triangle of North Atlantic, more astonishing perhaps if they had not adventured further on the wind system and discovered the larger Atlantic triangle bounded by the bulge of South America, the chain of West Indian islands, and Newfoundland with its rich fisheries. That is how it happened, and it was a similar small triangle between Portugal, West Africa and the Atlantic islands which served as a base for exploration into the south Atlantic and round the Cape of Good Hope into the Indian Ocean.

Spaniards from the Atlantic provinces immediately north and south of Portugal, Muslims from the Atlantic coast of Morocco, even Frenchmen from the Biscay region had similar opportunities, and indeed settled a few Atlantic islands for a short while in the fourteenth century, but the advantages of wind and distance out and home were marginally with the Portuguese; as it turned out, in the decisive century when a number of pressures were tending to force trade westwards into the Atlantic, it was the Portuguese who had fewest constraints.

Their kingdom was small and poor but united. They had thrown out Muslims from the more fertile regions of the Algarve in the thirteenth century; towards the end of the fourteenth they had thrown back invasions from Castile. Although the Castilian threat remained, that kingdom was occupied in struggles for eastern and southern Spain, and was drawn by these concerns towards the Mediterranean; it would be truer to say that the wealth of the Mediterranean system drew her that way; in any case Portugal was left relatively free from distraction during the earlier part of the fifteenth century when the vital bases for discovery were established. Another reason for this relative security was Portugal's poverty. Much of the country was mountainous and stony, much of the rest so unsuitable for agriculture that she had to import grain for her few towns. The majority of her small population, probably no more than a million at the beginning of the fifteenth century, subsisted in a barter economy balanced precariously between small-holdings and fishing, each complementing the other where the soil was too poor for prosperous agriculture and the coast lacked sheltered harbours, or even an extent of continental shelf necessary to support large-scale fisheries. With so few internal advantages it was natural that the Portuguese should have looked outwards, and facing the wrong way, natural that their powerful neighbour would not extend too much effort to subject them.

The positive direction for the drive outwards came from Lisbon. Here was one of the only two large sheltered anchorages in the country with the equally rare attributes of good communications with a fertile hinterland; the city had grown into a thriving international port of call on the regular shipping route from the Mediterranean to north Europe. With a population of 40,000 including a sizeable merchant class, it stood alone in the kingdom for size and wealth and was the only port with the combination of shipbuilding and ancillary industries and the financial contacts necessary for overseas expansion. Whether Lisbon merchants and Genoese and Florentine money, or King John's third son Henry, the legendary 'Navigator', were the most important influences in Atlantic exploration, it is certain that both sides played an essential part. Without the kind of finance and entrepreneurial drive which only the Lisbon merchants could supply, or the patronage which only the Royal house could give, the outward movement would have resulted in little more than piracy, seasonal fishing colonies and attacks on Muslim north Africa. All of these occurred at first; the initial drive outwards probably had more to do with the ending of warfare inside the country than with any positive ideas; as so often belligerent pressures and disciplines vented outwards when the internal struggle was over.

The first notable feat of the Portuguese, and of Prince Henry himself, was the capture of Ceuta (on the Moroccan coast just inside the Straits of Gibraltar) from the old Muslim enemy. This was in 1415 and it is evident that the Mediterranean, not the Atlantic, was the magnet: Ceuta was a splendid base for piracy and also a terminus for one of the camel caravan routes across the desert from central Africa. These overland routes ending at the north African ports played a vital part in the Mediterranean economy; European manufactures, principally textiles, were carried south to the markets for tropical west Africa or the Sudan, and there exchanged chiefly for gold dust and black slaves to be brought north to the coast. Much of the gold then found its way to the Levant, where it was used to pay for spices and Oriental luxuries, hence the overland routes were essential drive belts in the whole Mediterranean and world trade circulation. It is reasonable to assume that the Portuguese and their merchant backers studied the routes and sources of gold, learnt of the great rivers which flowed from them to the sea, and made a deliberate decision to tap them from the sea.

It is equally possible that they made a deliberate effort to tap the source of slaves. Negro slaves were not as valuable as white slaves from eastern Europe, but they were in demand for agricultural labour. Moreover sugar, dependent on slave labour, had been introduced into Spain and Portugal by the Genoese around the turn of the century and had already become an important export; landless Portuguese backed by sugar merchants were sailing out on the north-east trades to farm and plant in the Canaries.

Whatever the sequence of events and motives, which can only be guessed at now, by mid-fifteenth century the Portuguese had reached the Guinea coast and established regular trade routes in which gold, slaves and island produce were staples. It was not quite the same as the later triangular trade providing slaves for the West Indian and American plantations and sugar for Europe on the final leg, because the Canaries and Madeira lay upwind of the Guinea coast, hence the negroes were carried back to Portugal to be marketed. In other respects it was similar: cheap, manufactured trinkets and bowls, brightly coloured textiles, also horses were shipped from Lisbon to the west African coast and exchanged for gold, ivory and slaves – a horse was worth fifteen prime, young male negroes at the first trading post at Arguim some 450 miles south of the Canaries. This trade, though small in comparison with later years, was enough for the Portuguese to mint their first gold coinage since the expulsion of the Muslims – the Cruzado in 1447 – and it encouraged interlopers, notably Spaniards who were also settling the Canaries. The Portuguese, as pioneers, considered themselves entitled to an exclusive monopoly and fought the Spanish and any other 'trespassers' they found, meanwhile applying to the Pope for a ruling; they were obliged with a series of Bulls. These decreed that since the Portuguese king had acquired extensive maritime dominions which advanced the boundaries of Christendom and the work of God, he should be allowed to enjoy the benefits undisturbed; he was therefore granted sole and absolute lordship over the regions already opened, and those still to be discovered between Morocco and the Indies. Here in 1455 is the first documentary evidence of Portuguese ambitions to discover a sea route to the Indian Ocean, for the Bulls followed the suggestions of the applicants. It was spelled out the next year in another Bull granting to the Order of Christ ecclesiastical jurisdiction 'through all Guinea and past that southern shore all the way to the Indians'.[1] Whether the Portuguese, noting the south-easterly trend of the Guinea coast, thought they were on the way to rounding Africa, or whether they were trying to secure all possibilities for the distant future is not clear. There is little doubt that they believed it possible to circumnavigate the continent, for about this time European maps were appearing showing a sea passage connecting the Atlantic with the Indian Ocean; previously the European tradition had been to draw Africa extending southwards to join a great southern continent bounding the Indian Ocean, which was consequently represented as a landlocked gulf. The Chinese had maps representing Africa as circumnavigable as early as 1312.[2]

If the Portuguese really were interested in reaching the Indies at this time, they seem to have made little effort to do so. By 1460 when Prince Henry died they had penetrated no more than 500 miles – perhaps ten days' sailing with a favourable current and anchoring by night – down the south-easterly trend of the Guinea coast from the Gambia. They needed to go down almost as far again to round the corner of what is now Liberia to enter the Gulf of Guinea. Of course the trade winds had run out by this latitude. So had the money. Prince Henry died in debt. Moreover the Portuguese were having to protect their monopoly against Spanish and Moorish incursions. Whatever the causes, sustained exploration did not begin again until the king leased it out on a concessionary basis to an entrepreneur named Gomes in 1469; then it went ahead at an unprecedented rate. During the five years of the concession, the whole of the Gulf of Guinea into the Bight of Biafra and down to the Equator including the off-lying islands of Sao Tome and Fernando Po, were sailed, charted and opened to trade and colonists. More was done in the five years than in the forty-odd years of discovery in Prince Henry's time, and under incomparably more trying conditions. Alternating long periods of calm, violent squalls and variable winds, glassy heat, humidity and fever-ridden swamps at the mouths of the great trading rivers gave the area an evil reputation throughout the sailing era. It is interesting that exploration under the concession reached precisely the point – so far as there can be any precision – that the eastward and southward trend of the Guinea current meets the opposite-bound current coming up the coast and branching out westwards to run along the Equator towards South America; in short it reached the natural turning point for home. After this point current and prevailing winds are against further progress down the coast.

This period is significant not only because exploration was unmistakably linked to private trading profit in gold and slaves, but because the concession stipulated a discovery rate of one hundred leagues of coast a year; it was not simply a trading concession; the Portuguese Crown was determined on rapid advance. Were the Indies the goal? Had they been the goal earlier when lack of money halted exploration?

The question of finance leads to further speculation. There is little doubt that the capital required to mount such a spectacularly successful series of voyages over such distances in such adverse sailing conditions, freighted with sufficient barter goods to return the kind of profits it is known were made, was beyond the capacity of Lisbon alone, and it is tempting to see the whole movement down the African coast as part of the massive reorientation of Genoese capital that was taking place at this time as Genoa was forced out of the eastern Mediterranean by the advance of the Ottoman Empire.

Although Genoese capital had been moving westwards from much earlier – Portuguese and Atlantic island sugar as an obvious example – it was only after the fall of Constantinople to the Ottoman Turks in 1453 that her eastern position became impossible, and she had to make a massive switch of resources. With the fall of Constantinople she lost the whole of her Black Sea and soon her Aegean trade, particularly Caucasian slaves and alum that helped to balance her purchase of spices and eastern silks in the Levant, and during the next twenty years she lost most of the chain of eastern Mediterranean coastal bases which formed the other leg of the Levant operation. She sought to replace eastern silks with silks from Granada, Caucasian slaves with negro slaves from Africa, Asian and Aegean alum – vital to the major industry of textiles – with Italian alum, and she sought gold wherever she could from the overland routes and the Portuguese sea routes from west Africa. So far as Portugal is concerned, her domination of Lisbon's commercial life is evidenced by a petition of 1459 asking for the expulsion of Genoese merchants who, it was claimed, took Portuguese money without bringing any profit.[3]

What Genoa could not replace was her lost spice trade; this remained more than ever in the hands of Venice, which was better placed to resist the Turkish advance. Hence, if the movement of the Portuguese down the African coast in the 1470s was as concerned with finding a sea route to the Indies as it was with more immediate prospects of gold and slaves it could be presented as a Genoese move towards regaining the spice trade from her old rival. If this is too extreme, it is at least true that speculation about a sea route to the Indies was engrossing the imagination of sailors and geographers of Lisbon and Genoa, indeed all the Italian cities including Venice at this time. And whether or not it was a conscious drive for an alternative route to the lost eastern trade, by the time that route was found Portugal and the whole Iberian peninsula had become economic dependencies of Genoa; whatever the mixed motives of the 1470s the eventual outcome was that Genoa recovered her eastern trade via Portugal and the southern tip of Africa.

The most immediate result of the Gomes concession, however, was to establish the Portuguese and their Italian backers in a flourishing web of trade between Lisbon, a chain of fortified trading posts and slave pens (known as baracoons) off the great west African rivers, and the Atlantic island groups. All parts of the web were complementary: African slaves provided the labour for the island sugar plantations; the islands in the Bight of Biafra provided the coastal trading posts with fresh produce; the whole provided Lisbon with increasing quantities of gold, sugar, slaves and a variety of other tropical produce including a type of pepper found in Benin. It was a series of triangular trades, fore-runners of the rich trans-Atlantic triangular trade of the following centuries.

Exploration stopped at the end of the concession as war broke out between

Portugal and Castile, and the sporadic actions between Portuguese vessels and increasing numbers of Spanish intruders on the west African coast flared up into regular naval operations concerned with the seizure of bases in the Canaries and the control of Guinea trade. The Portuguese proved more than a match for their opponents at sea, and after four years of savage fighting the Treaty of Alçacovas, while allowing the Spanish their existing colonies in the Canaries, confirmed the Portuguese in the African monopoly they had been granted by the Pope; this was the first of a long series of European treaties concerned with colonies and trading spheres.

The next and final series of exploratory voyages began with the accession of King John II in 1481. These were shrouded in a secrecy which is unlikely now to be penetrated. At least there is no doubt that discovery of a sea route to the Indian Ocean was the prime motive, and immediate trading profits secondary to the long-term benefits of breaking into the Eastern spice trade at source. This can be deduced from the spies that King John sent overland through the Muslim world to report back on Indian Ocean trade and make contact with a legendary Christian kingdom ruled by Prester John, which was believed to lie in east Africa. The possibility of enlisting this Christian aid against Islam in the Indies had been envisaged in the Papal Bulls of Henry the Navigator's time; what distinguished the efforts made under John II was the duration of the voyages and the determination with which they were pressed against adverse winds and currents down the west African coast below the Equator. These differences may be explained by the secure system of bases and supplies which John's navigators enjoyed as far as the Equator, and the confidence in long oceanic passages which the Portuguese had acquired through the Gulf of Guinea and Atlantic island trade routes – also the heightened confidence of the Crown as the profits from this trade swelled each year. These differences may be sufficient to account for the greater endurance of John II's navigators in the infinitely more testing conditions they encountered without the need to assume that the voyages marked a new departure; in other words Henry could have been as interested in the Indies as the Papal Bulls, legend and the old Chroniclers suggest – in which case the epic voyages under John II were indeed the climax of a much earlier movement.

The highlight of this series of voyages was Bartholomeu Diaz's rounding of southern Africa in January 1488. The navigational details of the feat are lost; all that is known is that after crossing the Gulf of Guinea, then struggling down the coast some way past the latitude 21° 50' south, which had been reached by his predecessor, Diogo Cao (or Cam), perhaps to almost latitude 27° south, he either struck out or was forced out westwards from the coast. As the north-going current in this area can reach forty miles a day, and the prevailing south-east trades blow from a more southerly than easterly direction, this was the best thing he could have done; 400 to 500 miles sailing on a west-south-westerly course would have taken him past the southern limits of the trade winds into a region of variables in which he might have been able to make southing. He was subsequently driven south-easterly by a storm, or he reached the belt of westerlies – sufficiently storm-like for his small craft – and ran until he estimated that he was further east than his point of departure from the coast; in fact he had rounded the southern tip of Africa out of sight. After altering northerly he made landfall some one hundred miles east of the Cape, which he named Agulhas, and anchored in what is now Mossel Bay. He coasted on, soon convinced from the north-easterly trend of the land that he had indeed rounded Africa, then turned back, carefully recording latitudes for his successors.

Between that famous voyage of Diaz and the departure of Vasco da Gama ten years later, there is a remarkable silence, broken only by the westward voyages of Christopher Columbus under Spanish auspices.

Christopher Columbus was a living demonstration of the link between Genoa and Atlantic discovery. He was a Genoese by birth who went to sea, probably as a young man, in Genoese ships; he moved to Lisbon perhaps as early as 1470 when barely twenty, and became caught up in the ferment of excitement and geographical speculation attendant on Portuguese explora-tions in the Gulf of Guinea. He sailed on some of these voyages, whether as sailor or supercargo is not clear, and interested himself in map-making and the questions which naturally occurred to map-makers beyond the points of furthest discovery. Chief among these for Columbus, as it probably was for the Portuguese, was a sea route to the Indies and the fabled riches of Cathay, as Marco Polo had called China. He conceived the idea that they would be reached more easily by sailing west across the 'Ocean Sea' than by rounding Africa and sailing east. Whether this came to him first as a result of observations and hearsay during his voyages and a period spent in the Madeira islands, possibly also the Azores, or whether it was an intellectual concept derived from study and correspondence with Italian cosmographers, his justification rested equally on mathematical considerations of the circum-ference of the earth – which he conveniently underestimated – and on such evidence as a piece of carved wood found in the ocean 450 leagues west of Cape St Vincent, 'evidently drifted from the westward'.[4]

He interested John II in the idea, but failed to secure his backing. The reasons are as obscure as most of the rest of his story, but may have as much to do with Columbus's character as with the Portuguese commitment to the route around Africa; Diogo Cao had only reached latitude 13° south by 1484 when Columbus was turned down. The king did, however, send out one vessel behind Columbus's back to test the route but the crew lost heart in mid-Atlantic and turned round. Chagrined by the duplicity Colum-bus went to Spain to solicit backing. He arrived in the middle of a war. The kingdoms of Aragon and Castile, lately brought together by the marriage of their monarchs, Ferdinand and Isabella, were consummating the union with a crusade against the Muslim provinces of Granada (southern Spain) and although Columbus found the court as susceptible to his strange ideas as the Portuguese had been, the royal pair were too occupied with the war to commit themselves to a new adventure. We have glimpses of Columbus during the next seven years – following the itinerant court, regarded as a lunatic visionary, examined by members of a learned council who finally pronounced against his theories, corresponding again with John II of Portugal, actually in Portugal to watch the triumphant return of Bartholomeu Diaz, consumed with impatience, growing more obsessive, but still able to convince a few thoughtful men of influence. Finally in 1492, after Castile and Aragon had driven Islam from Granada and the whole Iberian peninsula had been regained for Christendom, one of these men persuaded the victorious dual monarchy to support Columbus.

He sailed from the little port of Palos on the Atlantic coast of southern Spain that August with three very small vessels provided by the port as a fine for some previous misconduct, and commanded by local shipowners experienced in the Canary Island trade. With such a small outlay and by the slenderest threads of chance which have not been detailed here, the newly-forged nation state of Spain acquired first claim on a continent whose existence was not even suspected. It might as easily have been Portugal. It was a logical extension of Portuguese activity in the Atlantic.

A major mystery about this voyage in which the larger islands of the Caribbean were discovered and the natives had their first taste of the lust for gold which drove the newcomers about from shore to shore like bees after nectar is that Columbus on his return, sailed to Lisbon and discussed his findings with John II before reporting back to the Spanish court. Columbus was sure that he had proved his theory. Although the natives of Hispaniola and Cuba were naked primitives as far from current ideas of the wealth and culture of the East as it was possible to imagine, the fact that the islands had been discovered just where his wildly inaccurate calculations had led him to expect Cipangu (Japan), taken together with native gold ornaments and indications of inland sources of gold, convinced him that he had arrived. It is doubtful if John II was equally impressed. Certainly John Cabot, a Venetian who had travelled in the East and who was in Valencia when Columbus passed through on his way to the Spanish Court, knew from the descriptions that the expedition had not reached the Indies. Cabot was fired to try himself by sailing in the same direction, but in higher latitudes where the earth had a smaller circumference, and he eventually found backing in England, setting off in the same year that Vasco da Gama sailed.

The cross-fertilisation of knowledge and ideas in all the early voyages of discovery is evident from all this, and the Portuguese who were at the centre of it all may easily be imagined to have preceded Columbus across the Atlantic. The distance between the Portuguese Cape Verde Islands and Brazil is little more than half the distance Columbus sailed, and much of it in the same north-east trade wind belt. A more southerly departure from off

Liberia before entering the Gulf of Guinea would have brought them there more surely on the south-east trades. All this is speculation, but it is difficult to explain aspects of Vasco da Gama's voyage without assuming that the ten years' silence between Diaz and da Gama was a deliberate silence behind which the Portuguese probed westerly. The diplomatic negotiations between Portugal and Spain after Columbus's return could be held to support this.

Ferdinand and Isabella, who may have taken Columbus's discoveries at his own valuation – at least as strategic stepping stones to the East – were immediately attracted by the promise of gold, fitted out another far more ambitious expedition equipped for colonising and mining, meanwhile appealing to the Pope for a monopoly. A series of Bulls similar to the early series concerned with Portuguese discovery drew a north–south line one hundred leagues west of the Azores and Cape Verdes, beyond which the Spanish crown was granted all rights of discovery and conquest. John II immediately addressed himself to moving this line further west, and on the pretext of protecting his African trade eventually secured an agreement by negotiation with Spain to have the line 370 leagues west of the Azores. The Portuguese were in a position to make things very difficult for Spain when it came to exploitation of Columbus's discovery – John II concentrated a large fleet to underline the point – and the result of these negotiations formalised in the Treaty of Tordesillas in 1494, reflected the strength of the Portuguese strategic position in the Atlantic. It may be that John's interest in shifting the line was caused by genuine concern to protect the wide loop of his Guinea and Cape Verde Island trade, more probably to hold as much as he could of the ocean his countrymen had made peculiarly their own. But it is interesting that the original line one hundred leagues west of the Cape Verdes just misses South America while the revised line places a considerable part of the coastline of that continent within the Portuguese sphere. This may have been fortuitous. The first discovery of South America may have been six years later during Pedro Cabral's voyage to India; it is just as easy to imagine that the Portuguese had far more geographical knowledge than we or their contemporaries credited them with – indeed it is difficult not to imagine this in the light of Vasco da Gama's voyage. And the question recurs: what was Columbus doing in Lisbon on his return from the Indies?

The vessels associated with the Portuguese voyages of discovery were caravels. These were probably a development of traditional Atlantic seaboard fishing craft with the high-angled bow and sweet sheer of boats built for the steep seas of an unprotected oceanic coastline. They never reached great size; the larger ones were perhaps fifty to sixty feet overall and they had lower and finer lines than the usual cargo-carrying sailing ships of their day. They were carvel-built, that is with flush, abutting hull timbers, and were decked throughout with a short raised poop or perhaps in the early days a light shelter rigged aft; they probably had a small, sheltered space under a raised forecastle deck as well. They were driven by a large, triangular fore-and-aft sail (lateen) set on a long yard from a mainmast about amidships, and one or two smaller lateens set from smaller masts abaft the main. Later in the fifteenth century some caravels had as many as four masts and some, caravels redondo, were rigged with square sails forward, lateens aft. However, it was the windward power of the pure, lateen-rigged caravel that the explorers favoured for the beat home from Guinea into the north-east trades; the leading edges of the sails, held rigid as wings by the yards enabled them to sail much closer to the wind than was possible with the loose leading edge (luff) of square sails. Caravels were renowned among all Atlantic sailors for their weatherly qualities, and having less weight and superstructure than large merchant ships, strained less and were more secure in storms.

The first point that distinguishes Vasco da Gama's voyage from those of his known predecessors is that his squadron of four vessels contained only one caravel; both flagships were *naos*: high-sided, bluff-bowed, square-rigged vessels rigged as barques; there was also a square-rigged storeship. This was a deliberate choice for the *naos*, *Santa Gabriel* (flag) and *Santa Raphael* were specially constructed for the expedition under the supervision of Bartholomeu Diaz himself. They were beamier and more capacious than caravels, had better accommodation in the high stern castles and were in these respects better suited to the proposed extraordinarily long voyage. However, they were inferior to caravels for a beat against the south-easterly trades south of the Equator, indeed it is doubtful if they would have been able to make any way against the northbound current. It is the change of ship type – so suitable for the course da Gama actually followed, so unsuitable for the courses followed by his known predecessors – taken together with the outward and public manifestations of confidence before his departure which suggest that some exploratory voyages must have been made across the south Atlantic, perhaps even around the Cape and into the Indian Ocean in the ten years before he sailed. It may be that the Indian Ocean pilot, Ahmād ibn Mājid, who left notes of 'Frankish' vessels wrecked off Sofala in what is now Mozambique, east Africa, two years before da Gama's departure was not confusing his dates.

The size and specification of da Gama's ships have been subject to as much speculation as Columbus's *Santa Maria*. They were small, perhaps as little as one hundred, perhaps as large as two hundred tons, perhaps eighty or ninety feet overall, perhaps more. If the most contemporary picture, made half a century later, is a guide, they had aftercastles rising three decks above the uppermost continuous deck, a high forecastle and very round bows; both fore and main masts carried a deep square sail (course) fitted with two sets of bowlines each side to keep the leading edge into the wind when beating, and a small topsail above. There was also a spritsail set below the bowsprit and a small lateen on the mizen sheeted to a boom astern. Like all sails of the time they were cut full and designed to fill with wind like bags rather than set taut and flat as in the heyday of the nineteenth-century square-rigger, and with the high sides and castles below it is doubtful if *naos* could have made any progress into the wind. They were steered by tiller from below the poop by helmsmen guided only by compass and orders shouted from above; there was another compass in a binnacle on the quarterdeck for the pilot and mates.

Compass course, estimated distance, observed latitude, these were the three components of Portuguese oceanic navigation. The techniques had developed with the extent of the discovery voyages, and by the last decade of the fifteenth century they had caught up with much earlier developments in the China Seas and Indian Ocean. Starting with Genoese pilots and a Mediterranean system based on coasting from port to port and headland to headland, expressing sailing directions as compass bearings and distances between ports and capes, and drawing charts on a similar grid of compass bearings and distances rather than co-ordinates of latitude and longitude, their oceanic voyages out of sight of land on the return loop had forced them to rely on the measurement of latitude by observation of heavenly bodies. The pole star was the first one used; its altitude was measured by quadrant, essentially a graduated arc with open sights and a plumb line suspended above the arc. When the sights were lined up on the star the altitude could be read off the arc where it was cut by the plumb line. This was not very satisfactory on a rolling and pitching ship, and was a long way astern of contemporary Chinese and Arab practice of measuring the *space* between the star and the horizon. At first the Portuguese did not translate their angular measurement into latitude, but grafted observation to their existing technique and treated each degree of altitude as equivalent to fifty miles of distance in a north–south direction, expressing their observations as distances north or south of their departure point. Positions on charts were expressed in degrees of altitude of the pole star – with rules to allow for its slight displacement from the true pole. Navigation out of sight of land consisted essentially of making sufficient northing or southing to bring the altitude of the pole star up or down to its known altitude at the destination, then if the winds were favourable, altering due east or west until the destination was reached. In course of time latitude replaced pole star altitudes on charts, but the destination-finding technique known as 'latitude sailing' remained unchanged, indeed it was used by all navigators for centuries until the development of accurate time-keepers allowed measurement of longitude.

The most striking example of the way navigation techniques followed the urge to discovery is found in the final thrust down the African coast below the Equator. Here the pole star was not visible, and there was no southern equivalent. The sun was the obvious replacement as visible everywhere and already used for noon observations, but its use was complicated by its apparent movement north and south of the Equator through the different seasons of the year. John II set up a commission of astronomers to solve this problem, and in remarkably short time they came up with tables allowing calculation of the sun's displacement from the plane of the Equator (declination) each day of the year. These tables were based on previous astronomical work, so the solution cannot be said to have been called into being by the demands of navigation alone; it was a nice blend of pure and applied science. This was in 1485. Bartholomeu Diaz was able to determine his latitudes around the Cape by observing the altitude of the sun at noon and subtracting the declination given by the tables.

With sun sights came the sea astrolabe; this was a wooden or brass ring graduated like the quadrant, suspended when in use by a cord through a ring at the top. A sight bar which pivoted at the centre of the ring had plates at either end with fine holes drilled through them. The sun's altitude was read by holding the astrolabe about waist-height and rotating the sight bar until the beams of sunlight from the hole in the upper plate fell on the lower. This suffered from the same errors as the quadrant aboard ship but allowed remarkably accurate calculation of latitude ashore.

It seems clear that both ship types and navigation techniques were called into being by the demands of discovery, not the other way about as usually assumed. Discovery was called into being by the search for wealth. Ostensibly it was a crusade for souls; if the Portuguese had built churches instead of baracoons, and sought conversions instead of slaves they might be believed. Missionary work followed half a century behind man-stealing. Ships, navigation and discovery were, so far as can be judged by results, tools in the search for wealth, and wealth not technical developments or religious crusade was the driving force behind the movement.

The other tool developed during the course of the voyages was the great gun – the weapon that was to become the supreme arbiter of sea power. From the second half of the fifteenth century, if not earlier, Portuguese caravels mounted 'bombards' which they used not only for defence against pirates and interlopers but for mounting in the boats with which they explored African rivers and estuaries. Bombards were tubes formed of wrought iron bars welded edge to edge and strengthened by rings of wrought iron fitted over while white hot so that they shrank as they cooled and held the barrel in a series of tight reinforces. These were lashed to a simple timber bed. The powder charge was packed hard into a separate 'chamber' shaped somewhat like an elongated beer tankard laid horizontally, its open end tapered to fit into what would now be called the breech end of the barrel. This was wedged tightly in place. The piece was fired by blowing on a lighted match – a length of line impregnated with an inflammable mixture – and putting the glowing end to a touchhole or vent filled with specially fine powder to transmit the fire to the charge within. Aiming was a matter of touching off when the course and roll of the ship brought the target into line, hitting largely a matter of luck outside very close range, indeed the guns' crews sometimes ran more risk than the enemy; there are numerous accounts of gunners and others of their own side succumbing to the imperfections of these 'built-up' pieces. James II of Scotland was one in 1460:

> And while this Prince, more curious than became him, or the majesty
> of a King, did stand near hand the gunners when the artillery was
> discharged, his thigh bone was dug in two with a piece of a mis-
> framed gun that brake in shooting, by the which he was stricken to
> the ground and died hastily.[5]

The workmanship and strength of metal used in the best examples which have survived was of a high order, but the separation of 'chamber' and barrel was a design limitation which the technology of the time could not surmount.

After firing, the wedges were extracted, the chamber removed from the barrel and replaced with another previously charged and rammed chamber after the projectile – usually a hand-shaped stone ball – had been loaded. The piece was then ready to fire again. Theoretically this was a swifter and far safer operation than serving the cast muzzle-loaders which succeeded these guns in the following century, and it is probable that breech-loading bombards were extremely quick-firing by comparison with their successors. The stone balls projected were often five inches or more in diameter, but the guns carried by the early caravels were probably half this calibre; it is difficult to imagine a really large piece mounted in a ship's boat, and we know this was the practice on the Guinea coast as early as the 1450s.

Similar heavy guns capable of breaking through masts and upperworks, although only exceptionally through the stout hulls of Western sailing ships, were appearing on Venetian and Genoese galleys at about the same date, but it is probable that the Portuguese took the development furthest in sailing ships, in the process inaugurating a new technique of sea fighting which they demonstrated with dramatic effect as soon as they reached the Indian Ocean; this was the stand-off artillery duel fought by groups of ships in close-hauled line ahead – a development that naval historians have generally credited to the Dutch or English a century later.

Lighter guns than bombards were also carried; they were constructed in the same way, but the chamber was secured on an extension of the breech, and they were mounted at rail height on an iron pivot or swivel. These probably fired iron or lead pellets cast on board, or any pieces of old metal, nails or scrap to damage flesh and bone rather than the structure of an enemy ship – although they could cut rigging and tear sails satisfactorily. Da Gama's flagship carried twenty guns, more than half probably bombards, but their size is not known.

The principal hand weapons at sea as for land warfare were spears, pikes, halberds or pole-axes, swords and crossbows, with a few firearms perhaps in the last decades of the century as the arquebus began to rival the cross-bow. The arquebus was a forerunner of the musket fired by a slow match gripped in pivoted jaws which were moved towards the flashpan by pressure on the trigger, via a wheel-lock mechanism. One history which has been found inaccurate in other respects states that firelocks had not entered the Portuguese service at sea in Vasco da Gama's time;[6] it is known however that Columbus asked his Spanish backers for one hundred for his 1495 expedition, and Portuguese fleets to the Indian Ocean certainly carried firearms by 1506.

The choice of da Gama to command the expedition of 1497 may be another indication of previous exploratory work. He was not a professional sailor of the type of Cao or Diaz, but a gentleman of the royal household, the kind of man who would be chosen to lead a diplomatic or warlike expedition. His mission, so far as can be gathered from his actions and the letters he is known to have carried, one for the Christian king, Prester John, one for the ruler of Calicut, the major spice *entrepôt* on the south-west (Malabar) coast of India, was diplomatic.

He was about thirty-seven years old, born in the coastal town of Sines. Of gentle, but not aristocratic or wealthy, parents according to one chronicler he had served in fleets before being selected for command by King John II; he was confirmed as Captain-Major of the expedition by John's successor, Manoel, who succeeded in 1495. Nothing more is known of his early life. His character may be deduced from the record as exceptionally able, firm and harsh, although probably no more cruel than his contemporaries. If he thought it his duty on one occasion to burn his plundered enemies alive in their own ship, or on another to cut off the lips and ears of a spy and have a dog's ears sewn in their place, this was by no means exceptional behaviour for Portuguese commanders in the Indian Ocean.

In his old age he was 'a very disdainful man and ready to anger, very rash, much feared and respected'.[7] Also in old age he was zealous for the king's service, scornful of those who became wealthy in the East at the king's expense and scornful of promotion by nepotism.

He would not give captaincies except to those who in war had shown
themselves as good soldiers; for he would give the honours of war to
those who had won them with their right arms, and however low a
man might be, he would show him more honour than a gentleman
Jew. This he used to say of many in public, for [he] was very haughty
in his speech . . . he inspired everybody with great fear.[8]

These glimpses probably bring us as close to the man as it is possible to get at this remove. Of one thing there can be no doubt; he was a leader of the utmost determination; his first expedition to the Indian Ocean is perhaps the most outstanding of all the voyages of discovery.

His squadron sailed in company with Bartholomeu Diaz, who was going out in a caravel to command a Guinea fort. They followed the usual outward track to Santiago in the Cape Verde Islands, where they anchored for a week, refitted and reprovisioned, then sailed south-easterly, still on the usual route for Guinea. Somewhere off the south-easterly trend of the coast before entering the Gulf of Guinea, bombards were fired in farewell salutes and while Diaz continued south-easterly on the track to the Gulf, da Gama headed south-westerly or perhaps south-south-westerly or southerly – who knows what shift of wind made him decide that this was the moment to make the planned alteration? He must have spent some days, perhaps longer, adrift in the doldrums, sails hanging lifelessly, lowering boats and towing towards catspaws glimpsed on the oily swell. It is all speculation. But the south-east trades for which he must have been aiming come substantially north of the Equator in the summer months, and once the squadron began to feel them they would have driven along steadily towards the coast of South America with rolls of foam under the bows and flying fish skittering before them. The further west they travelled the more the wind would have backed into the east allowing them to sail ever more southerly until they ran out of the trades and entered the region of variable winds between modern Bahia and Rio de Janeiro – presumably out of sight of the coast since the only eye-witness account of the voyage makes no mention of land until they had run back to the southern tip of Africa.

It is doubtful if they made this run back far enough south to get into the belt of westerlies that roar around the ocean below the tip of Africa, since they made their African landfall to the north of the Cape. Besides it was the practice even late in the following century to make easting as soon as the winds allowed it. An account from 1579 states that once across the Equator they trimmed the sails to make as southerly course as possible until they reached the latitude of the point (the Cape) 'which is 35° 30′ south and then take their course towards the east and so compass the point. But the wind served us so that at latitude 33° south we did direct our course towards the point'.[9]

However da Gama made it, after ninety-three days at sea, the longest recorded voyage out of sight of land to that date, his squadron reached the coast about half a degree north of the Cape of Good Hope, and eventually anchored in St Helena Bay. There they careened and scraped the hulls, made repairs, mended sails, took on fresh water and wood for the fires, and after only eight days weighed again and sailed south for the Cape.

The great south Atlantic loop they had made – which was followed in principle by all subsequent sailing vessels bound from Europe to the Cape – was a triumph of diet no less than faith. How many of the 150 or so men in the four vessels went down with scurvy is not known but it cannot have been too many since there was no mention of sickness in the eyewitness journal. And it is difficult to imagine how they would have been able to refit and sail in only eight days if a large number had been affected by the lassitude and weakness preceding the more revolting stages of the disease.

They spent almost a week tacking and filling off the treacherous coast in the vicinity of the Cape against the strong northbound current, but eventually rounded it and anchored in Mossel Bay. There they remained for a fortnight, emptying and burning their storeship before sailing on in early December. The next few weeks, during which they coasted easterly and northerly against a south-westerly current that often set them astern of their point of departure, exercised da Gama's resources of leadership and determination to the utmost. Water ran so short that rations were restricted to one pint a day, storms severely strained the gear, and scurvy began to take a serious toll. By the time they reached the Quillimane River towards the end of January the crews were in such bad state that they had to stay a month to rebuild their health. They were now on the outskirts of the Moslem trading area, finding in the town of Quillimane stone houses with Moorish arches and carved lattice windows, markets where silk, beaten brasswork and fine jewellery in the Arab style were sold by traders whose mixed Arab, Persian, Indian and native blood was unmistakable. These signs must have put fresh heart into da Gama.

His spirits were lifted higher at their next port of call, Mozambique. They had now reached the southernmost mart in the Muslim trade network, and from the merchants 'who spoke the same language as Moors'[10] and wore fine linens with cloaks of cloth of gold and other rich and elaborate workmanship, they learnt that further up the coast, gold, silver and spices were so abundant they could be collected in baskets. Asking the whereabouts of the kingdom of Prester John, da Gama was told it was northwards and a camel journey into the interior. As da Gama's mission was almost certainly to enlist Prester John's aid in the proposed attack on Muslim control of the spice trade, the news that his was an inland kingdom could not have been welcome. Of course it is possible that da Gama knew this already if the reports from John II's spies had got back.

A question which puzzles all historians – whether or not the spies' reports got home – is the total lack of suitable barter goods and presents for local rulers provided for the expedition, or even of gold and silver. Da Gama was sent into a trading area of known, indeed exaggerated, wealth and splendour to enlist local support and open negotiations with the ruler of the chief spice mart in the East, yet his backers, including some of the richest bankers in Europe, provided him with the kind of cheap textiles, brass bells and coral beads which were used for trade with the natives of tropical west Africa! This was an extraordinary lapse in a mission fitted out with such care, and despatched with the utmost confidence. It is a mystery. Da Gama received his first intimation of the mistake in Mozambique. Presenting the local sultan with hats, coral, hawk's bells and other trivia he found him 'so proud that he treated all we gave him with contempt, and asked for scarlet cloth, of which we had none'. Also at Mozambique the Portuguese had their first skirmish with the Arabs, who finding they were Christians and very obviously interested in spices and gold, laid an ambush for one of the watering parties. The Portuguese defended themselves successfully with bombards and crossbows from the boats and retired to the ships.

Previously da Gama had obtained two local pilots from the Sultan in return for one of his own men as a hostage for their safety; the hostage was one of several convicts the Portuguese habitually took for just such desperate occasions, and da Gama had no compunction about leaving him to his fate and sailing north for the regions where gold and spices could be collected in baskets. This section of the voyage was probably plain sailing as the winds are usually between south and south-east in March when he left Mozambique, and April when he came to Mombasa, the largest of the east African Arab cities; nevertheless his men were dropping down with scurvy again and the vessels were dangerously short-handed by the time they cast anchor off the island on which the city stood. News of the Portuguese presence had preceded them from Mozambique, and although they were greeted with every outward show of friendship it did not take da Gama long to discover that offers of spices were part of a plot to lure him into the harbour and overwhelm him. This information, extracted from two captives under applications of boiling oil, was confirmed by attempts made by swimmers to cut the ship's cables. He weighed and sailed north for the next Arab town of Malindi, a smaller, less favoured port whose ruler – fortunately for da Gama – was on bad terms with the Sultan of Mombasa. Here they received presents of sheep and fruit and found a welcome as potentially powerful allies against Mombasa; the thunder of their bombards had again preceded them. They were able to stay and restore their health before setting out on the final leg across the Indian Ocean for Calicut.

As da Gama's orders have not survived, it is not clear why he gave up the northward search for Prester John, and struck out for India. The south-west monsoon had set in by this time and either course would have been possible. Probably he had confirmation at Malindi that the legendary kingdom (Abyssinia) could not be reached by sea, and the dangers of leaving the ships for a journey inland had been made very clear by their previous experiences. In any case he managed to secure the services of a local pilot, and under this man's competent direction the little squadron sailed some 2,300 miles of ocean with the wind astern at an average of little less than 100 miles a day – some four knots – a good passage for such small, high-charged and by now rather foul vessels. They reached Calicut at the end of May.

Calicut was one of a chain of Hindu states along the south-west (Malabar) coast of India. It was the principal *entrepôt* for spices and Oriental wares, hence the most important city on the Malabar coast, whose *Samuri* – known by the Portuguese as the *Zamorin* – claimed authority over all the others. However as he was largely dependent on duties derived from trade, the mainly Muslim merchant community had enormous influence in his councils.

Here the scene comes into sharp focus again as the Portuguese squadron appeared literally out of the blue; the ships anchored some way along the coast from the open roadstead before the city, and da Gama and thirteen of his most trusted followers, attired in their most splendid robes, were rowed ashore under an array of banners to the sound of trumpets and guns. Met by a reception committee, including numbers of bearers for a palanqui for the Captain Major, da Gama was carried all the way to the city, and preceded by increasing throngs amidst the din of horns and drums, his own men behind him, he arrived at the *Zamorin's* palace an hour before sunset. Ushered through a series of doors to the audience chamber, the Portuguese found the potentate reclining (half-naked by their standards) on silken cushions on a magnificent couch covered and hung about with dark green velvet and holding in his left hand a golden spittoon, into which he projected husks of betel nut and squirted fine streams of juice through stained teeth. Servants, holding a hand before their mouth whenever they addressed him, kept their distance, others brought the travellers fruit, sweetmeats and water to wash their hands. After the courtesies the *Zamorin* asked da Gama why he had come; the Captain Major replied that he was an ambassador from the King of Portugal, who was lord of many lands and possessed of great wealth, exceeding anything in these parts; he came in friendship from the king his master, seeking trade between Calicut and Portugal.

The following morning his fine words rebounded. The tawdry collection of presents he had brought for the *Zamorin* – twelve pieces of striped cloth, four scarlet hoods, six hats, four strings of coral, a case of six washbasins, a case of sugar, two casks of honey and two of oil – were laughed out of court. The *Zamorin's* Factor told him that the poorest Arab or Indian merchants would bring more, and advised him that his wares would be unacceptable; if he wished to make a gift it should be in gold. Da Gama tried to retrieve the situation by saying that the presents were from himself not from his king, but the damage was done; he was kept waiting four hours before his next audience with the *Zamorin* and he and his men were treated to indignities and even imprisoned while on their way back to the ships. When eventually they were released and attempted to trade the goods they had brought for the pepper, ginger, cinnamon, cloves and other spices they found in abundance, they were offered such derisory prices by the Muslim merchants that they had to sell their shirts to buy sufficient to take home as samples. Finally, when da Gama wanted to leave, the *Zamorin* demanded payment for permission to do so, and the Portuguese had to seize some merchants and hold them as hostages to secure the return of a party of their own men whom the *Zamorin* had captured. In these circumstances, with the active opposition of the merchant community, it is not surprising that he was unable to find a pilot for the return voyage, and that he left at the wrong time, before the north-east monsoon. With hulls streaming weed the squadron drifted in calms or against contrary winds for almost three months before reaching the African coast. By that time they had lost thirty men to scurvy – the same number as succumbed on the outward passage – and most of the remainder were suffering from the tell-tale swollen gums and legs and blotched skin and extreme lassitude that marks the course of the disease; only some seven or eight men were left to work each vessel.

> If this state of affairs had continued for another fortnight there would have been no men at all to navigate the ships. We had come to such a pass that all bonds of discipline had gone.[11]

In such a state, near the end of their resources, they eventually made landfall near Mogadishu in early January and coasted down to Malindi, where the Sultan, still friendly, sent off the fresh food they so urgently needed; once again the fate of the expedition turned on the friendship of this ruler. When they finally sailed from the port, they burned the *Santa Raphael* as they had not enough hands to work three vessels, then made a slow progress down the coast, eventually reaching the Cape at the end of March. After that it was plain sailing, on the south-east trades, towards the Cape Verdes and the well-known loop home; the caravel arrived in the Tagus in July 1499, da Gama in the *Santa Gabriel* a month or so later; in all probability there were no more than sixty survivors in the two vessels.

Despite the cost in ships and lives, the narrow margin by which the expedition had avoided total disaster, the failure to make contact with Prester John, the evident hostility of the Muslim merchants, the humiliation of da Gama's treatment at the *Zamorin*'s hands, his inability to buy more than a token quantity of spices, despite all this the voyage was hailed as a triumph – as it was. King Manoel hastened to fit out a larger, more powerfully armed expedition to sail the following spring, writing meanwhile to Ferdinand and Isabella of Spain:

> we learn that they did reach India and other Kingdoms . . . that they entered and navigated its seas, finding large cities, large edifices and rivers and great populations, among whom is carried on all the trade in spices and precious stones which are sent on in ships to Mecca, and thence to Cairo where they are dispersed throughout the world. . . . And when the great trade which enriches the Moors of those parts, through whose hands it passes without intervention of other persons

shall in consequence of our ordinances be diverted so that henceforth all Christendom shall be able to provide itself with these spices and precious stones, this with the help of God, who in His mercy has ordained it, will cause our designs and intentions to be pushed with more ardour the war upon the Moors which your Highnesses are so firmly resolved upon, and in which we are equally zealous. . . .[12]

The letter, sent after the return of the caravel but before da Gama's arrival in Lisbon, catches the spirit of breathless excitement aroused by the news of this climax to the campaign of discovery. There is no dissimulation. Manoel's thoughts are written down in the order they must have occurred to him, 'all the trade in spices and precious stones which enriches the Moors . . . shall . . . be diverted . . . with the help of God', and almost as an afterthought an assurance that he is ardent for the Holy War. The tone of absolute confidence, on the face of it unwarranted by the puny results of the expedition and its desperate hazard, was echoed by Manoel's immediate assumption of the title, 'King of Portugal and of the Algarves on this side and on that side of the sea, in Africa Lord of Guinea, and of the conquest, navigation and commerce of Aethiopia, Arabia, Persia and India'!

Vainglorious as it sounded, the next few years were to demonstrate that it was based on a proper appreciation of what the voyage had revealed. The most important facts were that it was possible to make the voyage to India and back, and that the Indian Ocean craft in which the Muslim trade was conducted were ill-made compared with Portuguese vessels, and unarmed with either bombards or cross-bows. The significance of this was appreciated by everyone at Lisbon and soon by all Europe. Here is part of a contemporary letter from a Florentine resident in Lisbon to a colleague at home, dealing with the time spent by da Gama at Calicut:

During this time there arrived about 1500 Moorish vessels in search of spices. . . . They are of all sorts, large and small. Having only one mast they can make headway only with the wind astern, and sometimes are obliged to wait from four to six months for fair weather [in fact the change of monsoon]. Many of these vessels are lost. They are badly built and very frail. They carry neither arms nor artillery . . . some of these vessels are built without any nails or iron. . . . All the vessels as long as they remain in the city are drawn up on the beach for there is no port where they would be safe otherwise.[13]

This description suggests that most of the craft the Portuguese saw at Calicut were Arab dhows with the single huge lateen sail of the kind familiar to all subsequent travellers in the Indian Ocean. This rig makes it extremely difficult, though not impossible in emergency, to tack; the normal method of going about is to wear, and the normal method of sailing is to avoid going about for as long as possible. The dhow, in nearly all its forms, was a vessel evolved in and for a uniquely favourable monsoon system, guaranteeing a fair wind outwards on the south-west and homewards on the north-east monsoon – and vice versa for the east coast of Africa. Seldom needing to weather violent gales or beat into adverse winds it had not developed the stout construction of Atlantic sailing vessels. In 1939 Alan Villiers used much the same terms as the Portuguese in 1499: 'The trouble with these big dhows as I saw it was that they could not stand up to anything like a heavy sea, and it seemed to me they would quickly disintegrate in anything like weather.'[14] Many of the vessels trading to the coast of Africa and, it seems from the description, even to India had their hull timbers sewn together with coconut fibre (coir) instead of being bolted or pegged, and their sails made of coir matting, although it is evident from later accounts that there were also stout, multi-masted junk-rigged craft with flax or cotton sails; but these were chiefly employed on voyages east from India. In any case a later letter from the same Florentine describing the expedition being fitted out to follow up da Gama's voyage makes King Manoel's attitude and the reason for his confidence supremely clear:

> Should the King of Calicut not allow the Portuguese to trade in these countries, the Captain of the vessels is instructed to capture as many native craft as he can. In my opinion he will be able to capture as many as he chooses, for they are frail and so badly constructed that they can only sail before the wind.[15]

The other points revealed by the voyage were the actual routes taken by the trade and the extraordinary cheapness of the spices at Calicut; they could be bought for less than one-twentieth of the price they fetched at Alexandria, which was of course lower than their final prices in the markets of Europe. By sailing to the spice islands themselves they could be bought at half the price they fetched at Calicut. It is not surprising that Manoel – the Fortunate – could scarcely wait to send off another expedition. The riches of the East lay open for the taking.

CHAPTER 2

THE CONQUEST OF THE
INDIAN OCEAN

Command of the second expedition to India was entrusted to another young nobleman, Pedro Cabral. Only thirty-three years old, he was given the grand title, Admiral of the Indies. He was given ten king's vessels, and three were privately ventured, a mixture of ships (*naos*) and caravels and although the largest was probably under 300 tons all were heavily armed with bombards and swivels. His instructions were to sail to Calicut and open peaceable negotiations with the *Zamorin* to establish a Portuguese warehouse or 'factory' there. He was to do no injury to any ships on the way – not even Arab vessels – but he was to inform the *Zamorin* of the Holy War against the Muslims 'in order that all matters both great and small shall be clear and certain between us and him',[1] and tell him that while the Portuguese would respect all vessels at Calicut itself, Moorish vessels met at sea would be captured. He was also to say that 'it would further please us if he [the *Zamorin*] could exclude these Moors from his land and from trading in it, since please God, he will receive from us and ours all the profit which until now he has had from them, and much more.' Since Calicut was the principal seat of Muslim merchant power between the spice islands and the Red Sea, since the *Zamorin*'s chief advisers were Moors, and since Portugal had little that was valued in the Eastern trades, this was a breath-takingly highhanded even naïve, way to negotiate. King Manoel's letter to the *Zamorin* was equally naïve; almost the whole of it was taken up with declarations of the religious and evangelic purposes of the voyage – for da Gama had been misled by Hindu images into believing that the Malabar Indians were a Christian sect. But the desire for temporal profit broke through from time to time.

> wishing to fulfil as we ought that which the Most High God clearly
> shows us to be His will and service, we now send thee our Captain
> and ships and merchandise and our Factor who, by your pleasure, will
> remain there and perform his duties. . . . And if it should happen that
> owing to ill will and minds obstructive of good, which are never

lacking, we find in you the contrary of this [trade agreement], our fixed purpose is to follow the will of God rather than that of men, and not fail through any contrarities to prosecute this affair and continue our navigation, trade and intercourse in these lands, which the Lord God wishes to be really served by our hands, not wishing that our labour to serve Him should be in vain. . . .[2]

With such authority to break the Moorish monopoly, it was of course unthinkable that the Portuguese should turn back. But while the letter is a connoisseur's piece for transparent hypocrisy, there are sections revealing a genuine sense of the awe that was felt at the 'great mystery and novelty' of these voyages linking hitherto impossibly remote parts of the world:

We give praise to God because in our day and yours He has bestowed such favours on the world that we are not able only to know through hearing, but to see and know by sight and by intercourse to unite and also be neighbours.

The written instructions Cabral received were immensely detailed; there is one relating to the tactics of capture at sea which marks a significant turning point in naval history.

If on the voyage you encounter any ships of Mecca and it appears to you that you are able to capture them you are to try to take them, but you are not to come to close quarters with them if you can avoid it, but only with your artillery are you to compel them to strike sail and launch their boats.[3]

This defines the coming-of-age of the great gun in naval warfare; instead of taking enemy vessels in the time-honoured way by boarding and entering, Cabral was ordered to conduct a stand-off artillery duel, in this case an annihilation since the enemy had inferior guns or none at all. This was probably a special instruction based on the frailty of the Indian Ocean craft, and the need for the Portuguese, so far from home, not to hazard their men – indeed the purpose is explained thus later: 'that this war may be waged with greater safety, and so that less loss may result to the people of your ships.' Nevertheless, a similar movement towards using broadside armed sailing ships as mobile artillery batteries to break up opposing galley formations was taking place at this time in the Venetian fleet in the Mediterranean, and as it is unlikely that an entirely new method of warfare would be specifically ordered, it seems certain that by 1500, when these instructions were written, the stand-off artillery battle was a well-tried and proven tactic; the conclusion is supported by the consummate stand-off tactics practised by da Gama on his next voyage.

Cabral sailed in March 1500, and taking da Gama's advice, made his south-westerly alteration to cross the Atlantic from the Cape Verde Islands instead of from somewhere between them and the Gulf of Guinea, thereby crossing the Equator further west – about 30 degrees – and making the first recorded landfall in South America, some 200 miles south of where Bahia now stands. He raised the Portuguese flag and claimed the land for King Manoel – who might have done better to concentrate his efforts here; there were gentle souls to be saved. Sailing after a few days, he again followed da Gama's advice to take a

circular course until they get the Cape of Good Hope directly east
. . . in this way it appears to him [da Gama] that the navigation will
be shortest and the ships more secure from worms and in this way even
the food will be kept better and the people will be healthier.[4]

Unfortunately the fleet was beset by storms, four of the ships were taken aback and turned right over, and the others were scattered into three groups which made their way separately into the Indian Ocean. All three passed far south of the Cape and made their alteration north on natural signs of the presence of land. One of the groups united with Cabral's group at Mozambique and the fleet, six vessels strong, made a coasting passage up to Malindi. The Sultan was as friendly as he had been to da Gama – for the same reasons – and Cabral obtained fresh provisions and pilots for the final leg to Calicut, which he reached on the tail of the south-west monsoon on 13 September, scarcely more than six months out of Lisbon; this was a considerable improvement on da Gama and can be ascribed to his good advice; it was marred, of course, by the loss of half the fleet.

After months of protracted negotiations, hindered by the Arab merchants, the *Zamorin* granted permission for the Portuguese to trade, and made a house available by the waterfront with a garden and a wall around for use as their factory. In view of Cabral's instructions and the deadly hatred between Muslim and Christian it was not to be expected that the established merchants would take kindly to these interlopers, and it was not long before the inevitable happened; quarrels between Portuguese and Arabs ashore, perhaps caused by the merchants withholding spices, or charging higher prices, or giving preference to their own kind, perhaps caused by Portuguese arrogance, or their capture of a Muslim vessel – whichever it was, the Arabs raised a mob which stormed the 'factory' and slaughtered between forty and fifty Portuguese; only some twenty escaped by swimming to the ships' boats. When the *Zamorin* failed to support Portuguese protests, Cabral exacted reprisals against the Arabs himself, taking their vessels in the port and burning them after plundering and killing the crews. Then turning his attention to the *Zamorin*, whom he suspected of treachery and siding with the Arabs, he sailed up and down before the city bombarding, 'so that we slew an endless number of people, and did them much damage, and they fired from on shore with very weak bombards.'[5] So it was war between Portugal and Calicut. Given Cabral's instructions it is difficult to see how there could have been any other end to his mission.

Afterwards Cabral sailed south to the port of Cochin where the Rajah, nominally a vassal of the *Zamorin*, but actually jealous of his wealth and power, welcomed the Portuguese for the same reasons as the Sultan of Malindi had welcomed them, as enemies of the too-powerful neighbour, and as most potent allies; the noise of their bombards had reverberated along the whole coast. They loaded spices, sailed north to complete the cargo from another of Calicut's rivals, Cananore, and not staying to give battle to a large fleet that the *Zamorin* had raised against him, sailed for home. Another vessel was lost on the way, so that only five laden ships reached Lisbon in the summer of 1501. These were filled with sufficient pepper, cinnamon, lac, ginger, cloves and other spices, bought at sufficiently low prices to keep Manoel and his merchant backers at fever heat.

It was also sufficient to alarm Venice. The spread of the Ottoman Turks and the disintegration of the Mogul Empire which lay across the overland trade routes from the East had stopped the flow of spices and Oriental wares from this direction during the fifteenth century and forced practically the entire trade into the sea routes across the Indian Ocean, chiefly to the Red Sea, thence overland to Alexandria or the coastal ports of Syria, Acre, Beirut or Tripoli. Venice was the major European buyer at these ports, all of which were under the control of the Mamluk Sultan of Egypt and Syria, hence the Portuguese assault in the Indian Ocean struck equally at Venice and the Sultan. Their initial reaction was slow, no doubt because at the time of da Gama's epic voyage Venice was fighting a naval war against the Turk in the eastern Mediterranean, and a land war to maintain the Italian city states against French overland assault – and of course da Gama had not interfered with trade.

Cabral's voyage was a different matter; news of his destruction of spice ships and his bombardment of the principal spice mart sent prices soaring – from sixty-two up to one hundred ducats a cargo of pepper at Venice.[6] The Sultan threatened Manoel with the destruction of the Christian holy places in his Syrian empire unless he desisted, and appealed to Venice for help in fitting out a fleet for the Indian Ocean. Manoel, assuming that the Sultan would not wish to forgo his dues from the lucrative pilgrim trade to the Holy Land, took no notice, and Venice was too immersed in her own wars to help; instead she suggested the Sultan seek timber and guns from the Ottoman Sultan. He did so, and prepared for the construction at Suez of a great fleet of galleys on the best Mediterranean pattern, armed with the great guns that were an Ottoman speciality.

This was the position when da Gama, now Dom Vasco, was placed in charge of the next expedition to India. He was burning to avenge his own humiliations from the *Zamorin* and his merchants – since compounded by their destruction of the Portuguese factory – but the chief purpose of the voyage was to place Portuguese power in the Indian Ocean on a permanent basis by taking out sufficient force to leave a squadron behind when the main fleet sailed for home with its cargoes. This Indies squadron was to be based on one of the friendly Hindu ports, Cochin, Cananore or Quilon, and was to direct the entire trade of the Indian west coast away from Calicut to these ports by means of patrols, blockades and a system of licences; any ships bound to or from any other port or without a licence (*cartaz*) were to be taken, plundered and destroyed. Considering the distances involved – if reckoned in units of time, the six months' voyage out is equivalent to three times around the world at present-day speeds – and considering the scale of losses on the first two expeditions, this must surely rank as the most audacious plan of conquest ever conceived. Two considerations alone saved it from fantasy: the most important was the overwhelming superiority of the gunned Portuguese ships – the floating castles described in the Introduction to this book – the other was the local jealousies which enabled them to rely on friendly bases. Without these, particularly the first, on which the second really rested, all the Portuguese oceanic navigation and shipbuilding techniques, all their ardour as faithful soldiers of Christ, all their lust for gold and spices, all their desperate cruelty would have been quite insufficient. Without the disparity in strength at sea the plan could not even have been considered.

Da Gama sailed in March 1502 with ten ships of burden and five caravels rigged with square sails for the passage. A second squadron of smaller ships under the command of one of his relatives followed in early summer. All these vessels were heavily armed:[7] the smaller ships mounted six bombards on the uppermost continuous deck, two on the quarterdeck, eight falconets and numerous smaller swivels on the poop and forecastle. The larger ships had far heavier batteries whose details are not recorded. The caravels, small as they were, mounted four bombards on deck, six falconets and ten smaller swivels on the quarterdeck and in the bows; the bombards and falconets were struck down below during the voyage. In the main fleet under da Gama there were some eight hundred soldiers, including a large number of crossbowmen and many gentlemen adventurers like those who were to follow Columbus's discoveries in the West.

The fleet followed Cabral's loop across the south Atlantic close to the South American coast, and down to the belt of westerlies below the Cape, altering course northwards again on an estimated position. They lost one vessel to a storm on the east African coast; subsequently they were met by the squadron which had sailed after them, and progressed up the coast in force, exacting tribute and submission under their guns from Mozambique, Kilwa and Mombasa before making their departure in the now established way from Malindi and arriving on the Indian coast at Dabul some 350 miles north of Calicut. Here the caravels were re-rigged lateen style, the heavy artillery was swayed up from their holds, and all was prepared for a campaign of extortion and terror down the Malabar coast.

The spirit and purpose of this campaign is conveyed in da Gama's reply to an ambassador from Batticola who came aboard as the Portuguese were working towards that town, having devastated one coastal province to the north.

This is the fleet of the King of Portugal, my sovereign, who is Lord of the sea, of all the world, and also of this coast, for which all the rivers and ports which have shipping must obey him and pay tribute for their people who sail in their fleets, and this only as a sign of obedience in order that thereby the ports may be free and that they may carry on in them their trade and profit in security, neither trading in pepper, nor bringing Turks, nor going to the port of Calicut because for any of these three things the ships that shall be found to have done them shall be burned with as many as may be captured in them.[8]

In this case da Gama accepted tribute of 1,500 loads of rice annually for the Portuguese officers and crews – an inferior quality for the latter – and having seen the first yearly instalment aboard, he left the province in peace.

Terror was an integral part of the campaign, especially it seems against Calicut. The flavour of the revolting proceedings here is illustrated by the fate of a fleet of mainly small vessels which appeared in the offing laden with rice for the town while da Gama was establishing a blockade after yet another bombardment. Having captured the craft and plundered as much rice and butter as his own ships could use, he ordered the hands, ears and noses of the prisoners to be hacked off, their legs bound together and their teeth knocked down their throats lest they bite through the cords. He then had them bundled into one of the captured vessels, mats and dry leaves spread over them, the sails trimmed for the shore, and finally as the craft were cast off, the leaves were set on fire. Another vessel loaded with the severed members was sent after it, unlit, towards the shore. There are other versions of this and other all too 'human' atrocities committed by da Gama or his second-in-command Vicente Sodre; while part of a personal campaign of vengeance against Calicut for the humiliations he had received there, the real purpose was to make the name of Portugal so feared throughout the Indian seas that no vessel would dare to disobey the trade regulations imposed.

The immediate effect was to sting the *Zamorin* into furious war-like preparations; he vowed to the Muslims that he would expend all the resources of his kingdom on vengeance, and started the construction and assembly of vessels of all types from rowing craft to proas and large ocean-going dhows along all the rivers of the province, appointing a Commander-in-Chief, Coja Kassim, whose brother had been killed in a vessel plundered by the Portuguese and set alight on da Gama's orders to burn crew and passengers aboard. Kassim knew that his fleet would stand no chance against the Portuguese broadsides in a manœuvring battle at sea and he planned to catch da Gama while loading for the homeward passage, board the ships and set them alight with torches carried for the purpose. However da Gama, loading at Cochin, was warned of the preparations by the Rajah, who advised him to leave at once without going up to Cananore to complete his cargoes and provisions for the homeward passage; he would find all he needed at Cochin.

Da Gama's reply is significant for any study of the development of tactics. He said that he had come expressly to avenge the wrong done to Cabral by the people of Calicut, for which purpose he had brought caravels 'which are so good at fighting that they are sufficient for whatever fleet Calicut might possess.'[9] This phrase and the course of the subsequent action are clear pointers to the development of the stand-off artillery battle in Atlantic waters before the Portuguese entry into the Indian Ocean, which had seen few caravels before this second expedition of da Gama's. Caravels were lightly armed compared with the ships of burden – four bombards only against eight in the smaller ships, while the larger ones were 'much more equipped with artillery'.[10] They were also smaller and lower, hence more easily entered with fewer men to repel boarders, and without the armed castles at bow and stern which served as citadels for *naos* when entered. The only advantages the caravels could possibly have possessed were greater speed and significantly better performance into the wind – exactly the advantages which the English enjoyed against the galleons of the Spanish armada later in the century. But these are only advantages if the intention is to force a stand-off artillery action. While it is possible that this was a tactic developed for the particular enemy in the Indian Ocean, da Gama's words – assuming they were reasonably correctly reported – seem to imply that caravels were already recognised as the best fighting vessels; moreover he had them re-rigged as lateen caravels at the same time as their heavier guns were brought up from below and mounted; it is known that John II's lateen caravels had been famed for their bombards mounted so low they sent their shot 'skimming over the water'[11] as well as for their handiness.

Da Gama went on to tell his ally that he hoped he would fall in with the Calicut fleet. 'I shall take upon it a part of the vengeance which my heart longs for.' It is to be wondered exactly what untold indignities he had received there, or what exactions might have sated his lust for vengeance, for any rational balance sheet of injuries must have shown Calicut in debit.

For nothing in the world would I desist from returning to Cananore to take the ginger which is brought there. For if I did not go there and were thus found wanting by the King of Cananore, I should be committing so great an error that the reputation borne by the Portuguese would be lost for ever. I would sooner die a thousand deaths than that anything should be found wanting in me for that which befits the state of the King, my sovereign.

He sent for the squadron of caravels under Sodre, which was employed on blockade and patrol, and when the fleet was concentrated – bar a few ships already loading at Cananore – sailed north towards Calicut, sending the squadron of five caravels and two or three of the least laden small *naos* under Sodre ahead and close inshore, following himself rather more to sea-ward with the main body of laden ships of burden. Before sailing da Gama had instructed the captains 'they were by no means to board, but fight with the artillery'.[12] If it became necessary to take in sail they were to brail the canvas up rather than lower the yards – presumably because these would interfere with the guns and provide useful grappling and boarding ladders for the enemy – and he cautioned them to provide numerous tubs of water about the decks to put out fires, which would be their greatest danger. In short both sides were well aware of the tactics their opponents would attempt.

By this time the Calicut fleet had been reinforced by a fleet of Red Sea dhows, and the command had been taken by a warrior emissary from the Sultan of Egypt, Cojambar. Exactly how many large dhows and how many smaller sambuks, proas and rowing craft there were in the combined fleet is impossible to say; all Portuguese accounts differ and these are the only ones available. The King of Calicut apparently boasted he had 20 vessels for every one of the Portuguese – which would amount to a fleet of over 350. Cochin spies warned da Gama that the odds were ten to one against him – 180. Portuguese accounts vary from 29 to 70 vessels in the main squadron, with numerous smaller craft astern. Whatever the figures, the Portuguese must have been outnumbered, probably greatly, because of the resources available to the Muslim merchants and the known and feared strength of the Portuguese ships and guns; a small fleet would have been ludicrous for such an object. The dhows were equipped with guns of a sort but these were small and very weak compared with the Portuguese weapons, some indeed had wooden barrels, and 'threw their shot like bowls'[13] – presumably in a lazy arc as in the game of *boule*. Their missile weapons were bows and arrows.

The Portuguese sighted their sails in the morning somewhere between Cochin and Calicut; they were heading southwards, arranged in a long line stretching back over the horizon 'for so the Captain Cojambar had ordered it that they might make more show'. Probably they were strung out because of their differing sizes, rigs and sailing speeds; large dhows of which the advanced squadron was formed are fast sailers. The wind was off the land – on the starboard hand of the northbound Portuguese – and directly Sodre

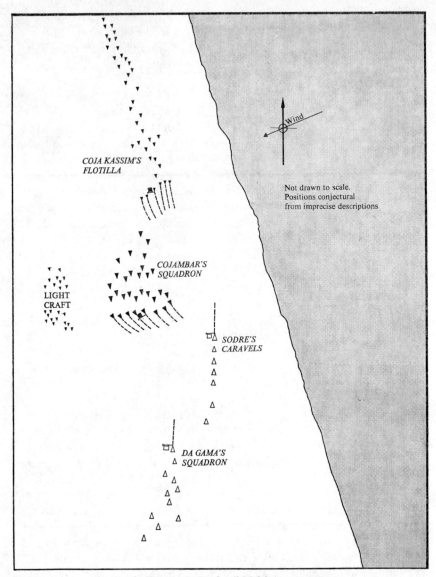

COJA KASSIM'S
FLOTILLA

Wind

Not drawn to scale.
Positions conjectural
from imprecise descriptions

COJAMBAR'S
SQUADRON

LIGHT
CRAFT

SODRE'S
CARAVELS

DA GAMA'S
SQUADRON

Battle diagram 1: Battle off Malabar coast, 1501

saw the approaching fleet he hauled up as close to the wind as he could –
again a highly significant move in any study of tactical development. It is
possible, as one account has it, that the move was ordered by da Gama, or
was the result of consensus in a council of war summoned on first sight of
the enemy fleet; this would be more in keeping with battle conventions of
the time.

The dhows and lesser craft which were hung with flags and banners of

Islam wherever there were halyards to hoist them came on with a tumult of
shouting and dinning gongs and horns. Sodre's caravels, cleared for action
and without flags, sailing close-hauled 'one astern of the other in a line . . .
under all the sail they could carry',[14] raced for the windward position,
leaving the few ships of the squadron astern and to leeward. As they
reached the enemy main body which was probably bunched in lines abreast
by this time, the line of caravels was well to windward; they opened fire,
each with its two lee (port) side bombards, at Cojambar's flagship. The
range was short enough for effective shooting and of these first ten shots,
which may well have been directed so that they ricocheted over the calm
surface, one or more hit Cojambar's mast and brought it down, another
went through his poop timbers, and others hit three separate vessels low
down, causing them to fill and sink. The gunners re-loaded and continued a
rapid fire: 'they made such haste to load again that they loaded the guns with
bags of powder which they had ready for this purpose made to measure so
that they could load again very speedily.'[15]

Very soon the dhows and smaller rowing craft became tangled in confusion as men from sinking craft leaped overboard and attempted to climb
up the oars or sides of others; the caravels brailed up their sails and lay off,
firing into the thick of them. 'It was not possible to miss . . . they shattered
many [vessels] killing many people on account of which there were shrieks
and cries among the Moors.' The wind completed the work, driving the
Muslim vessels further seawards as da Gama's heavy ships reached the
scene and joined in the work of destruction, also 'sailing in file one after
the other as the Captain Major had ordered'.[16]

The caravels and Sodre's light ships loosed their sails again as the second
wave of the enemy, perhaps 70 to 100 sail, mostly light craft led by Coja
Kassim, held on towards them, intending to close and board. The wind was
freshening however, and the caravels, while not turning aside, were able
to keep their distance and pour in a destructive fire from bombards and
swivels, sweeping down the yelling, white-robed masses on Kassim's flagship – which did however manage to put one shot into a Portuguese vessel,
killing the captain and wounding others with splinters. During this phase
the caravels either could not keep to windward of all the enemy because
Kassim's smaller craft were closer inshore and many were under oars, or
they did not bother to try, but keeping steerage way, sailed amongst them
all firing bombards from both sides into the enemy hulls between 'wind and
water', and swivels at the men massed on deck, and in the process cutting
rigging, bringing down masts and yards, destroying the outboard rope and
beam steering gear. In return they received small shot and showers of arrows
which damaged their own sails and rigging, but could not penetrate the
timbers behind which most of the men lay hidden. Only the swivel gunners
were exposed and they formed the bulk of the Portuguese casualties.
Arrows quivered from the bulwarks and masts like porcupine quills.

By the time Sodre's squadron had worked right through the fleet, they had wrought such destruction on the flimsy craft that Kassim was beating a retreat towards the shore, leaving behind a trail of disabled hulls and shattered timbers, and drowning men clawing at the debris. The remnants of Cojambar's dhows were also moving away in whichever direction they could to escape the fire of da Gama's main body. The Portuguese tacked and steered after them; the caravels sailing close enough to get up with them, aimed at leisure without distraction, and sent several more to the bottom. The ships were not able to sail close enough to the wind, which in any case was beginning to drop; before long it died away altogether. The Muslims had their larger vessels towed towards the shore by rowing craft, and the caravels did the same in pursuit, while da Gama, 'seeing that the business was certain',[17] had his ships' boats armed with falconets and swivel and twenty cross-bowmen in each and sent them to join the chase. So the battle ended in isolated boarding actions over a wide area in which the fire of the guns and cross-bows from the boats drove the enemy off the becalmed or towing vessels, which were then plundered and burned.

About midday a sea breeze sprang up and da Gama fired a gun and hoisted a flag signal of recall, meanwhile setting course for Cananore, 'giving to the Lord great praise for the great favour He had shown him'. Sodre, not content to let the victory pass without a secular demonstration, had the caravels take a number of enemy vessels in tow, and sailed with them to Calicut, where they were made fast to one another and set alight on the sea breeze so that they drove ashore; the caravels fired into the vessels and into a crowd which gathered on the shore to watch. So ended the first serious challenge to the Portuguese in the Indian Ocean. How many of Cojambar's vessels were destroyed is not known, but da Gama lost not a single ship, nor even a boat, and Portuguese casualties were light. It was a massacre rather than a battle, but it should stand out in naval history as the first recorded sea battle fought to a pre-arranged pattern as a stand-off artillery action by squadrons sailing in close-hauled line ahead.

In the same year on the east African coast, a single Portuguese ship commanded by Ruy Marques, which had become separated from an outward-bound fleet, cruised off Zanzibar Island, and captured some twenty dhows laden with ivory, tortoiseshell, honey, rice, coir, silks, cottons and suchlike. The Sultan of Zanzibar sent 4,000 men in a fleet of canoes against him; Marques armed just two ships' boats with swivels and these killed thirty-four men in the leading canoes at the first discharge, and soon put the rest to flight. Marques followed, and landed in Zanzibar, forcing the Sultan to pay tribute and become a vassal of the King of Portugal. The Atlantic-gunned sailing ship was quite simply irresistible in the Indian Ocean. To ask why this should have been so is to become lost in some of the large questions touched on in the Introduction to this book. It is understandable that China, which had developed guns, oceanic navigation and stout, multi-masted ships so much earlier than the West, and had made forays into the Indian Ocean with enormous fleets in the thirteenth century should have turned inwards later; she needed little from the area, and was in any case a territorial power with all the territorial opportunities and problems to distract her from the sea. The Japanese, who preyed on Chinese shipping, had not settled their own internal problems either; feudal lords were fighting for power. But to ask why the Far Eastern system as a whole did not take either the gun (the instrument of conquest) or the wealth-accumulating process (the drive to conquest) to the stage that both were taken in the West in the fifteenth century is to begin another study altogether. Several answers have been attempted. If the story of Portuguese expansion in these pages is more or less as it happened, the real answer to the problem must lie in the Mediterranean. It was in the Mediterranean that the first European guns were developed and the wealth was accumulated to support the Portuguese mercenary sailors on their spectacular career of conquest – and the Spanish as well. Most of the proceeds of both went straight back to the Mediterranean. 'Born in the Indies, passing away in Spain, buried in Genoa, Sir Money is a powerful Knight', a poet commented.[18]

The simple answer to the question of West and East may be that the Far East did not have its own Mediterranean Sea; in the temperate zone where the strange alchemy worked in the West through the catalyst of the short Mediterranean trade routes, there was only a great expanse of land bordered by a great expanse of ocean. The Japan Sea led only to Japan; it did not give the Japanese that middleman position between trading areas which the Italian city states enjoyed.

However it came about, there is no doubt that so far as warfare was concerned the Mediterranean and its Atlantic offshoot were areas of high pressure, the Indian Ocean a very low pressure area by comparison, and directly the Atlantic system expanded around the tip of the continent that separated the two it blew through the Indian seas with hurricane force.

That second expedition of da Gama's was a success on a scale which justified the most extravagant prior assumptions of King Manoel. On the coast of east Africa the most important centres of Arab trade, Mozambique, Kilwa, Mombasa and Zanzibar had been chastened and made tributary to Portugal – the Sultan of Malindi thereby given demonstration of the wisdom of his original choice! On the Malabar coast of India the most prosperous spice mart, Calicut, had been even more humiliatingly treated, and the Portuguese had established trading posts and begun fortifications at Cochin, Cananore and Quilon. The system of shipping licences and terror by which the Portuguese intended monopolising spices, taxing all seaborne trade and diverting it to their vassal ports had started remarkably well; while the Portuguese fleet returned to Lisbon in 1504 with nearly 2,000 tons of spices, mainly pepper, Venetian galleys on their 'liner' route to Beirut and Alexandria the same year found practically none.[19] The system of piracy and 'protection' which was supposed to make the whole enterprise self-supporting had begun equally well; from Zanzibar to the Red Sea, and on the opposite coast from Dabul to Cape Comorin at the southern tip of India, native shipping and coastal ports had been plundered and destroyed or forced to render tribute in gold or local produce. It had all been accomplished with trifling losses, and a squadron of caravels had been left on the Indian coast to maintain the position until the next outward fleet arrived.

In some way the success was illusory, resting as it did on the sheer speed with which da Gama's original voyage had been followed up, and the stunning effect of the bombards. The whole area had been knocked temporarily off balance. Later, as forces regrouped to restore the balance and ways were found to circumvent the patrols, the Portuguese had to stretch over a far wider area at a far higher cost to achieve far less absolute control.

The debate over this problem began surprisingly early considering the initial success; its main lines were established by the first Portuguese Governor of India, Francisco d'Almeida (1505–9) and the 'Great' Affonço d'Albuquerque (1509–15). Almeida believed that control of the ocean should be maintained by naval force alone; acquiring territory ashore and maintaining fortresses would drain away the wealth won at sea, overstretch the limited resources of manpower in operations which contributed nothing to wealth, and involve them in ever more costly land wars to hold what they had won. Albuquerque, on the other hand, believed that 'a dominion founded on a navy alone cannot last',[20] and advocated a system of secure fortress bases at Socotra Island to command the straits leading to the Red Sea, Ormuz to command the Persian Gulf, Diu in north-west India to command that rich trading area, and strong forts to protect the 'factories' established on the Malabar coast and command the sea routes from the East. Circumstances led him into other adventures, and a far wider diversion of force, for which he was constantly criticised by the King's advisers, concerned like Almeida, with economy and profit. Albuquerque was unrepentant. To complaints about the cost of maintaining Goa, his most lasting achievement, he replied that the acquisition of this fortified city

> did more for your Highness' *prestige* than all the fleets which have come to India . . . if those of your council understood Indian affairs as I do, they would not fail to be aware that your Highness cannot rule over so extensive a territory as India by placing all your power and strength in your marine only.

Albuquerque knew that in the long run the Portuguese position rested as much on prestige as physical domination; 'if once Portugal should suffer a reverse by sea, your Indian possessions have not power to hold out a day longer than the kings of the land choose to suffer it.'[21]

King Manoel veered from side to side in this debate, which was more a matter of balance than a clear-cut 'blue-water' versus 'fortress defence' argument. Matters were largely decided by the temperament and force of the Governor and his reaction to immediate events, and it was Albuquerque, justly called the Caesar of Portugal, who gave the eastern empire its shape.

> This great captain was a man of middle stature with a long face fresh
> coloured, the nose somewhat large. He was a prudent man and a
> Latin scholar, and spoke in elegant phrases; his conversation and
> writings showed his excellent education. He was of ready words, very
> authoritative in his commands, very circumspect in his dealings with
> the Moors and greatly feared, yet greatly loved by all.[22]

His portraits show a full, black-bearded face of immense determination; his actions reveal complete ruthlessness, cruelty, overpowering strength of personality, arrogance and contempt for those who lacked his own steel, reckless personal courage, and that power of instant decision in action which distinguishes so many great commanders. His will was indomitable, and he possessed a cunning streak which served him in his dealings with his own captains as much as with enemies and allies; his exploits are as amazing as any in the extraordinary story of Portuguese conquest.

Born near Lisbon in 1453 to noble parents, and educated in the fashion of the time, at Court, he fought against Islam in the Mediterranean and became chief equerry to John II. His first visit to the East was in 1503 on behalf of King Manoel to advise on future policy in India. Impressed by the difficulties of protecting the isolated trading posts established by da Gama against the armies of hostile inland rulers, he conceived a vast scheme of strategic fortresses which would not only control the areas where shipping routes had to concentrate, but would be secure against the largest land armies for long enough to enable reinforcements to come by sea. There was nothing remarkable in the idea; the system of seaside fortresses succoured by naval power was the essence of the whole system of Mediterranean naval warfare, and such fortresses were naturally built at or near those narrows and headlands where shipping lanes converged. What distinguished Albuquerque's plan – as it distinguished the Portuguese conquest itself – was its enormous oceanic scope and the audacity with which it was carried through.

He sailed with an outward-bound fleet under Tristan da Cunha in the spring of 1506 as commander of a squadron to be based on the island of Socotra off the entrance to the Red Sea; he carried secret instructions that he was to assume the position of Governor-General of India three years later when Almeida's term was to end. Almeida, who had sailed the previous year, was not told of this. The fleet, under da Cunha, arrived in east Africa and after carrying out what had become statutory punishments of the enemies of the Sultan of Malindi, sailed northwards for Socotra on the south-west monsoon of 1507 with pilots provided by the grateful Sultan. The small Arab fort on the island was captured in a short time, Albuquerque contributing to the victory with a characteristic departure from da Cunha's plan when an opportunity was presented by a calming sea to land a force close to the fort. Afterwards the Portuguese went in procession to a mosque near by, where they held mass, 'and not without the tears of our men, to behold in a land so remote from Portugal the name of our Lord Jesus Christ reverenced in that house of abomination.'[23]

After building a stronger fortress and garrisoning it, da Cunha departed for India with the main body of the fleet in August, leaving Albuquerque with a squadron of five and a small storeship to patrol the area; Albuquerque immediately sailed for the Persian Gulf to take Ormuz. This fabled city which commanded the narrows leading to the Gulf was the principal *entrepôt* where the sea routes from India and the East met the land routes of Persia, Syria, Turkestan and all Asia Minor; thus although it was built on a barren, sun-dried island of rock salt producing nothing – except pearls from the neighbouring waters – it was a byword for wealth and luxury; 'If all the world were a golden ring,' the Arab saying went, 'Ormuz would be the jewel in it.' The Kingdom of Ormuz held the whole of the opposite coast of Trucial Oman and Muscat, and Albuquerque planned to lead up to the assault on the island by sacking the tributary ports along this coast, both to prevent them assisting Ormuz and as a deliberate policy of terrorism to weaken resolve in the capital.

So it was that towards the end of August the little port of Quryate just south of Muscat was sacked and burned to the ground and those of its inhabitants who survived the slaughter had their ears and noses cut off by the Portuguese and despatched to Ormuz as a sign of the approaching conqueror. Four days later the squadron dropped anchor off Muscat itself. This was a larger, more elegant port, second only to Ormuz as a trade mart for the overseas routes to that area; it faced a horseshoe-shaped harbour sheltered from all winds by cliffs and crags behind. Directly the Portuguese entered, two delegates came aboard and, signifying their willingness to become a vassal of Portugal, begged Albuquerque to spare the city. Albuquerque prevaricated to give his captains a chance to sound around and survey the fortifications. The Arab submission was equally a ploy to gain time for after further negotiations over the following days an army of some 10,000 men arrived from the interior. Immediately the Arab mood changed; they even attacked a Portuguese watering party. Albuquerque responded by sending two of his ships close up to the high, earth-packed rampart that bordered the harbour with orders to bombard, and calling his captains to council, told them he was determined to attack and destroy the town. Asked their opinion the captains replied 'that in a matter so completely agreed upon and determined there was nothing to advise about'.[24] The cryptic reply suggested to Albuquerque that they considered the attack ill-advised!

The solid earth ramparts of the harbour were carried up both sides of the city to the hills behind, and the numbers and confidence of the soldiers within evidently daunted them. However Albuquerque knew that to back down now would be to destroy the moral ascendancy on which he set such store, and he sent them back to their ships to prepare for an assault on the morrow.

The following morning before dawn the drum sounded on the flagship and boats armed with swivels and filled with arquebusiers, cross-bowmen, lancers, sailors and engineers with scaling ladders, pulled across the still water to join Albuquerque and his men at arms. From his ship they made for the harbour ramparts, branching out into two divisions as they went. Met by showers of arrows and stones, they cleared the way with gunfire and cross-bow bolts, set up scaling ladders in the smoke and stormed the wall in two, widely separated places. After fierce mêlées at lancepoint, the Arabs behind scattered; the Portuguese joined forces again inside and stormed through the streets of the town behind the flying soldiers and citizens of all ages and sexes, maddened by blood lust, slaughtering indiscriminately and continuing the pursuit beyond the houses and into the hills above. Later, as the sun climbed and the rocks shimmered with heat, they returned, tacky with sweat and blood and parched with thirst. Albuquerque had defences prepared in case of a counter attack, and then gave the town over to plunder and rape. When an Arab came down from the hills under a flag of truce to beg him not to destroy the buildings, he replied that they might ransom them in gold before noon the following day. Directly the hour had passed he gave orders for the town to be burned, the vessels in the harbour destroyed, and ordered gunners with axes to cut down the supports of the mosque, 'a very large and beautiful edifice, the greater part of timber, finely carved, and the upper part of stucco'.[25] Afterwards it was set alight.

> Now as our people had many Moors, men and women, prisoners,
> whom they did not expect to have any need of and could not carry
> away Albuquerque gave orders that their ears and noses should be cut
> off, and that they should then be liberated.[26]

It would be interesting to know the real number of defenders and attackers to be able to form some idea of the numerical superiority against which the Portuguese guns, arquebuses, cross-bows and armour could triumph on land. The figure of 10,000 for the relieving army was given by Albuquerque's natural son, who hero-worshipped him; it is unlikely to have been more than a coloured guess. However, the *total* complement of Albuquerque's ships amounted to less than five hundred.

Despite their remarkable technological superiority and the successes with which the Lord was endowing them, a spirit of disaffection was already evident among Albuquerque's captains; the lack of enthusiasm for the attack on Muscat had been a symptom. Whether it was because of Albuquerque's autocratic methods, or a fear that he was using them as tools in a mad, personal war against the entire kingdom of Ormuz when they could be taking far easier plunder by patrolling at sea; whether it was the suffocating heat and continuous, glaring rock and sea scapes which made them long for cooler coasts, Albuquerque had to call them together and threaten the leader of discontent with severe penalties. He made it clear that whatever they might say, he was determined to go to Ormuz, first destroying all its tributary ports in order that no enemies should be left behind him.

So the squadron sailed up the coast, receiving the voluntary surrender and vasselage of some towns and villages, storming and sacking others, using the young Arabs they captured as slaves for the heavy work about the ships, hacking off the ears and noses of all who were too old or unfit to work. In Ormuz, meanwhile, an immense fleet and army were being gathered to meet them.

Albuquerque received news of these preparations – which he tried to keep from his captains – but even he must have been astounded by the sight which met them as they rounded the eastern hills of the island at sunrise one morning in late September and came in sight of the splendid anchorage before the city. It was thronged with some 250 craft, many of them small, oared galleys, but 60 of them large vessels, one of some 1,000 tons, far larger than anything in the Portuguese squadron. The whole, immense fleet was decked with flags, and as they approached slowly under the lightest of zephyrs across a burnished sea, they saw that all the vessels were packed with armed men, mostly archers, wearing armour made of overlapping plates; thousands more armed men, many on horses, were crowded along the shore, the sun darted light from lance heads. Horns, trumpets and drums competed with 15,000 voices in a prolonged dissonant greeting as the squadron approached. At a council aboard the flagship, Albuquerque's captains suggested that on this occasion he should listen to advice instead of acting on his own conclusions, since Ormuz appeared very different from the other places they had destroyed.

> As Albuquerque had been many days wearied by their importunities
> he replied that he confessed it was a very serious undertaking, and one
> which required great caution; but as they were now got into the place,
> they wanted a good, determined spirit rather than good advice. So he
> refused to hold any more conversation with them upon the subject,
> but he ordered them to set their larger sails and keep on sounding the
> depth.[27]

All that day they sounded in, coming to anchor in late afternoon on either side of the three largest native ships, which they saw were armed with the usual short Indian Ocean artillery. The Portuguese flagship and larger vessels came to on the seaward side, the smaller vessels on the landward side of the Arab heavy ships; inshore of them were rows of small galleys armed with two short guns at the prow, and piled high with bales of cotton to protect the rowers, and inshore of them smaller rowing boats full of armed men. 'The shouting on land and ships was so great one would think the world had come to an end.'[28] At another council at which they could scarcely hear themselves speak for the din, Albuquerque repeated his determination to fight and asked his captains their opinion on how he should proceed. 'He did not ask if he should do it, but how he should do it.' The captains, seriously alarmed at taking on such a multitude in a confined space without the possibility of manœuvre, advised him to open negotiations first. This was done, and an ambassador came aboard. He was greeted by Albuquerque and his captains in their most splendid dress, seated on plundered carpets draped over benches on the quarterdeck, the ship's company drawn up at arms. Albuquerque immediately assumed the role of conqueror; he had been sent by the King of Portugal, Lord of the Indies, to seek the friendship of the King of Ormuz; if the king were willing to become a vassal of Portugal he would serve him with his fleet against his enemies. 'If he be unwilling, let him know that I will surely destroy all his fleet, and take the city by force of arms.'[29]

The ambassador returned ashore and reported the message, adding that he believed the Portuguese were bragging to hide their fear – certainly true of most of the captains, who immediately took Albuquerque to task for his harsh bearing.

'Gentlemen, I am not the man to achieve so important an affair as this with dissembling and sentiment. I trust in the Passion of Jesus Christ, in whom I place all my confidence to break the spirit of these Moors.'[30]

By now the reputation of the Portuguese was such that the King of Ormuz, a young man in his teens, decided, despite overwhelming preponderance in numbers, to await a fleet and an army on their way to aid him from another part of the kingdom; he responded to Albuquerque's demands by keeping negotiations on the boil with all the arts of Eastern diplomacy. Albuquerque had known from the first that he would have to fight; after three days of prevarication he issued an ultimatum to expire the following dawn, and the next morning before daybreak, had his ships' boats lay out anchors near the largest enemy vessels so that they would be able to warp up close to them. The Arab craft responded by hauling in on their own cables, whereupon Albuquerque sent the flagship's boat with fifty armed men, who succeeded in hooking a grapnel to the stem of the 1,000 tonner. As morning broke with no word from ashore, he had his flagship heaved alongside the great vessel and fired a broadside, the signal for the rest of the squadron to follow his example.

Once in action, his captains lost their fears. The anchorage echoed to the roar of their bombards; smoke drifted slowly across sinking native craft, Arab sailors and archers leaped overboard, armoured men sinking like stones. For a time the action was severe and confused, the Portuguese repelling boat attacks from every quarter with falconets, swivels and arquebuses, while firing into the larger enemy vessels with bombards. As in da Gama's action off the Malabar coast, the balls shattered the light timbers of the native craft, while the Arab guns made no impression on the Portuguese hulls or on the men behind the bulwarks; only the exposed swivel gunners and arquebusiers were wounded by showers of arrows.

After the violence of the initial clash, as the smoke gradually cleared, Albuquerque realised that once again his guns had given him the victory. Everywhere around them native craft were sinking or retiring or being abandoned in confusion; the water was alive with thrashing white cottons. Calling out to his ships' captains to send boats to follow up the victory, Albuquerque clambered into his own skiff and led the assault on those native craft out of range of the ships' guns, and on any swimmers they could catch in the sea. There were stiff fights on the decks of several of the further vessels, but Portuguese firearms prevailed, and the battle ended with Albuquerque's men using their lances as harpoons to spear shoals of swimmers making wildly for the shore. Even the cabin boys and cooks joined in with grapnels, tearing at the bowels of the men in the water; the sea became 'so tinged with blood that it was a fearful thing to look at'.[31]

The victory in the anchorage was followed up by the ships' boats cruising along the shore, destroying all Arab craft they came upon, and bombarding and devastating the suburbs outside the city walls, until eventually a white flag was run up from a tower of the castle. This was followed by a deputation to Albuquerque carrying the king's submission. It was then sunset. The Portuguese had been fighting all day.

Albuquerque was now in quite as delicate a position as before the victory. Although the king and his counsellors were 'much broken down, like people who are conquered and overthrown',[32] according to the Portuguese officers whom he sent to negotiate terms, his own losses were so great that he dared not land a force lest the Arabs guess how few men he had. Moreover, the captains were more determined than ever to end the war and sail for India, and he had lost any faith he may have had in their judgment. He determined to remain on board his ships and put on a brave show, demanding an extravagant tribute from the king, and land on which to build a castle. Both demands were eventually conceded, and after a treaty had been signed he felt it safe to land with his captains and gentlemen to take formal possession for the King of Portugal, a ceremony attended with much pomp, to the thunder of the ships' broadsides. Crowds of natives, many blowing or beating instruments, the rest shouting 'Portugal! Portugal!' preceded the procession, 'and it seemed as if the world would come to an end with their cries'.[33] The splendours of the occasion were somewhat marred by the rise of many bodies to the surface of the bay, and a scramble from the Portuguese ships to strip and loot them of valuables, ornamental daggers and other weapons.

With the treaty behind him, Albuquerque set about constructing the new fortress to maintain the position he had won, using local stone masons and labourers with his own men as overseers. The physical work went well, but he was defeated in the end by the disloyalty of his captains. As the weeks drew out and all hope of catching the northbound traffic for the Red Sea vanished with the change of monsoon, they became openly mutinous and started inciting their petty officers with tales that Albuquerque planned to cheat them out of their shares in the plunder. Albuquerque pleaded with the men, begging them not to ruin the great enterprise on which they were embarked for Portugal, but he was forced to give in to demands for immediate payment of shares in the loot of the coast. Calling his captains together afterwards he lectured them angrily about putting lust for prizes before duty to Portugal, and replaced the leading malcontents. It is remarkable that he appears never to have used capital punishment even under the most severe provocation. Matters had gone too far in any case; the Arabs were well aware of the extreme tension within the Portuguese camp, and it was not long before co-operation was withheld and watering parties from the ships were attacked. Albuquerque responded with another bombardment, followed by a blockade to break resistance by preventing water from reaching the city. This was the last straw for his captains; three deserted, sailing their ships to India, where they laid complaints about his insatiable appetite for an altogether fruitless war before Almeida; the complaints coincided exactly with the Governor's own views.

With only three vessels left, all short-handed, Albuquerque was forced to leave Ormuz with the castle unfinished. He sailed back to relieve the garrison on Socotra, and was deserted on the way by yet another captain, losing with him the ship carrying the supplies intended for the garrison. Arriving at Socotra he found the men at their last gasp, sustaining themselves on palm leaves and wild fruit, and he had to send his one remaining consort to Malindi for fresh provisions. He himself took the flagship to lie in wait for the traffic expected from India on the north-east monsoon; he sighted just four vessels and caught one small dhow with little merchandise. Meanwhile the captain he had sent for provisions was also cruising after prizes on his own account, and it was only the arrival of two ships fresh out of Portugal that prevented disaster to the Socotra base.

There can be no doubt that despite the astonishing victory at Ormuz, Albuquerque's first campaign was quite as profitless as his captains alleged. Whether the support of those same captains would have allowed him to complete enough of the fortress and leave enough men to hold it is an open question; so is any consideration of whether it was his own autocratic habit or the avarice and indiscipline of his captains that caused the break up of the squadron. Discipline was not a quality that distinguished the Portuguese, officers or men at the time; they were wildly individualistic, seeking personal reputation before everything. Their successes were not due to better order than their enemies; their failures were all marked by fearful indiscipline.

After wintering and refitting at Socotra, Albuquerque took his few ships back to Ormuz to complete the work begun the previous year. He found that Almeida had expressly repudiated all his actions, and that reinforcements of Persian archers, reputedly among the best soldiers in the world, were arriving to protect the island city and take it under the Persian wing. Immediately he was drawn in to more desperately fought land actions to prevent them crossing from the mainland, and although he succeeded in routing them, it was at heavy cost. His position was made worse by storms which scattered the squadron and damaged his already deteriorating ships; they had no protection at all against the ravages of the worm of those waters. Finally he sailed for India without having accomplished anything more; this was in 1509, and he presented Almeida with his secret instructions to succeed as Governor of India. Almeida had him thrust into a cell in the fortress of Cananore. Had he died during his months of confinement in this noisome prison it is unlikely that he would be remembered today – certainly not as the first great oceanic strategist – a criticism not of the man so much as of the divided Portuguese aims in the Indian Ocean.

The most significant event of 1508, while Albuquerque had been attempting what was surely impossible with his small resources, was the first Portuguese defeat at sea. This occurred in the mouth of the River Chaul just south of Diu on the north-west coast of India. The great fleet of galleys which the Sultan of Egypt had been constructing to the best Mediterranean pattern to throw the interlopers out of the Indian Ocean, had at last been completed and had sailed for India under Hussain al-Kurdi. The plan was to combine with a fleet of local craft provided by the Muslim Sultan of Gujerat, to await the departure of the homeward-bound Portuguese fleet on the north-east monsoon, and then sail down the Malabar coast, join forces with the *Zamorin* of Calicut and destroy all the Portuguese factories. The fleets had combined at Diu and were about to start out when news came of the arrival of some Portuguese ships at Chaul. Hussain put to sea and caught them at anchor in the river.

The Portuguese squadron, which had arrived quite fortuitously on a routine patrol against Arab, or any other kind of shipping not licensed by Almeida, consisted of three ships and five caravels under the command of Almeida's son, Lorenzo. Probably the young Lorenzo could have forced his way down the river and escaped by night on the ebb tide as his captains advised; the odds were probably not so much greater than those over which Albuquerque had triumphed, and Hussain could not bring his full force to bear because of the narrowness of the channel. Almeida, however, decided to fight – perhaps because he believed that flight would compromise Portuguese moral superiority, perhaps because he had been criticised by his father for failure to press an attack on Calicut earlier, perhaps simply because he thought he could win. Whatever the reasons, the Portuguese squadron remained in the river, repelling wave after wave of galleys and small craft with their broadsides and fire arms for the best part of three days, succumbing only when the men were so weary they could no longer load fast enough to keep out repeated attackers from every direction. The final scene on the deck of the flagship was a fitting climax to epic resistance; Almeida, his leg broken, had himself tied to the mainmast to keep himself upright, and continued to shout encouragement to his surviving men, who formed a ring around him as the enemy scrambled over the bulwarks from all sides. No quarter was expected. After the Portuguese behaviour else-where in the Indian Ocean no quarter was sought; death fighting was preferable by far to being taken prisoner.

Only two of the caravels escaped from Chaul. As for the Muslim fleet the exact numbers are not known, nor are the casualties in men or galleys, so again it is difficult to assess the point at which Portuguese technical superiority could be neutralised by sheer numbers. Nor is it possible to explain why it turned out that the Portuguese defeat at Chaul had the same eventual result as a victory. Hussain returned to Diu, no doubt to refit his damaged ships and replace the considerable numbers of men he must have lost during the three days' battle, but he never sailed from the port again. Whether this was because he had been so impressed by the Portuguese defence that he had no stomach for it, or whether there were other more political or logistic reasons is not altogether clear. The fleet of magnificent galleys of Dalmatian oak and pine, mounting Turkish bronze guns, lay gathering weed during the whole of the north-east monsoon season, and their crews and fighting men dispersed. When Almeida himself arrived in the spring of 1509 to avenge his son's death, he was able to sail into the harbour and board and burn every vessel with scarcely a fight. This annihila-tion of the grand Sultan's fleet at Diu marked the end of the last serious attempt to turn the Portuguese out of the Indian Ocean by local naval force. Perhaps it was simply a postscript to Chaul; perhaps the younger Almeida's defeat had been the real turning point.

Albuquerque was released from prison in October 1509 when a fleet under command of his nephew arrived from Portugal with confirmation of his appointment as Captain General and Governor of India. Almeida de-parted, and the next five years during which Albuquerque's genius was allowed free reign, saw the framework of the Portuguese eastern empire established.

His first task was to chastise Calicut once again. But his long-term aims remained the establishment of strong advanced naval bases at the mouths of the Red Sea and the Persian Gulf, both to control these key funnels and to prevent Muslim warships from entering the Indian Ocean; 'the best way is to seek them there and not let them get out and set foot in India where for a certainty they would command the assistance of the Moors against us.'[34] Accordingly he sailed in February 1510 with a fleet of twenty-three vessels and some 2,000 men, intending to call at Socotra, then enter the Red Sea and seek out a new fleet which the Sultan of Egypt was reported to be assembling. However, he was still on the Indian coast when he fell in with a pirate chief named Timoja and learnt from him that some Moors who had escaped from the destruction at Diu had gone south to Goa – some three hundred miles north of Cochin – starting there the construction of another fleet with which to throw the Portuguese out of the Indian Ocean 'so that the spices would go again to Mecca and Cairo as they used to in the old days'[35] – a remark which is testimony to Almeida's policy of continuous naval patrol. Timoja, who hoped to gain the lordship of Goa for himself (as a reward for assisting the Portuguese), told Albuquerque that there was dissatisfaction and strife within the city since the death of its Rajah; now was the ideal time to take it. He went so far as to promise that the Portuguese would only need to anchor in the river for the keys of the fortress to be handed up to them. Albuquerque debated a long time, but finally could not resist the opportunity. He sailed back down the coast to Goa with Timoja's forces, and after a successful joint attack on one of the forts commanding the river entrance, anchored within. Everything went much as Timoja had forecast and by the beginning of March the divided city was in Portuguese hands with scarcely another shot fired.

Goa was an island surrounded by river, marsh and salt-water lagoons. There were several shallows which could be waded at low tide, but these were guarded by strong towers – also, it was said, by alligators that had acquired a taste for human flesh, for it was the custom to feed them with prisoners of war. Besides forming a splendid moat, the river provided the city with a deep, sheltered anchorage; there was a flourishing ship-building industry on its banks, and it was the principal harbour for the region, and the terminus of trade routes from the interior, in short an almost ideal base for a sea power, marred only by an unhealthy climate and an exposed bar at the river mouth which was impassable in the early months of the south-west monsoon. These disadvantages were outweighed by Goa's natural defences, and Albuquerque immediately set about strengthening the fortifications and building granaries and great storehouses for rice, intending to use it as the victualling base for the Malabar coast factories as well as the principal refitting and refreshment port for the fleets.

While this work was going on he attempted to open negotiations with the Shah of Persia for an alliance against the Sultan of Egypt, suggesting that the combination of Portuguese fleets and artillery by sea with Persian cavalry by land would enable the Shah to gain the 'lordship of Cairo and all its kingdoms and dependencies'. He titled himself:

Affonso D'Albuquerque, Captain General and Governor of India, on behalf of the very high and very powerful King Dom Emanuel, King of Portugal and of the Algarves on this side and on that side of the sea, in Africa Lord of Guinea, and of the conquest, navigation and commerce of Aethiopia, Arabia, Persia and India, and of the Kingdom and Lordship of Goa, and of the Kingdom and Lordship of Ormuz.[36]

Here in one letter is the essence of what may be called 'sea power diplomacy', its principles, first prestige – gained by the mastery by numerically insignificant forces of a rather useless element, the sea, and second – the offer of this unique control to tip the military/territorial balance in the area. Alas for Albuquerque's grand ideas! His emissary was poisoned in the island city of Ormuz over which he claimed lordship, and he and all his force was expelled from Goa by the return of the son of its former ruler, who forded the river with troops while the Portuguese were destroying rafts he had constructed in another place. Once again the precariousness of any Portuguese land base was exposed. Having retreated to the ships they were forced to remain in the river between artillery fire from the forts and the bar which was lashed by the south-west monsoon. Their water and provisions ran out and only night raids ashore for cattle and fresh produce kept them from starvation before, in mid-August, they finally escaped over the bar, decimated by scurvy, dysentery and fever.

Albuquerque was not the man to accept such a defeat. Portuguese prestige, and with it their whole position on the coast, was at stake; with the arrival of a fresh fleet from home he sailed for Goa again in November. This time, although the ruler was away again on campaign, the city was defended by numerous mercenaries, including cavalry, and the Portuguese were met with the severest resistance they had encountered yet, 'so well fought was it indeed on one side and the other, that for a long space of time each side thought that it had gained the victory'.[37] Eventually the fortress commanding the town was taken by storm and the defenders fled. Portuguese losses are given as 150 killed and wounded against 2,000 of the enemy killed, a disparity which can only be accounted for by the superiority of their firearms and heavy armour over the arrows of the enemy.

After the victory, the city was given over to plunder and rape in the customary way, and Albuquerque gave orders that all Moors were to be put to the sword:

men, women and children . . . for his determination was to leave no seed of this race throughout the whole of the island . . . for four days continually they poured out the blood of the Moors who were found therein; and it was ascertained that of men women and children, the number exceeded 6,000.[38]

The second capture of Goa had tremendous moral effect; the great Sultan of Gujerat offered the Portuguese a site for a fortress in the port of Diu, Albuquerque's original choice for an Indian base, the *Zamorin* of Calicut sent an embassy to congratulate him on his victory and offer him a site for a fortress in Calicut, and the Sultan of Egypt, when brought the news by one of his commanders, apparently gave up all hope of defeating the Portuguese, and stopped work on a second great fleet under construction at Suez; there were other reasons for this decision, but Goa and the collapse of the Gujerat alliance were clinching arguments. Meanwhile Albuquerque, who intended to make the city his seat of government in India, once again set about strengthening its fortifications and completing the great storehouses, using stones from the mosques for the purpose. And realising that the shortage of manpower must be a continuing weakness of the Portuguese empire he encouraged his men to marry the daughters of principal Hindus and distributed land and property among the couples to give them a good start. He also sent out patrols to divert all sea trade away from the neighbouring ports and into Goa with the intention of making it the chief mart on the coast.

After establishing the city as an impregnable fortress, he had intended to resume his voyage to the Red Sea, but the affair took so long that the favourable north-east monsoon was ending by the time he sailed. He made for Malacca instead. This was the principal *entrepôt* for the spice trade in Indonesia. Commanding the narrow straits which formed the shortest and most convenient route between the Indian Ocean and China seas – being, as it were, at the end of the monsoon routes of both these areas – it was also a principal market for all the luxury goods of the East. Muslim merchants had been attracted here as early as the thirteenth century, and it had long been a Muslim Sultanate similar to others bordering the Indian Ocean, settled with merchant communities of various nationalities, principally Arab and Gujerati; it was the most prosperous and populous of them all, wealthier even than Ormuz. The Portuguese, also naturally attracted there as soon as they reached the Indian Ocean, thought it the first city in the world. The Muslim merchants resented their arrival – and in view of Portuguese activities in the Indian Ocean they had very good reason to fear it – and they persuaded the Sultan to attack the interlopers ashore. Several Portuguese were killed, several captured and held prisoner. It was to avenge this 'treacherous' attack that Albuquerque directed his course there. There can be little doubt, however, that he would have been drawn to the conquest of this focus of Indonesian spices at some time.

Albuquerque's fleet of eighteen sail arrived in the roads in early summer 1511 with banners flying, trumpets sounding, bombards firing blank, in the customary manner, and the customary round of dissimulation that passed for negotiations began while both sides weighed up the strength and determination of the other. Albuquerque would not conclude peace until the Portuguese prisoners had been released, the Sultan would not release them until peace had been concluded! Albuquerque allowed this to continue for five days while his ships were put into fighting order, then he started destroying Gujerati ships and some houses along the shore. The Sultan released the prisoners but by now – and almost certainly from the first – Albuquerque was determined to add the Sultanate to the Portuguese strategic system.

It is the headquarters of all the spices which the Moors carry every year hence to the Straits without our being able to prevent them. But if we deprive them of this ancient market, there does not remain for them a single port, nor a single situation so commodious in the whole of these parts, where they can carry on their trade in these things. For after we were in possession of the pepper of Malabar never more did any reach Cairo except that which the Moors carried thither from these parts, and forty or fifty ships which sail hence every year laden with all sorts of spices bound for Mecca cannot be stored without great expense and large fleets, which must necessarily cruise about continually in the offing of Cape Comorin. I hold it very certain that if we take this trade of Malacca away out of their hands Cairo and Mecca are entirely ruined and no spices will be conveyed to Venice except that which her merchants go and buy in Portugal.[39]

The city was built on both sides of a river. The Portuguese plan of attack was to take and hold the bridge which joined these two halves, thus splitting the forces within, which they had been warned numbered over 2,000 fighting men, well provided with artillery and matchlock firearms, although their principal missile weapons were arrows and poisoned darts fired from blowtubes. Albuquerque's men-at-arms could not have numbered more than some 1,500, but he was confident that the power of God was greater than that of the Sultan of Malacca and after awaiting a favourable saint's day, launched the attack with ship's boats manned and armed as usual. After hard fighting during which the Portuguese lost some seventy wounded who subsequently died from the poisoned tips of the native weapons, they gained the bridge, but repeated counter-attacks by the Sultan's men led by elephants of war, together with lack of shelter, difficulties of supply up the river between enemy-held banks, intense heat and sheer exhaustion defeated them in the end; reluctantly Albuquerque withdrew to the ships. It was not until several days later when he had prepared a junk with artillery, gunpowder, grenades and provisions to act as a mobile strongpoint, and floated it down to the bridge at high tide that the Portuguese were able to maintain themselves between the two halves of the city. The fleet and the boats supported landing parties with a continuous bombardment, and after several days of sortie and devastation, the Sultan fled. With him all organised resistance collapsed.

The customary slaughter of Muslims followed, after which Albuquerque set about constructing a fortress in his usual mode, using local slave labour, and stone from the mosques and 'sepulchres of bygone Kings' as the foundation materials. The fortress was built to command the anchorage, and so close to the water that it could be provisioned at high tide by ships alongside. He appointed a captain for the garrison with powers as governor of the city and to command a squadron of eighteen vessels he intended to leave to maintain Portuguese supremacy in the area. At the change of monsoon he sailed back for India with the remaining four ships.

In India he was greeted on the one hand with news that Goa was under siege and in desperate straits, and on the other with complaints from King Manoel about the great expense and unhealthiness of the place. Albuquerque replied to the king that its capture had done more for the Portuguese influence in the East than all the fleets that had gone out, and 'as for the extraordinary expenses of which these idle fellows write to Your Highness, the mere dross of India is so great that if the Portuguese possessions be properly farmed by your officers the revenue from them alone would suffice to repay a great part of these.'[40] With the arrival of fifteen fresh ships from home, he set out to relieve his seat of government.

He raised the siege, reinforced the defences, and early in 1513 sailed at last on the mission to the Red Sea which had been his chief preoccupation since becoming Governor of India. The Socotra base which he had established with da Cunha, had proved unsatisfactory because of its distance from the Straits, and he had orders from the king to take Aden instead; this port was far better placed to command the narrows of Bab el Mandeb which lead into the Red Sea, and enjoyed a naturally strong defensive position entirely surrounded on the land side by a range of high peaks. It was a thriving *entrepôt* for Indian and African trade, the southern terminus of Arabian caravan routes, and as populous as Lisbon itself. The Portuguese campaign in the Indian Ocean had actually enhanced its prosperity as dhows attempted to evade the Portuguese patrols by sailing at the wrong season and discharging their cargoes at Aden instead of continuing up the Red Sea to their usual ports of transhipment for Egypt and Syria. It is not surprising that when Albuquerque arrived there at the end of March the city looked flourishing and very strong. The harbour front was bounded by a continuous, high masonry wall with towers at intervals, and this was carried up to the encircling jagged hills, each of which was surmounted by a tower flying a banner. Flat-roofed houses packed within shimmered in the heat.

Albuquerque wasted less time than usual on negotiations before attacking, and it seems certain that he neglected a proper survey of all approaches. Whether this was because his previous string of successes had made him over-confident, or whether it was because of a warning from his pilots that the prevailing easterly winds would not allow him back once he got to the westwards is not clear. The attack was launched in the usual way in armed boats before dawn on 25 March and the whole force was concentrated on the single gate in the harbour wall – apart from a small party sent up the hills outside one side wall. Things began to go wrong almost at once: the boats grounded outside effective range, and the men in their heavy armour had to scramble forward as best they could, slipping down or between rocks, the arquebusiers soaking their powder so that the volleys which normally opened the way for assault literally misfired. The gate proved to be walled up on the inside, and because of the shallow water approaches no guns could be brought up close enough to make a breach. Special scaling ladders which had been constructed aboard the ships to allow six to mount abreast began to collapse under the weight of armoured men rushing up without order. When halberdiers were instructed to support the one remaining ladder from beneath, it broke, despite their efforts and many were wounded or crushed. Thus, although several Portuguese succeeded in gaining the top of the wall and forcing their way in to one of the towers, they could not be reinforced, and eventually had to retire before an overwhelming concentration of missiles and fire and smoke weapons. About midday Albuquerque remarked philosophically that the hour of Aden was not yet come, and ordered a withdrawal.

As both Portuguese and Arabic accounts ascribe the result to the Deity, it is again not possible to form an estimate of the point at which sheer numbers could overcome the superiority of Portuguese arms and armour; it seems certain that Albuquerque had some 2,000 men with him for the assault, and on previous form this ought to have been ample. Perhaps the inability to force a breach in the high wall, and the failure of the scaling ladders are sufficient to explain this, Albuquerque's only permanent defeat. Also the plan of attack was hasty and ill-prepared, unlike his earlier, more deliberate campaigns, and he did not stay to make a second attempt on the town or blockade it into submission, probably because of shortage of water in the fleet. Also he was anxious to press on into the Red Sea before the favourable easterlies failed in order to seek out the new fleet of the Egyptian Sultan. This is what he did, becoming the first Portuguese commander to pass through the Straits of Bab el Mandeb. To mark the occasion the ships were dressed over all and quantities of gunpowder expended on salutes.

It is an indication of Albuquerque's roving mind that while in the Red Sea he played about with ideas for transporting workmen to Ethiopia to cut a new bed for the Nile to divert it from Egypt, and so desolate 'the land of Cairo', and another for an overland expedition to sack Mecca and 'carry off the body of the false Prophet'. In fact it was too late in the season to penetrate far, and after experiencing variable winds the expedition returned, having achieved nothing – but they took some brief satisfaction from destroying merchant shipping in Aden harbour before setting course for India.

There Albuquerque at last settled the affairs of Calicut by conspiring with the *Zamorin's* brother to poison the *Zamorin*, whose offer of a site for a Portuguese fortress had come to nothing. The brother succeeded and immediately granted the Portuguese the shore site they required. As usual Albuquerque had the fortress constructed with a gate looking to seawards through which it could be supplied by boat.

His last campaign in 1515 was a similar but far more delicate operation in Ormuz, where the young king whom he had defeated so many years back had been toppled by a usurper backed by Persian forces. His handling of this situation showed that whatever the cause of his failure at Aden, it was not due to failing powers. The subtlety of his diplomacy and the cunning with which he first had the usurper assassinated to put the former king under obligation to himself, then persuaded him that all the guns in the palace should be removed to the fortress which he had started on his previous visit, show the touch of a master, and make a tale worthy of *The Arabian Nights*. When he left Ormuz in November that year the island was firmly under Portuguese control with a puppet king pitifully anxious to seek Portuguese advice on every matter.

By that time Albuquerque was a sick man. He died on the voyage back to India, not however before intercepting letters from home which revealed that his enemies had found favour with the king, and a new governor had been sent out to succeed him, together with new captains of the fortresses in place of his own appointees, and that his policy of acquiring advanced bases had been rejected. It was a bitter blow. He took it as philosophically as his defeats in battle, only writing to the king to ask that his natural son should be ennobled as a reward for his own services to Portugal. 'And as for the affairs of India, I say nothing, for they will speak for themselves and for me.'[41]

An English naval captain visited Ormuz 350 years later:

I found immense water tanks, with fresh water in them in plenty. They were in perfect repair, and with their arched and groined roofs supported on heavy pillars appeared like the crypts of some great cathedral. From the tower of the fort we had a good view of the surrounding plain, and could well trace the marks of splendour which was gone. Out into the sea on both sides of the peninsula which the fort terminated ran the foundations of old warehouses, streets and squares as far as the eye could stretch inland, even to where the red and white pinnacles of the mountains closed the view and the plain together. . . . The round watchtower stood out in sad loneliness, and further away the ruins of the Cathedral of Santa Lucia seemed to try to bear it company.[42]

With Albuquerque's death the first storm of Portuguese conquest came to an end. He had attained three out of the four fortress bases which he had come to believe essential for Portuguese control, Ormuz, Goa, Malacca, besides the string of tributary ports and fortress factories down the Malabar coast of India, the Muscat coast of Arabia and the east coast of Africa from Sofala to Mombasa and Malindi; only Aden had defeated him; affairs in India and the East and the seasonal change of monsoons had prevented him spending sufficient time there. Perhaps this failure was as important for the long-term success of the Portuguese in the Indian Ocean as his most important achievement in founding Goa, for Aden and the Red Sea route acted as a safety valve through which spices continued to reach the Middle East, and the area settled again into a kind of balance, which would have been impossible, perhaps, had his plans for a total Portuguese monopoly been realised. Albuquerque was criticised in his time and has been since for raising costly and isolated hostages to fortune all over the Indian seas; Aden would have been the most costly and isolated of all, for it was closest to the Muslim seat of power, while the Red Sea was, in terms of reliable winds, as far away from Portuguese reach as China. Albuquerque's successor, Lope Soárez d'Albergaria, followed his track into the Red Sea in 1517 to strike at an Egyptian fleet concentrating at Jiddah, the port for Mecca, but he was unable to prevail against the shore defences and galleys combined, and was forced to withdraw. The Red Sea remained firmly in the Muslim sphere, and Aden itself was eventually taken in 1538 by a force of Ottoman Turks after that empire had advanced southwards making Syria, Iraq and Egypt tributary to the Sultan at Constantinople.

With the powerful Turkish presence in the Red Sea and Indian Ocean, the Portuguese had to make the alliance with Persia that Albuquerque had aimed for; in so doing they opened another leak in the spice monopoly (via the Persian Gulf) so that before mid-fifteenth century both the old spice routes to the Middle East were working again just as they had before da Gama's appearance. In the 1560s Portuguese spies estimated that some 30–40,000 *quintals* (roughly, a quintal is equal to one hundredweight) of spices were passing through Alexandria alone;[43] adding the quantities coming through the Syrian ports, it appears that the ancient spice routes had recaptured the advantage for the annual quantities sent around the Cape to Lisbon were probably no more than 25–40,000 *quintals*. Venice, which in the early days of Portuguese disruption of all the traditional routes, had sent buyers to Lisbon, was back as the major European buyer in the Levant, and was taking more than she had the previous century. By the 1580s the Portuguese share of spices had declined further, and the Levant/Venetian route dominated the trade.

The Portuguese were always over-stretched in the Indian Ocean; Albuquerque's grand strategic vision was not the reason, which had more to do with the success of their novel weapons of naval warfare – novel to the

Indian Ocean – hence their overweening confidence and grasping ambition; combined with the extremely small population of the home base – probably never more than one and a half millions – they naturally overreached themselves. In the 1530s they began seriously colonising the coast of Brazil which Cabral had claimed, establishing their most lasting source of wealth in sugar and the slave trade on a vast scale. They also sent out great fishing fleets to Nova Scotia, where seasonal colonies were established to fish the Grand Banks; their Gulf of Guinea factories and baracoons prospered, not only in the trade to South America, but supplying ever-increasing numbers of slaves to the Caribbean and Spanish American colonies. In the East, they pushed Albuquerque's boundaries wider by settling bases in the spice islands themselves, and entered the China trade, eventually gaining a base in Macao after first disgracing themselves by plunder and pillage in the established tradition. They also built factories along the coast of Ceylon. None of this extraordinary spread can be blamed on Albuquerque; his plans were an early symptom of it all, but they actually laid the foundations without which it would have been a very much flimsier structure.

In fact the Portuguese eastern empire was far more widely spread than its geographical extent implies; because of the monsoon system its extremities were separated by seasons rather than miles of ocean. The Malacca fortress and squadrons came under constant attack from local coalitions mounting vast fleets and armies, and was often close to disaster before relieving forces could reach the area. Goa, the centre of the whole system, was out of action for one-third of the year, and when it was at its peak of activity as a naval base in the north-east monsoon, could not be reached from the African coast bases. None of these extraordinary disabilities was Albuquerque's doing, but it was largely due to them that there was seldom a period when some Portuguese establishment somewhere was not under dangerous local concentration, and had to be reinforced directly the monsoon changed. It was this diversion of resources from trade control, especially when it occurred, as it often did around Malacca and the spice islands, that caused Lisbon merchants to suffer as much as Levantine merchants in the days of Portuguese disruption.

Equally important as an explanation of the Portuguese failure to maintain their monopoly in spices was their trade system. Unlike the Venetians, who fitted out State fleets but auctioned the ships to merchants who bought as cheaply as they could and generally acted within the disciplines of the market, the Portuguese kept spices and other important commodities as a Crown monopoly and sought to keep prices high, using the profit to pay for their eastern empire. Thus prices at Lisbon and Antwerp – where they established their market for north Europe – were generally higher than prices in the Levant. More important, Portuguese colonial servants, who were always underpaid, had no commercial incentives; put another way it was a system that encouraged colonial administrators to become traders on their own account; the eastern empire became a byword for venality, and it was here that the major leaks in the spice monopoly occurred. As early as 1524 Vasco da Gama, ennobled as the Count of Vidiguiera, was sent out as Viceroy to stamp out abuses and restore the king's fortunes. In marked contrast to his first arrival on the Indian coast as a barbarian whose gifts were scorned, he came in great state, served by men bearing silver maces followed by pages with gold neckchains and a retinue of equerries and finely dressed body servants, guarded by 200 liveried soldiers with gilt pikes. 'He was a very disdainful man.'[44]

> He was very zealous for the King's revenue, he used to say that men came to India poor and enriched themselves, and he was very ill-disposed towards those of the King's officers who were rich . . . he ordered it to be proclaimed that no one should navigate without licence, under pain of death and loss of property and those who owned ships should make contracts and shipments with Kings Factors.[45]

He died in India on Christmas Eve 1524 before his attempted reforms could have any effect. But however many similar Viceroys the king may have found, the temptations and potential loopholes and vast distances of the Eastern system were too great for any reformers. Men went to the East in search of riches, and the colonial empire which had been formed to seize a monopoly in spices changed gradually into one which flourished by controlling and taxing and taking part in all the most lucrative trades of the area, including spices to Mecca! It became very much a hybrid empire, dependent on the fleets and fresh blood sent out by the Portuguese Crown each year, yet driven by local, commercial forces and grasping for personal riches. Although the Portuguese were lords of Malacca and the spice islands, hence with a hand on the throat of Venice (as one early Portuguese account put it) the grip was removed as the fingers dipped into the profits to be made in the Eastern system.[46] Venice ended the sixteenth century as she had ended the fifteenth, queen of spices.

CHAPTER 3

THE MEDITERRANEAN CENTRE

While Albuquerque was laying the foundations of Portuguese power in the East, the Spanish successors to Columbus were colonising the large islands of the Caribbean, and exploring mainland central America. In 1513 Balboa pushed across the Panama isthmus and sighted the Pacific. In the following decade Magellan sailed into the Pacific around South America and, more important, there began that series of overland marches and conquests by a few adventurers in search of gold that was to establish Spanish dominion over Mexico, the isthmus and most of South America except for Portuguese Brazil. Like the Portuguese conquests the movement owed its success primarily to gunpowder arms and the exploitation of local rivalries. It was accompanied by similarly repellant atrocities. In other respects it was very different. The most advanced civilisations the Spanish overthrew were technically far behind the peoples the Portuguese came up against and it was a land, not a naval or trade conquest; the empire won was territorial with capitals mostly far inland (apart from the Caribbean) and it was settled by men who were given a stake in the land – for which they were required to share in the defence of the colony. The sea, far from being the reason and basis of their existence became for most Spanish Americans nothing more than a distant highway over which they imported European wares and exported their own surplus.

In the first quarter of the sixteenth century this trade was not of great value; the gold obtained mainly by panning and plunder was less than the Portuguese had from their Guinea establishments, and the hides, dye-woods, cochineal, sugar and tobacco sent home by planters, while important to the merchants of Seville, was not sufficient to over-stimulate the greed of sea rovers; the first interlopers were Portuguese traders with negro slaves from west Africa whom the colonists needed to replace the natives that were dying under their system of forced labour. Probably the most dangerous area West Indian fleets had to sail was around the Azores on the homeward route, for there pirates and privateers lay in wait for returning Portuguese spice fleets as well; it was off the Azores that the first real treasure haul was made in 1523 by a fleet of privateers from Dieppe who cut out several galleons carrying Cortez's loot from the palace of Montezuma. This opened many eyes to prospects on the Spanish 'Main', and the second quarter of the century saw the beginnings of that harassment of Spanish shipping and possessions in the Caribbean that was to make the area notorious for centuries. Most of these were rovers from the French Biscay and Channel ports. In 1537 the same house of Ango of Dieppe, whose privateers had taken much of Montezuma's treasure, devised what is perhaps the first of those large-scale plans to capture the annual treasure fleet from the isthmus that were to recur time and again in the calculations of pirates and statesmen. They succeeded in taking nine of the fleet with much bullion. By this time silver was being mined in Spanish America, but it was not until midcentury after the discovery of immensely rich fields in Peru (1545) and Mexico (1546) that the value of the silver consignments took off, displacing gold as the most important part of the treasure and becoming in the imagination of Europe – bankers, statesmen and sea rovers alike – the chief sinews of Spanish strength, and as one history of the Caribbean succinctly puts it, 'the focus of envy'.[1]

Before that happened, and before the Portuguese sugar plantations in Brazil also 'took off' rather later in the century, the Mediterranean remained the centre of the world, and the spectacularly wealthy and cultured Italian city states remained the centre of the Mediterranean. Braudel defines the focal point of the world economy at this time as 'a narrow urban quadrilateral, Venice, Milan, Genoa, Florence'.[2] It was to this trading and financial heart that the new nation states, Spain, France and Ottoman Turkey, were drawn. These extensive territorial powers were – like the oceanic expansion of Portugal and Spain – the product of gunpowder weapons, principally siege artillery which enabled armies of the territorial centre to break down distant bases of resistance. Each of the three new nation states had a different speciality: the Ottoman Turks, whose fighting strength was in light cavalry and archers had developed cast, bronze, siege pieces to spectacular size; the French had taken developments in the opposite direction and produced the lightest, most mobile artillery suitable for use in the field; Spanish strength lay in the fire of mass arquebusiers.

The three powers pressed in from north, east and west on the Italian centre, in the process acquiring major ports – Constantinople for Ottoman Turkey, Marseilles for France, Barcelona for Spain – hence some of the compulsions of commercial and naval power, which they could back with greater resources than the individual city states. The result was a remarkable increase in the size of the major war fleets, which could not be matched by the two former naval powers, Venice and Genoa, and at the same time a turmoil of changing alliances between groups of city states and between them and the rival nation states which were encroaching on their independence. Genoa, which had been investing in Spain and Portugal throughout the previous century, ended up firmly in the Spanish orbit in 1528, bringing with her the most sophisticated financial institutions and relationships as well as a powerful galley fleet under the most experienced sailor of fortune, Andrea Doria. As Spain had acquired with Barcelona a sea empire comprising the Balearic Islands, Sicily and Naples, with galley squadrons based on these colonies, she became undoubted mistress of the western Mediterranean. She had also acquired by dynastic marriage the Netherlands, Austria, Hungary, Milan and most of Lombardy as well as leadership of the loose confederation of Germanic States known as the Holy Roman Empire (the Empire). More accurately, Spain had been acquired, for it was the Habsburg Maximilian of Austria whose flair for marriage policy had brought about the union of these amazingly separated territories, and it was the Habsburg Charles (V of Spain) who inherited them in 1516, knowing nothing of Spain, unable even to speak the language. However, Spain became his power base, and it was from here that he attempted conscientiously to weave the broadening silver thread from the 'New World' into the diverse strands of his inheritance. He was the first modern Emperor of the West. Genoa, which had lost much of her independence, became the financial capital of the West, whose financiers supported governments with loans and speculated in gold and silver and foreign exchange.

Venice, on the other hand, retained her independence, but gradually lost her power. The most recent historian of the Republic sees the turning point in 1503, when she made naval base concessions for peace with Turkey in order to devote herself to the new power balance brought about by the rivalry of France and Spain in Italy;[3] as a result she became caught up and bled in territorial struggles. This turn towards the land, away from the sea, was not made without fierce, internal argument; it was contrary to the policy of centuries, and for this reason may be regarded as a necessity rather than a simple mistake in priorities, especially as the same sudden switch from a habitual 'blue water' policy was made by later sea powers confronted with similarly ominous continental developments. In any case she lost to the Ottoman Empire the greater part of her chain of seaside fortresses in Greece and the Aegean. This Turkish presence at the very gates of the Adriatic, the gulf she had considered her own for centuries, was followed by the Ottoman conquest of Syria (1516) and Egypt (1517), so that the entire Levant trade had to be conducted through ports of the Ottoman Empire. Of necessity then she had to keep on good terms with Constantinople – despite the fact that Turkish expansion at sea was the greatest danger to her remaining island colonies and naval bases. As she could not hope to match the resources that the Ottoman Empire could direct into fleet building, her diplomacy veered between concessions to Turkey and alliance with the naval powers of the western Mediterranean, principally Spain. Her situation was complicated by the sharp religious division across the area; she was in the Christian camp, nominally committed to the Holy War against the Infidel, and her galley squadrons were at the very front line of resistance to the Islamic Ottoman advance in the eastern Mediterranean, yet the Ottomans were her essential partners in trade! It was a consummate balancing act.

Had the issue been decided entirely in the Mediterranean, Venice must have become tributary to one or other of the great empires at either end of the sea. But these were of course hybrids – basically territorial states that had acquired sea power – and a large share of their resources went on territorial campaigns. Spain in the west was engaged in a continuous struggle with France; Spain in Austria-Hungary was engaged in the same struggle with France, but also with Ottoman Turkey pressing up from the Balkans along the Danube; Ottoman Turkey was also engaged with Persia on her eastern borders, and mounted attacks on the Portuguese in the Indian Ocean from her Red Sea and South Arabian bases. Spain was similarly harassed overseas by French assaults on her Caribbean islands and 'treasure fleets'. Consequently neither of the two great naval powers in the Mediterranean could ever put forth full strength in the area for any length of time, and Venice as incomparably the strongest naval power of the second rank played the balances with skill and success, using largely mercenary troops in Italy, and maintaining a huge reserve fleet in addition to her active squadrons. In the early sixteenth century the reserve was fixed at fifty galleys; by the 1540s it had risen to the astonishing figure of one hundred, a quarter of which were supposed to be fitted out and ready for sea at short notice. The increase was due chiefly to a heightening of the Mediterranean naval struggle as a new naval power grew up on the Berber (Barbary) coast of north Africa under the leadership of the redoubtable Barbarossa, or Kheir ed Din.

Barbarossa, meaning 'Red Beard', was a nickname held by two brothers in succession. They came from the Greek island of Lesbos, taken by the Turks in 1462, and were the sons of a soldier who had been settled on the island as a reward for services in the Ottoman armies – whether he was a Turk himself is doubtful – and an island woman said to be the widow of a priest; the brothers were brought up as Moslems. They probably went to sea young, which is to say that they became pirates, since trade and piracy were mixed as opportunity offered in every sea, particularly in the politically contested eastern basin of the Mediterranean; certainly Aruj, the eldest, was captured at sea by a galley of the Christian Knights of St John, and subsequently served as a slave at the oars until released, probably by ransom. Little more is known of his early career or that of his younger brother, Khizr – the future Kheir ed Din. At some time after 1500 both appeared at Tunis as owners or perhaps shareholders in two galleots – little more than long, open boats with perhaps fifteen benches of oarsmen. This was a time when the Moors, expelled from Granada by Ferdinand and Isabella, were taking their revenge by piracy on Christian shipping from bases along the north African coast; it was ideal pirate territory with sheltered lagoons and harbours and reef-strewn channels, well placed along the flank of western shipping routes, and Tunis itself was ideally situated off the narrow strait connecting the eastern and western basins of the Mediterranean below Sicily. Its Sultan sheltered corsairs in return for ten or twenty per cent of the plunder. It was here that the brothers brought their first rich prizes at about the time, 1505, that Spanish records begin to mention Moorish corsairs off Sicily. Nerve, tactical sense, cunning, total ruthlessness, together with gifts from the goddess of fortune brought them quick success; within six years they were men of property and owners of a corsair fleet of eight galleots.

By this time Ferdinand of Spain had reacted to the Barbary menace by naval blockade and assault on the principal strongholds; he had taken Mers el Kebir, Oran, Mostaganem, Ténès, Algiers, Velez, Bougie, and was constructing a powerful fortress on an island just off the entrance to Algiers harbour to exact tribute. His Italian campaigns deflected him from continuing the work and establishing himself in strength along the whole coastline, however, and pirate squadrons continued their operations, particularly around Tunis. By 1510 Aruj and Khizr had prospered sufficiently to set up their own independent base, and they moved south to the island of Djerba. Other corsair leaders, many of them Christian renegades, were attracted to their flag, and over the following years expeditions went out every spring to ravage not only the shipping, but the ports and coastal provinces of Sicily and Italy. 'Barbarossa' and the names of his principal captains became synonyms for terror throughout the western Mediterranean, and among sailors of the Atlantic nations who ventured through the Straits of Gibraltar. Capture meant an oar bench, or the slave markets of the Ottoman Empire.

Within a few years the brothers felt strong enough to attempt the Spanish-held section of the Algerian coast nearer to the rich shipping lanes of the West, and after making two unsuccessful attacks on Bougie, settled in 1514 for the nearby harbour of Jijil (Djidjelli), some 150 miles east of the Spanish stronghold at Algiers. Two years later Ferdinand of Spain died; the inhabitants of Algiers marked the occasion by inviting a local Berber Sheikh, Selim ed Teumi, to relieve them of their Spanish oppressors. Selim was eager to oblige, but lacked the naval force or artillery to overcome the fort at the harbour entrance, and he called on the corsairs at Jijil to fill the gap. It was the chance the brothers had been waiting for; sending a force of sixteen galleots with artillery along the coast under Khizr, Aruj marched overland with a force of 5,000, mostly local Moors stiffened with a core of his own Turks. Before joining Selim, he invited another corsair chief called Hassan, lord of the neighbouring port of Shershell, to help with the reduction of the fortress. When Hassan came to discuss the proposition Aruj killed him. Sheikh Selim suffered the same fate soon after they joined forces inside Algiers – some versions have it that he was strangled with a towel while bathing by Aruj himself. The brothers were now in control of the port, and although the light guns of the galleots failed to reduce the Spanish fortress offshore, Aruj had himself proclaimed Sultan of Algiers.

That was in 1516, the same year that the Ottoman Sultan, Selim I, conquered Syria; Turkish power was expanding simultaneously along the eastern and the south-western shores of the Mediterranean, and there is little doubt that the new Sultan of Algiers corresponded with Constantinople. It was no planned Islamic advance though; in both cases it was Islamic Turks – also Greeks and renegades – against their brothers in the Prophet; in both cases it was a strike at trading riches rather than against Christendom; what was happening here, as in the Indian Ocean, was that new forces equipped with gunpowder weapons were taking over the older Islamic position at the centre of the board, where local sheikhs and sultans had not adapted sufficiently to the new modes of warfare. It is notable that it was arquebusiers who formed the core of the force with which Aruj, the new Sultan of Algiers, expanded his dominions westwards in 1517, taking the port of Ténès from an Arab who had raised the country against him as the new oppressor, and pursuing the routed forces to the inland trading post of Tlemcem, which he also made his own and fortified. It was near Tlemcem that a Spanish expedition sent to retrieve their now tenuous hold on the coast, caught his force in the open in 1518. Aruj, to his great credit, stayed to fight alongside his own men, although he might have escaped, and he was killed. But for the second time the Spaniards failed to follow up the opportunity to rid the whole coast of corsairs; the legend and awe of the name Barbarossa, and his Algerian dominions were allowed to pass to the younger brother.

The second Barbarossa, Khizr, had auburn, not red, hair. He was a well-set-up man, 'portly and majestic' with a great bushy beard and remarkably heavy eyebrows and long lashes. To Moslems he was Kheir ed Din, 'Protector of the Faith'. He proved quite as cunning and ruthless as Aruj, and after surviving a Spanish assault in the following year, which was actually defeated by a violent summer storm destroying the expeditionary fleet, he extended and consolidated his hold along the Algerian coast, finally in 1530 taking the Spanish fort of Algiers with the aid of huge siege pieces sent from Constantinople. By then he ruled an independent power, the terror of the Mediterranean. It was about this time that the battle for the central sea began in earnest, and he was called to Constantinople by the Sultan, now Suleiman 'the Magnificent', to reform the Ottoman fleet and become its High Admiral. In the next forty years, up to the climax of the struggle at Lepanto, the naval forces employed in the Mediterranean increased at least threefold.

The conventional Mediterranean warship was still the galley, a sharp, low craft with a waterline length of something over 130 feet, eight times the beam and a draft of only four and a half feet. Instead of the ram of classical times a metal-shod spur to scatter opposing oars and act as a boarding ramp extended from dead flat forward lines of the hull; aft there was a sweet rise in the sheerline up to the poop where the commander, officers and nobles took their station under elegant canopies. A rectangular rowing frame extending some two feet over each side was mounted above the hull with groups of thole pins for the oars arranged in three along it; this was known as an *alla sensile* or 'simple' arrangement whereby three men on each rowing bench each worked his own individual oar; the oars varied in length from twenty-six to over thirty feet according to the rower's position. The benches, twenty-four a side on a standard galley, were set at a slight angle, and sloped up towards the centre line for the convenience of the oarsmen; the two sides were separated by a central, raised gangway or *corsier* running from bows to poop. In rowing, the men rose from their bench, placed one foot towards the bench in front of them and stretched as far forward – in fact towards the stern – as they could before dipping the blade in the water; then they fell back on the bench, using weight, thigh and body muscles in the pull. It has been estimated that the maximum speed that could have been obtained under oars was about seven knots in short bursts of not more than twenty minutes;[4] the best sustained speed was not more than four knots, and cruising speed probably under three. However, they were rigged with a large lateen sail from a single mast about one-third of the length from the bow, and could sail considerably faster with a fair wind than their maximum speed under oars.

It follows from this that galleys were little use in open ocean conditions where gales could overset their narrow hulls, a heavy swell could swamp them, where tidal streams and currents might run as fast as the oarsmen could propel the craft in a normal watch, and where regular trade winds gave the advantage to specialised sailing craft. They were certainly no use for long ocean passages as the combination of massed rowers and fighting men (over 200 all told) and narrow hulls meant that they could not be provisioned and watered for more than a twenty-day cruise; within a fortnight at sea the need to water dictated the course. It is not surprising that galleys were not developed on any oceanic seaboard except briefly and experimentally. In enclosed seas where winds were variable and calms frequent, tides and currents light or non-existent, and where shelter, water and food could be readily obtained at convenient intervals galleys were in many respects better suited than the cumbersome oceanic sailing vessels – evidently for they survived thousands of years, and continued to survive the 'oceanic' age in the Mediterranean, Baltic, Red Sea, Persian Gulf, Black Sea and various lakes and island groups.

Their two chief functions were the transport of armies and siege artillery, and the attack and defence of trade; the two were more often than not interrelated, since the galley's very short endurance made both trade attack and defence dependent on bases along the trade routes. Mediterranean naval warfare, therefore, was largely concerned with attack and defence of the seaside fortresses which protected the bases, and galleys were used as assault landing craft rather more than as warships to fight other warships. When they did fight a naval battle it was nearly always as the result of a siege campaign for an important naval base.

There were, nevertheless, variations between the different national craft due to differences in strategic roles. Ottoman galleys were built for offence against trade and bases, hence were lighter and swifter than Spanish and other Western galleys which were built for trade defence; the few Algerine galleys were also light, but the corsairs preferred the smaller and even swifter galleots. Venetian galleys seem to have been swifter still under oars, although not under sail; as the Ottoman navy was revitalised under Kheir ed Din, they became heavier and were fitted with a platform raised some five feet above the bows, extending the width of the hull, which was built up with light bulwarks before battle to act as a redoubt for massed arquebus and cross-bow men; this was in line with prior Spanish and Western practice generally. Ottoman galleys had a light protection around the poop but no similar redoubt at the bows, again suggesting that their role was attack on trade and amphibious assault rather than battle with other galleys. Another vital difference contributing to these variations in weight and speed was that most Algerine and Ottoman galleys employed paid, or conscript, oarsmen who were a part of the fighting complement, whereas most Spanish and Western galleys employed convicts or slaves, each with one leg chained, who took no part in fighting; consequently they had to carry more soldiers. The Venetians also employed paid, professional oarsmen, carrying in addition a select corps of arquebusiers chosen for their performance at a shooting range. However as the size of warfleets and individual galleys increased towards the climax of the 1570s, all states were driven to greater use of slave and convict oarsmen, and this dilution of skill and willingness led to a different system of rowing; three, four or even five men sat at a bench and pulled the same huge oar. These are generalised comments; there were, in fact, differences in each of the fleets between commanders with different preferences, and there was much debate and experiment especially in the matter of increasing speed as size and weight were forced upwards in the heightening struggle; there was also much debate about whether slave or free oarsmen had the balance of advantage. So far as hygiene went, slave-driven galleys were noxious; the men were chained to their rowing positions and never allowed from it; the bottom boards and bilges became foul; and, like the later slaving vessels of the Atlantic, slave-driven galleys could be smelled several miles downwind.

A battle between galley fleets remained, as it had always been, a soldier's battle on the water. The object was to disorganise the opponents with missile weapons in the final stages of the approach just before closing, and as the vessels came together to feed as many men as possible aboard the enemy to overcome them in hand-to-hand combat. The sides and spread oars were the most vulnerable parts of galleys, hence the attack was always head on. The opposing fleets approached one another in disciplined fleet line abreast, each usually formed of three squadrons whose vessels followed the movements of their flagship (capitana) in the centre of each; the capitanas took their directions from the Commander-in-Chief at the centre of the centre squadron, who made his wishes known by flag and sail signals, and by despatching small, oared 'fregatine' from which verbal orders were shouted. Behind the front line, whose wings were often advanced or retarded deliberately to form a crescent to attempt or defend a flank attack, there was usually a small reserve squadron whose duty was to go to the aid of hard-pressed sections of the front after battle was joined; they fed in their troops over the sterns of the embattled galleys. This system had evolved and been brought to a peak of disciplined perfection over thousands of years; there were no tactical surprises to be achieved, only advantages of position, wind or numbers.

The chief advantage a commander could gain was to mass greater numbers than the enemy, thus allowing an attack on the vulnerable flanks; if this could be achieved in the open sea, victory was practically certain and annihilation probable. However an outnumbered fleet would not stay for a set-piece battle if it could be avoided; a favourite defensive posture was to pass a stout hawser from galley to galley to prevent the enemy breaking through the line and backing oars to beach sternfirst, then landing men and guns to protect the flanks. But the best defensive posture was inside a naval base where the mobile galleys and fixed fortress guns sealed the approaches and defended each other. As the latest study makes clear,[5] Mediterranean naval warfare was based on the intimate mutual dependence of galleys and seaside fortresses, both for offence and defence, and the possibilities of a campaign were determined by the galley fleets' endurance; since they were so heavily manned and could only carry substantial provisions in accompanying sailing ships, which usually found it impossible to conform to the galleys' movements, and since there were few ports with the facilities for large-scale provisioning, the radius of action declined as fleet size increased. All the rules of the game were well established and well known to all commanders; nevertheless strategic surprise could be achieved as there were always a number of important targets within effective range. Also as naval campaigns were limited by the weather to the spring and summer months it was possible to achieve surprise by an early start; the more centralised Ottoman navy nearly always moved off before the Spanish and Western fleets – probably due in part to more favourable spring weather conditions in the eastern Mediterranean.

As for weapons, these were soldiers' weapons with the same national specialities as in the armies ashore. First in point of delivery, though not importance, were guns – by now cast bronze cannon types as well as the earlier, built-up wrought iron pieces. The new guns were cast as one, hence had to be loaded through the muzzle, but they were more powerful because larger charges could be used. A heavy piece, throwing anything from a 30-pound up to a 50-pound cast ball, was mounted on the centreline just behind the short forward deck (usually on a box carriage that slid back along a trough below deck level in recoil). In the 1530s this was flanked by some four, light breechloading swivels mounted atop stout vertical posts. The heavy, Spanish and Western galleys also carried a pair of medium, cast guns, perhaps 9-pound or even 18-pounders, one on either side of the heavy piece. As galleys grew in size the armament increased so that by the 1570s Spanish galleys – always in the van with heavy batteries – mounted two medium pieces on either side of the central cannon at deck level, and numerous light swivels on posts from the raised fighting platform above. It can be seen why they were slower than Ottoman and Venetian craft. Ottoman galleys, like Ottoman armies, tended to rely on one monster stone-throwing piece with perhaps a few medium or light guns; in any case they lacked the raised fighting platform for the secondary battery. Venice developed a compromise between the two, but acquired the most formidable reputation for accuracy; it was said that their gunners could hit another galley at 500 yards. It is impossible to believe that this kind of shooting was anything but a once-in-a-thousand chance for the bores of early cannon were not accurately cast; moreover to reach 500 yards the pieces would have had to be elevated some five degrees, and unless the range was correct to fifty feet or less the ball would have passed over the low hull or failed to reach it. And, it is difficult to believe that ricochet shooting would have been effective at such a range. Perhaps these long shots were attempted when in chase of Turkish raiders, but in a set-piece fleet or squadronal action the batteries would not have been fired until so close that it was almost impossible to miss, fifty yards, or less. Here we come to a decided tactical consideration; the dense smoke from the guns would quickly clear from a fleet to windward, but drift down and temporarily blind the men of the fleet to leeward in the vital moments before contact.

After the artillery, it was the turn of the arquebusiers, cross-bowmen and archers. Here there were equally great national differences. Spanish and Western galleys relied on matchlocks and cross-bows in about equal proportions in the 1530s, but firearms gained rapidly until they all but ousted crossbows in the 1540s. The Turks also used firearms, but clung on much longer – and with good reason – to the composite long-bow for which their armies were famous; this was a weapon of formidable accuracy with a much faster rate of fire than cross-bow or arquebus, and able to penetrate any armour at fifty yards. It was no doubt the devastating sustained flights of arrows from this weapon that caused the adoption of protected redoubts over the bows of Western and Venetian galleys; the oarsmen had some protection from leather shields hung along the sides. The barrage of arquebus pellets, bolts and arrows during the final burst of speed preceding the collision of the fleets was followed on impact by hurled ballast stones, grenades, fireballs discharged from short wooden tubes (*trombe*), quicklime to blind, blazing tar, liquid soap and oil to make the opponent's decks slippery, sharp, star-shaped metals to pierce feet, while the air was rent with awful cries to inspire terror. Then it was the boarders with lance and half-pike for thrusting, halbert, sword and scimitar for hacking, shield for parrying; free oarsmen, wearing breastplates and helmets took up weapons from below their benches and joined in the swaying mêlée. In Ottoman-Venetian clashes, no quarter was given.

While galley warfare was much as it had always been since long before gunpowder weapons, which merely increased the shock of impact, the galley itself was no longer supreme at sea. Guns had devalued it as a type, by conferring advantages on sailing vessels, whose sides, unencumbered by oars, could mount far more powerful batteries and numerous light swivels. Galleys with their light hulls and massed ranks of exposed oarsmen could not approach a well-handled, gunned, sailing ship without being fearfully mauled and often sunk. They could not themselves mount equal batteries without interfering with the propulsion unit – massed oarsmen – nor could they add thick protective timbers like a sailing ship's sides without becoming heavy and sluggish under oars; in short, musclepower was inelastic; it could only be increased by adding men, which meant a further increase in size and weight of vessel, further overcrowding, and an increased drain on provisions. Sailing ships were not caught in this cycle of diminishing return. The larger they were, the more canvas they could spread, the more power they could take from the free wind, and the more guns they could mount; moreover the power unit did not interfere with the batteries, nor require more men, and all hands except the swivel gunners and a few sail-handlers perhaps were protected by the massy sides. Galleys were as powerless against them as the Indian Ocean dhows against the Portuguese caravels.

All the maritime powers of the Mediterranean had large, heavily gunned sailing vessels by this time. Genoa seems to have started the trend to great size for merchant vessels in the fifteenth century – it has been said because of opportunities provided by three- and four-masted rig – square sails on fore and main, lateen on mizen and bonaventure mizen – but it is more likely that the changes in rig distinguishing what is known as the 'carrack' were the result of a drive for increased size. In some cases this was for military advantage, in Genoa's case it was for economy in the long-distance, bulk-carrying trades to which she turned her attention after being driven from the eastern Mediterranean. It is probably significant that the striking increases in size took place as bombards and breech-loading swivels were becoming more numerous and giving the advantage to defence. Certainly Genoese carracks of the last half of the fifteenth century were the largest vessels seen until then in the Mediterranean – between 500 and 1,000 tons (with some monsters up to 2,000 tons) and illustrations of the type show massed swivels all along the rails. The Venetians, while specialising in heavy, merchant galleys for their high-value liner trades, also built large carracks, some of more than 1,000 tons. These were armed with batteries of guns and used in conjunction with galleys in naval battles against the Turks as early as 1499. By this time huge carracks were being built in every maritime state in Europe, from England in the north, and Portugal in the west, to the Mediterranean powers; in addition to broadsides of mixed bombards and the new cast cannon, some of immense size, these great ships mounted literally hundreds of light swivels in tiers along the rails of towering castles at bow and stern.

By the 1530s even the Knights of St John based on the island of Malta had one of these great vessels as their flagship. This had no less than eight decks including the castles, and was said to carry provisions for six months at sea. She was so heavily timbered she was believed unsinkable and was sheathed with six tiers of metal, those underwater being lead with bronze screws – antedating British Admiralty copper sheathing by two and a half centuries. She antedated British Admiralty victualling by a longer period, having her own bakeries aboard providing 'excellent white bread'! She mounted some fifty heavy guns and the usual tiers of massed swivels in the castles; she also carried a fifteen-bench galleot on deck with other ship's boats and towed another astern. 'But what crowned all was that the enormous vessel was of incomparable swiftness and agility, and that its sails were astonishingly manageable.'[6]

In 1535 this prodigious war machine – whose merits may have been exaggerated in the handing down – was responsible for breaching the walls of the fortress of Goletta in Tunis Bay, making possible its capture and the subsequent capture of Tunis itself by Charles V of Spain. This is an indication that great ships were not simply defensive castles, but had an important offensive role in the Mediterranean system.

They could not, however, overcome galleys if the galleys held off upwind or in shallow water, nor because of the fickleness of Mediterranean winds could they guarantee arrival in such good time as galleys might make with the help of oars, hence they were not true 'capital' ships. They existed in a separate system alongside the galley fleets, often impinging, but never obtaining that superiority which naval historians define as command at sea. It has been argued that this 'stalemate' period between the old and the new type of warship was caused by lack of sufficient guns – several squadrons of galleys could be armed with the guns of each great carrack – and that it was the increased availability of guns later in the century, together with shortages of manpower and provisions, which they consumed in such quantity that doomed the galley. It is more likely that it was the decline of the whole Mediterranean area in relation to the new Atlantic economies that doomed the galley to a subsidiary role, for of course, it survived in its own special conditions down to the age of steam. A contributary factor, probably, was the improved sailing and handling characteristics of the galleon developed out of the carrack by the Atlantic nations.

Certainly it was not simple conservatism that prevented the sailing war-ship from being adopted in place of galleys in the Mediterranean. Venetian admirals had experimented with combined great ship and galley fleets since at least 1499, attempting to draw Ottoman galleys against the broadsides of a line of carracks and nefs ahead of their own galley formation; they failed because the Ottoman commanders were not fools, and the different handling qualities of great ships and galleys made it impossible to combine the two types with sufficient precision to form the desired order *and* catch the enemy fleet.

The Venetians had rather more success with a hybrid broadside-sailing galley called the *galleassa* (galleass). This was a direct conversion of the merchant or 'great galley', which had served so well as cargo liner in the fifteenth century. It was over 150 feet in the hull, longer than any but the largest admiral's galleys (*reals*) with a length/beam ratio of 1 to 6 instead of 1 to 8. There were capacious holds beneath the rowing deck, and stern castles rising three decks above. It had two or three masts, the largest for-ward, all were lateen rigged. The rowing frame was wider and heavier than that of a galley, and built up with a bulwark giving protection for bow-men, or later, swivel gunners between each group of oars. As a merchant-man the oars were worked on the same trireme *alla sensile* system as galleys, but when converted numerous experiments were held with four, even five oars to a bench to try and give it a better speed. About mid-century the new style of rowing with one single oar manned by a complete bench of oarsmen was adopted; the benches were long enough for five oarsmen, but it is doubtful if they were usually manned by this number; in any case the galleass remained sluggish and clumsy compared with the traditional 'light' war galley. Its advantage was in the heavy batteries it mounted in bow and stern and the swivels ranged along the whole broadside. Once again it proved difficult to co-ordinate galleys and galleasses in fleet movements because of their differing speeds and handling, but there were some suc-cesses, notably at Lepanto. In the open ocean its compromises doomed it, for it had neither the heavy broadside nor the sailing performance of the Atlantic warship nor the mobility of the galley. However, its combination of qualities suited certain Mediterranean conditions, for it survived in Venetian fleets and was copied by other Mediterranean powers. It did not survive as a merchantman – no doubt because of the compromises that made it ineffective on the ocean. The last of the famous Venetian convoys to Flanders sailed in 1533, and the Levant voyages ended in 1564; carracks took over the carriage of spices.

It can be seen that behind the centuries-old tactics and rules of strategy governing pure galley fleets and trade war, the great gun had wrought a ferment of change and innovation.

The struggle for the Mediterranean was never a simple matter of Christianity against Islam; it was more of a struggle between the two great empires of Spain and Turkey counterpointed by the feud between Spain and France and the extraordinary alternating hostility and mutual dependence of Turkey and Venice. When the two conflicts coincided and France joined with Turkey against Spain, or Spain joined with Venice against Turkey, the alliances were never satisfactory because each partner had different objectives; it was no part of Charles V's plan to smash Turkish naval power so decisively that Venice would become undisputed master of the eastern Mediterranean, nor was it Venice's idea to assist Charles to gain control of all Italy by helping him against his French rivals or the Algerine corsairs who interfered with his lines of communication. In short, the two halves of the sea each supported its own system of trade rivalry and conquest, and the powers of the other half, together with small independent squadrons from the Knights of St John, the Papal States of central Italy, the Princes of Savoy, Tuscany and Monaco, were called in by subsidy and diplomacy to tilt or redress the balance when it was threatened.

What complicates the naval struggle further, making it unintelligible on occasions, were the underlying commercial motives of the Western commanders. A large part of the Spanish fleet was not built or maintained by the Emperor, Charles V, or by his successor, Philip II. It was hired from independent, or quasi-independent, mercenary commanders who owned and operated their own squadrons. These commanders, and to a lesser extent their officers and crews, combined private trade with their contractual fighting duties – and of course piracy. Free oarsmen were allowed to carry their trade wares beneath the rowing benches, officers were allowed larger chests of private ventures, while the commanders themselves seem to have speculated in galley- or even ship-loads of cargo, which they were naturally at pains to protect. Besides cumbering the decks, hampering the speed, even diverting the course of different sections of the 'Spanish' fleet, these commercial ventures also affected commanders' enthusiasms for fleet actions which might result in loss or damage to the galleys representing their capital! Not surprisingly there was often more shadow-fighting and intrigue than all-out warfare.

The best-known example of a mercenary commander whose actions cannot all be explained in terms of naval strategy or tactics was Charles V's 'Captain General of the Sea', Andrea Doria. He was a Genoese noble and patriot – introducing further complications in terms of the centuries-old rivalry of Genoa and Venice. An experienced soldier of fortune he had commanded many of Genoa's independent expeditions against Tunis and the Barbary corsairs before entering the service of Spain. The terms of his first contracts of 1528 and 1529 and those of his successor Gian Andrea Doria, brilliantly analysed in Guilmartin's study of galley warfare,[7] indicate the essential commercial basis of their operations. They were paid a fixed sum per galley per month, which worked out at slightly above the cost of a similarly operated Spanish galley. In addition an interest at 14 per cent was paid on arrears, a significant provision indicating that the Dorias expected to finance their own operations while the Spanish Crown scraped together the money to pay them; it was a capitalistic, entrepreneurial venture. This is underlined by the concessions their contracts entitled them to, the most important of which were the export of precious metals from Spain, 'a remarkable clause in view of Spain's preoccupation with preventing the outward flow of bullion',[8] and freedom from taxes on the purchase of Sicilian wheat; this last was estimated to cost the Spanish Crown 9,000 ducats in 1571, one and a half times Doria's official salary. No doubt his own profit was many times greater than this.

The first clash between the reformed Ottoman fleet commanded by Kheir ed Din and a Christian coalition commanded by Andrea Doria illustrates the complexity of the Mediterranean trade/warfare system.

It was preceded by rising waves of violence in which both great empires at either end of the sea carried the war into their opponent's domain. This was partly a result of the unbalancing effect of the growth of Kheir ed Din's power and his ambitions to extend it to Tunisia, partly the result of the ambitions of Suleiman the Magnificent in Austria-Hungary. To take the pressure off Hungary in 1532 Charles V despatched Andrea Doria to ravage the Turkish outposts in Grecian waters, a task which the sixty-six-year-old Captain General undertook with enthusiasm and great success. It was the next year that Kheir ed Din was called to Constantinople to reform the Ottoman fleet, hitherto regarded chiefly as a mobile pontoon for Ottoman armies – the typical product of a territorial power. He overhauled the dockyards at Constantinople with ruthless energy, appointed his own, experienced, commanders and sailed the following summer with a transformed fleet that was to make the Ottoman navy as feared as his own corsairs had been. He struck first at Reggio in the Straits of Messina, taking the town and enslaving the inhabitants. Then he sailed up the Italian west coast, bypassed Naples and ravaged the coastal towns of the Papal States, lying some time watering off the mouth of the Tiber itself. Then, despatching the slaves and captured treasure to his master at Constantinople, he turned southwards and fell on the unsuspecting city of Tunis, whose Sultan fled as soon as the sails appeared. Now master of the whole of the most strategically important section of the north African coast flanking Spanish communications with Italy and Sicily, he sent the Ottoman galleys back to Constantinople and started building a new fortress on the island of Goletta, which commanded Tunis harbour.

Charles V responded in 1535 with a huge expedition collected from Spain,

Genoa, Naples, Sicily and the Knights of St John at Malta. This was the occasion on which their great flagship's batteries breached the walls of the new fortress on Goletta. Tunis fell soon afterwards, aided by the revolt of no less than 12,000 Christian slaves within. Kheir ed Din, who had provided against disaster by moving his corsair galleots to the port of Bone, was warned of the preparations, it is said, by Charles's inveterate rival, François I of France and he made his escape. The city meanwhile was given over to an insensate extended orgy of rape and looting by its 'Christian' deliverers, after which Charles V reinstated the former sultan as a Spanish vassal.

Had the Christian expedition pursued Kheir ed Din with determination instead of being allowed to indulge animal lust at the expense of the unfortunate Tunisians, or had it attacked and taken his Algerian strongholds, it is possible that Mediterranean history would have been given a different twist. This was Spain's third missed opportunity to fulfil what one authority has called her geographic destiny on the north African coast. As it was, Kheir ed Din, apparently against the counsel of his captains, made an immediate counterstroke with his corsair galleots against the Spanish Balearic Islands. He took Port Mahon in Minorca, destroyed the defences of this great natural harbour and carried off some 6,000 Christians to slavery.

The following autumn, 1535, Kheir ed Din sailed for Constantinople, probably to offer his services to the sultan in return for a fleet and artillery to recapture Tunis, probably also to suggest an arrangement with France to further that campaign and his general anti-Spanish designs in the western Mediterranean; in fact François I – whose Gasconades included 'The Monarchy of Christendom shall rest under the banner of France, as it was wont'[9] – had allied himself with Suleiman a decade before during an earlier Ottoman push into Hungary, and was already negotiating with the Grand Turk for trading rights in the Levant. These were granted that same year, together with the essential guarantees for the safety of French traders and property in the area; in return Turkish fleets were granted the use of French ports, principally Marseilles. But the Tunisian expedition – if this was indeed suggested by Kheir ed Din – did not come off. Suleiman had more pressing naval needs nearer home. The Venetians had been retaking their former Greek and Ionian bases, even indulging in piracy against Ottoman vessels, and in 1536 Andrea Doria, too, swept into the Ionian Sea, capturing a small Turkish squadron and enslaving its crew. In 1537, therefore, Kheir ed Din was despatched at the head of a huge fleet of well over one hundred sail of galleys and galleots for Brindisi on the heel of Italy; the intention was to take the port and in concert with a Turkish army marching overland for embarkation in Albania, sail and ravage up Italy. The attack on Brindisi failed, and the joint campaign was transferred to the Venetian stronghold of Corfu on the opposite side of the strait leading into the Adriatic. This, too, failed after a siege lasting until the autumn, but Kheir ed Din took his revenge by ravaging the lesser Venetian bases in the Ionian and Aegean, returning in triumph to Constantinople with '400,000 pieces of gold, 1,000 girls and 1,500 youths' among the spoils.

Encouraged by the profits, Suleiman sent him out again in 1538 with a similarly huge fleet of perhaps 150 galleys and galleots. Again he ravaged through the Aegean, demanding tribute or men for the oars from the islands sacked in the previous campaign, ravaging others that had escaped before as he worked his way down towards Crete, whose capital, Candia, was a major Venetian base for the Levant trade. Meanwhile the size and aggressive strategy of the new Ottoman navy had induced Venice, Spain and the Papal States to come together in a Holy League to restore the naval position; none of them alone could muster such numbers. Overall command of the League fleet was given to Charles V's Captain General of the Sea, Andrea Doria. Kheir ed Din heard of the concentration that was taking place while he was coasting along Crete sacking and taking men from the villages and he accepted the challenge, heading north-westerly to meet his old enemy.

Andrea Doria's moves and motives in the subsequent campaign are hung with large questions. He maintained to the commanders of the other contingents that he had secret orders from Charles V; he was probably referring to instructions not to fight unless certain of victory. But was there more to it than this? It must be remembered that Venice was not only the traditional trade rival and bitter enemy of Genoa, but was the ally of Charles V's continental enemy, François I, who had negotiated a trade treaty with the Ottoman Empire the previous year. And Venice herself was in the Ottoman trading sphere. There was thus every political reason for Charles and every commercial reason for Andrea Doria, the Genoese entrepreneur, to see Venice humbled. Their only real interest in the Holy League was to prevent Turkish naval power spilling over into the western Mediterranean again, where the Algerian and French naval bases provided a formidable axis across all the Spanish/Italian lines of communication. Charles was also concerned in his role as Holy Roman Emperor to keep in good favour with the Pope (the Lutheran struggles had begun in Germany) and also to divert the Ottoman territorial attention from the 'Empire'. On the other hand a question arises over his and his Captain General's relations with the Grand Turk. Not only was Doria negotiating on his behalf with Kheir ed Din during the campaign, but recent studies have pointed to the curious fact that the sole remaining Genoese possession in the Aegean, the island of Chios close to the Turkish shore off the Gulf of Smyrna, was never threatened by Ottoman forces during Doria's lifetime.[10] The suggestion is that he struck some bargain with Suleiman to preserve it for Genoa.

The truth of the whole affair was probably buried with the protagonists, and interpretation of the only campaign in which the two greatest admirals of the day met in fleet action will remain speculative. There is no doubt that Doria was extraordinarily dilatory about bringing his squadron to the fleet rendezvous at Corfu. The Venetian squadron was there first; the Papal squadron joined in the middle of June, but it was not until 7 September that Doria appeared with his Spanish and Genoese galleys! Then he insisted on waiting for a force of some fifty sailing vessels (with Imperial soldiers and artillery) which did not arrive until the 22 September; finally he was forced to wait for a favourable wind. When at last a northerly started to blow on 25 September, he had three weeks at the most before the expected break in the weather which would mark the end of the campaigning season. These are hardly the actions of a commander eager to defeat the enemy in decisive battle!

Yet if he did have some arrangement with Kheir ed Din, the latter failed to take full advantage of it. Having ravaged his way up the Ionian to the Gulf of Arta, a deep inlet in the coast of Greece some fifty miles south of the Venetian and Papal ships at Corfu, he took up a defensive position inside the narrow, winding entrance which was commanded by the guns of the Turkish-held fortress of Prevesa; there he waited for Doria. This was playing the game by the rules. He could not threaten Corfu because of the Venetian and Papal squadrons also defensively arranged and almost equal to his own in strength, nor could he safely bypass Corfu and ravage Italy or the Adriatic lest he find a superior concentration across his route home when Doria finally joined. Whatever the purpose of Doria's negotiations and delays, the effect seems to have been to produce stalemate, certainly so far as Italy and the western Mediterranean was concerned, while the Ionian and Aegean had undergone another frightful summer of terror. In this light it is possible to see the campaign of Prevesa, always held as a tactical victory for Kheir ed Din, as a brilliant strategic coup for Doria, an admiral of Machiavellian subtlety. If Venetian suspicion and anger are any guide this is as good an interpretation as any.

The great allied fleet of some 130 full-sized galleys (fifty-five of which were Venetian) together with at least seventy-five Venetian and Imperial sailing ships of varying sizes loaded with troops and guns, arrived off the entrance of the Gulf of Arta and came to anchor in the lee of Prevesa Point on the 25 September. They could no more hope to go across the bar and up the tortuously shoaled channel under the guns of the fortress into the semi-circle of Turkish galleys across the entrance than the Turkish craft could thread their way out into the midst of the allied, broadside sailing ships and heavier galleys. The key to the situation lay on land. If the allies could take the fort of Prevesa they would be in a strong position, able to beach their galleys before the weather broke, sink blockships in the channel and trap the Turks inside the Gulf. If they failed to take the fort they would be forced to abandon the position for lack of water and provisions if they were not actually destroyed by storm as so many Western armadas had been on the north African coast. It was late September, as the experienced Mediterranean sailor Ernle Bradford puts it in his study of the battle, 'a period when

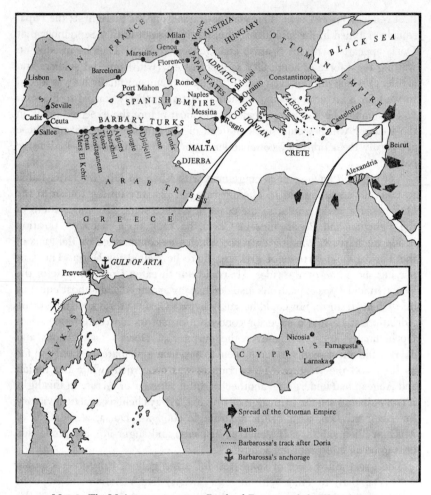

Map 2: The Mediterranean centre, Battle of Prevesa and the War of Cyprus

the Mediterranean is notoriously unstable. This is the month when the calm conditions of summer break down in gales, violent electric storms and dangerous local phenomena like waterspouts.'[11]

Both sides naturally realised the crucial importance of Prevesa itself, and both Commanders-in-Chief were urged in council to land troops and guns, Doria to lay siege to the fort, Kheir ed Din to establish lines along the shore to prevent the Christians from landing siege guns. Western accounts suggest that Doria overruled all opinion to land, arguing that if the fleet were caught by one of the north-westerly gales likely at the time of year, the troops ashore would be left unsupported and at the mercy of the Turks. If this was his reason, why had he waited so long for the troopships in the first place? An Ottoman account suggests that the allied galleys did attempt to land siege forces near the fortress on 26 September and were repulsed. There was certainly a movement of Turkish troops along the neck of land south of the fortress on that day and a long-range, partial galley action off the Prevesa narrows, but no major land engagement took place. That same night Doria decided to weigh and sail south, probably to seek the shelter of the island of Levkas and draw Kheir ed Din out from his strong, defensive position. Yet the defensive position could have been turned into a trap, and the suspicion remains that if it had been the Algerian coast, he would have landed in strength to lay siege to the fort, sheltering his galleys afterwards. He was in fact obeying his instructions from Charles not to risk the fleet except for certain victory; gales were a far greater risk than the Ottoman galleys.

Once Kheir ed Din realised on the morning of the 27 September that the allied fleet had departed and was steering south and would not be able to put back against the light, northerly wind that was blowing, he lost no time in putting to sea himself in chase. Meanwhile the allied sailing vessels, which had widely varying characteristics, became strung out along the iron-bound coast of Levkas; the allied galleys were ahead of them, and thus to the south, with some ten miles between them and the rearmost sailing ships. The Turkish fleet, which kept close to the shore at first, in case they might need to take up a defensive position sterns to the beach, caught up with the stragglers about sunset (according to some accounts) and began to engage. Other accounts have the engagement starting the following morning after the wind had gone round into the south. In any case, the main bodies of the galley fleets never came to grips and the principal action was in calms or in light airs between the Turkish galleys and the Imperial sailing ships to the north of the allied galleys; the highlight was the defence of the Venetian sailing flagship, a great galleon like that of the Knights of St John, sheathed with metal and mounting heavy batteries. This vessel seems to have become the focus of the Turkish attack. She lay scarcely moving, her mainmast cut down by an early shot, holding her fire until the enemy approached so close the gunners could not miss, then discharging a horizontal barrage whose balls ricocheted over the calm water, leaping and splintering oars and light hulls, swathing paths of blood and bone through the packed men. Wave after wave of galleys attacked from both sides, but were punished so severely that Kheir ed Din finally held them back for a longer-range artillery duel. While this and other isolated actions were taking place Andrea Doria lay off to the south until late in the afternoon, when he ranged up to seawards of the Turks, but failed to close. The following day he retired towards Corfu, leaving Kheir ed Din in possession.

It is impossible to gain a clear tactical picture from the different accounts and the welter of accusation afterwards. Whether Doria deliberately held off as the Venetians believed, or whether he thought it impossible to form the immense fleet of galleys – which would have stretched several miles – in battle order among the scattered sailing ships and individual mêlées, or whether indeed the fight went more or less according to plan with the Turkish forces drawn against the broadsides of the sailing ships and so disorganised that they declined to come on against Doria's galleys must remain speculative. It may be significant that Kheir ed Din apparently concentrated on the great Venetian galleon, and Doria apparently failed to bring the main body up to support. On the other hand Venice was the prime Ottoman target, and it was always the aim in early sea battles to capture the enemy flagship. The battle, if it can be called such, was indecisive with the Christians losing perhaps seven vessels and a few Turkish galleys damaged or sunk, but there is not enough hard information to provide answers as to whether Andrea Doria deliberately held his hand, or whether he was genuinely unable to bring his heavy line against harassing guerrilla tactics by squadrons of the lighter Turkish craft attacking isolated stragglers. Kheir ed Din had learnt his trade as a corsair; he would not have risked his outnumbered galleys (about 90 against 130) and galleots in a set-piece action against the heavier Spanish and Western vessels.

Prevesa has gone down in history as a humiliating defeat for the superior Christian fleet under Doria, the result of which was thirty-five years of Ottoman naval ascendancy in the Mediterranean, and a legend of Turkish invincibility at sea. This is to mistake the fragmented nature of the Mediterranean struggle as well as the nature of galley warfare. The result of the campaign was satisfactory for Charles V and Andrea Doria, who continued as his Captain General at Sea into his ninetieth year! It was not so satisfactory for the Papal States, and it was a bitter defeat for Venice, which was forced to make a humiliating, separate peace with the Turks two years later. She retained from her network of strategic bases in the Aegean only Crete, and Cyprus further east. The Holy League was, of course, dead from the moment Doria withdrew from Levkas.

Venice had not been removed from the board however. Her trade with the Levant actually increased, for the campaign leading to Prevesa coincided with Ottoman expansion eastwards into Iraq – bringing Suleiman into conflict with Persia – and southwards down the Arabian peninsula to the Yemen which became an Ottoman Pashalik in 1537 – bringing the Turks further into the Portuguese sphere. Aden was taken in 1538. With the entire Red Sea trade route secured within the Ottoman Empire, and the Gulf spice routes also flowing as a result of the Portuguese and Persians coming together against the Turks, a new Indian Ocean balance was struck; Venice as the major European trader with the Levant was the major beneficiary, and she soon recaptured her former dominance in the spice trade. At the same time she expanded her navy. Venice was trade rival as well as trade partner of Turkey and could never know when she would become the target of Ottoman expansion again. She extended her already enormous arsenal and fixed her reserve fleet at no less than one hundred galleys and four galleasses.

While this uneasy neutrality lasted in the eastern basin, the Turks transferred their attention to the West. It was the combination of huge amphibious expeditions mounted from Constantinople, corsair squadrons operating from the North African coast, and the French alliance enabling Turkish fleets to replenish at Marseilles that caused the Turks to be so feared at sea after Prevesa. It stemmed from Prevesa only in the sense that Doria's conduct had made it impossible for Venice to work with Spain. It was Venice's absence from the anti-Turk forces that was the major factor allowing Turkish predominance; this had as little to do with the military result of the battle – after which Kheir ed Din actually lost many more vessels to storms than Doria had lost in the fighting – as it had to do with Christianity or Islam.

The naval war settled into a series of amphibious assaults to gain, retake or defend the bases useful for the struggle for the western basin of the Mediterranean. It was not a struggle for 'command' as in naval historical dogma, but for the capture of bases from which attack and defence of trade and coasts could be mounted. Consequently the fleets which were far too unwieldy, costly and limited both in seakeeping and endurance to be used for trade warfare were not the primary objective for the opposing fleet; they occasionally became involved and they sometimes went on devastating coastal raids after slaves and plunder, but the real object of the major campaigns was always a strategic fortress; their locations tell the story, Algiers, Tripoli, Bougie, Djerba, Malta, Tunis. In the end the Turks failed to add any vital bases; the defence of Malta in 1565 was an epic of resistance by the Knights before they were relieved by a Spanish squadron. But Charles V and his successor, Philip II were just as unsuccessful in north Africa. This was a more costly failure since the corsairs – as ever a motley mixture of all the seafaring races, Christian or Islamic – plundered unchecked and were the terror of all shipping and all the coastline of the western Mediterranean, spilling out through the Straits of Gibraltar down the Moroccan coast and up into the Atlantic as far as the English Channel.

This spectacular rising tide of piracy coincided with an equally spectacular rise in the wealth coming from the New World after the discovery of the great silver deposits of Mexico and Peru, hence with a rise in French piracy in the Atlantic and Caribbean. The Dutch and English joined in. Everywhere Spanish wealth was the focus of envy, and on land, Charles and then Philip, were engaged against the Turks in Hungary, against rebellious Protestant states in Saxony and Flanders, and against France in Italy and the north. The lawlessness in the Mediterranean was just one of a continuous series of challenges to Spanish imperial authority, and neither Charles nor Philip could concentrate their full attention on it. In this respect the Algerine corsairs occupied much the same position in the western basin as Venice occupied in the east; both were engaged in the exchange – whether by force or trade – of high-value products originating a long way from the

Mediterranean; both owed their freedom to the distractions, chiefly land-ward, which drew the attention of their powerful territorial neighbours. It is significant that both powerful neighbours were less interested in commercial profit from the exchange of goods than in taxes on the exchange, or Crown monopolies; far less interested in the sea than in the land. They thrashed out in every direction; Venice and Algiers survived and prospered.

This pattern was only permanently disturbed when the Mediterranean was invaded by Atlantic seafarers, but there were temporary deviations, the most spectacular of which was the war of Cyprus leading to the campaign of Lepanto.

The immediate cause of the war was the desire of Sultan Selim II, succes-sor to Suleiman the Magnificent, to take the island of Cyprus. It was not a novel idea; Suleiman himself had been much occupied with it in his later years; a lone Christian outpost within the crescent of the Ottoman Levant, and scarcely more than fifty miles from the Turkish coast, it was a standing offence to Islam. For the same geographical reason it was an easy prey. It was also seething with discontent against Venetian rule, and agitators in-cited the oppressed to call in the Turk – not caring perhaps that Turkish misrule was quite as certain to reduce the colony to chaos and misery.

The Ottoman Empire was, of course, an expansionary organism; just as sea powers had a built-in compulsion to extend their markets, it had a built-in need to acquire territory for revenue and for manpower, and the fact that the manpower was needed both to produce the revenue and be expended in the armies and fleets from which the expansion derived was itself expan-sionary! It was also a cause of the man-stealing raids by Turkish fleets, particularly in the Greek islands and coasts, but also in the western basin. Whether the acquisition of Cyprus was a part of the Ottoman expansionary mechanism, or a logical extension of their naval hold on the eastern Medi-terranean, whether Selim was simply ambitious for a glorious campaign to throw the Christians from the 'Rock' and establish himself in the tradition of his 'Magnificent' predecessor, a temporary cessation of the wars in Persia and Hungary allowed him to concentrate on the question in 1569. He was advised of the economic importance of maintaining friendly trade relations with Venice, and of the danger of provoking another Christian League; while on the other hand a 'war party' pointed to the ease with which the island could be taken; there were also wildly exaggerated stories of an explosion and fire in the Venetian arsenal in September 1569, decimating the reserve fleet; in fact only four galleys had been completely destroyed.

For whatever reason or impulse, Selim decided to take the island. The Venetians, alerted to the preparations by their ambassador in Constantinople, were divided in their response; a 'peace party' in the senate, very conscious of the huge Venetian investment along the shores of the Levant, wished to cede the island to Selim in return for compensation along the Adriatic shore of Albania; the Doge, the elected President of the Republic, was one of these. Even those determined to resist disliked the idea of the Western alliance it implied. This was because of their rooted suspicion of Spain and their distaste for anything which might bind them to protect Spanish possessions in the West if the Turks should switch their attack. To the call of Pope Pius V to join with the Christian West in a Holy War they replied that they wanted men, munitions and money rather than an alliance.

In the end it was only the Pope's success in convincing them that the aid of Spain and the minor Christian Princes would enable them to save Cyprus that reconciled them to the idea of another Holy League. These serious divisions on policy (in both the Turkish and Venetian camps) and the probability that the vital decisions really turned on the whim of Selim and his warriors, and the religious fervour of the Pope, illustrate the nature of the Mediterranean balance and suggests an answer to the riddle of Lepanto – that is, the apparent lack of effect, let alone decisive effect, from such an obviously decisive battle! The whole war was an aberration. Religion for once was allowed to interfere with the delicate balance between the two halves of the sea. The course of the first year's campaign reinforces the interpretation. While a Turkish armada of between 120 and 160 galleys, backed by innumerable galleots, fustas (even smaller oared craft) and transports to a total of 350 sail or more, landed an army (including cavalry and a siege train) unopposed on the south coast of Cyprus in Larnaka Bay on 1 July, the Christian alliance squabbled. Venice had conceded that the Pope should appoint the Commander-in-Chief of the League fleet, but was deeply suspicious of his choice, Mark Antony Colonna, who had estates in Naples and was in the Spanish orbit. Philip II of Spain was also objecting to the appointment on the specious ground that there was as yet no fleet to command. In fact he was distracted by rebellions in Flanders and in Spain itself, and by the possibility of the Turkish force being diverted to his own coasts if Venice should make a separate peace with Constantinople. She had done this on previous occasions, and it was far from an unfounded fear this time. Paradoxically it was only when word reached Philip that Venice was about to come to terms with Selim that he decided to support the alliance to prevent the Turks from transferring their full weight against him in the western Mediterranean. Even so, he did not commit himself – except in public – to the Papal aim to smash the Turk, or to the Venetian aim to save Cyprus; the fleet he sent amounted to no more than forty-nine galleys, nineteen of which were hired, the greater part from Gian Andrea Doria – great nephew and heir of Charles V's Captain General – and it is generally believed that he gave Doria instructions to preserve the ships! It would be surprising if he had not; his support was a show to keep the Turk from the West.

The name Andrea Doria was, by itself, almost sufficient to split Venice from the alliance; his actions seemed designed for that purpose. He dallied at Messina, maintaining that his squadron had no orders to join the allies.

When at last he received direct orders from Philip on 8 August, he dawdled the short distance to Otranto, where the Papal squadron was waiting, but failed to pay the usual courtesies to Colonna as Commander-in-Chief. Colonna went to see *him* instead, and was told that although he, Doria, had orders to sail under the Papal flag he was also bound not to risk the King's ships, and he produced a variety of reasons for not joining the Venetians. How much his delaying tactics owed to his secret instructions, how much to the fact that his galleys represented his inheritance and his capital is not clear. The Venetian commanders thought it the latter after a taste of his entirely negative attitude when all elements of the fleet had at last combined in Suda Bay, Crete, on 31 August; they asked Colonna, whose consummate diplomacy was the only factor holding the fleet together, to inform Doria that they would stand security for his galleys to the extent of 200,000 ducats and the cost of repairs. Colonna refused to deliver such an insulting message and Doria continued to obstruct every council. It was only after it had been agreed that his squadron need not take its turn at rearguard duty, and should sail separately from the rest of the fleet that Colonna managed to move the force a few miles to Candia. It was while they were here on 9 September that Nicosia fell. This news did not reach them until a fortnight later, by which time they had reached Castellorizo on the Turkish coast halfway between Crete and Cyprus. They turned back, the different national divisions making their separate ways home.

The campaign had confirmed Venice's worst fears about Spain. They had made prodigious efforts themselves, raising enormous sums through the sale of offices and other means, recruiting nearly 60,000 troops, impressing thousands for the oars of 140 galleys and eleven great galleasses which were fitted out and armed by June, only to see the splendid force rot away in idleness through the summer; 20,000 men were lost by disease before the Spanish and Papal contingents joined. The alliance would have collapsed as it had in almost identical circumstances after Prevesa had it not been for the Pope's fervour and diplomacy. Once again he brought the two incompatibles together; this time definite conditions, which amounted to a naval alliance with a fixed fleet strength and fixed shares of expenses were agreed before the formal treaty was signed on 25 May 1571. The decisive change in the arrangements however was the appointment of Don John of Austria, Philip II's half-brother, as Captain-General of the Holy League fleet; Colonna was appointed second-in-command.

Don John was twenty-four years old and eager for glory. To the rancorous suspicions which divided the fleet he brought the fire of chivalry and crusade; knights and noble adventurers flocked to his standard, and the balance swung from commercial and strategic considerations to chivalry: 'the last Knight of Europe takes weapons from the wall, the last and lingering troubadour to whom the bird has sung . . . *Domino Gloria!*'[12]

He was unable to concentrate the allied fleet any faster than the previous year, but once it was assembled he made it clear that he intended to fight; he was unable to subdue the enmity between the different national contingents, but he neutralised it by dividing their vessels and dispersing them throughout the different squadrons, and in his Battle Orders he placed Colonna in the Papal Capitana on the right of his own flagship and Sebastian Veneiro, the Venetian Commander-in-Chief on the left. So far as tactics are concerned, the most interesting point about his dispositions is that the six Venetian galleasses were to lead into battle in pairs half a mile ahead of the front line galley squadrons so that their batteries could break up the enemy formation before the lines clashed. The sailing ships with the fleet were to serve the same purpose if the wind permitted; otherwise they were to send their troops by boat to the sterns of the galleys.

The Holy League fleet of some 207 galleys, over half of which were Venetian, and six Venetian galleasses, together with storeships, light rowing craft and a few great galleons, sailed from Messina on 1 September after a round of religious ceremonies; each vessel was blessed by the Pope's Nuncio as it left the harbour, Consecrated standards cracked from the Capitanas, 'then the tuckets, then the trumpets, then the cannon and he comes, Don John laughing in the brave beard curled'.[13]

By this time Cyprus had fallen. The last Venetian stronghold at Famagusta had put up an epic defence through the winter, spring and early summer under an inspired commander, Mark Antony Bragadin. In the final weeks of July, with the provisions exhausted, every horse, donkey, cat and rodent eaten, they threw back assault after assault at hand-stroke. The Turks who lost thousands of soldiers, reported the place defended 'not by men but by giants'. But by 1 August, with their stock of gunpowder down to just seven barrels and no sign of the allied relief force they had been expecting week after week, the defenders could hold out no longer. The Turkish commander, Mustafa Pasha, granted Bragadin honourable terms of surrender, paying flowery tribute to his defence. His courtesy concealed the passions of a monster. Bragadin had no sooner come out to meet him than Mustafa had his entourage seized and bound and personally cut off the Venetian commander's right ear, after which the left ear and nose were removed and Bragadin was ordered three times to extend his neck for an executioner's sword that never fell. Over the following days as a red veil of unspeakable savagery descended on the unfortunate Christians within the walls, Bragadin was subjected to every indignity the Pasha's childishly sadistic mind could conceive. Finally as the culmination of a Mahommedan festival, he was taken to the public square, stripped and flayed alive while Mustafa taunted him for his Christian faith. He was already weak and he soon died, it is said with a prayer on his lips. His skin was afterwards stuffed with cotton and straw, dressed in his garments, mounted on a cow and paraded through the streets, and subsequently round the island, as a symbol of the fall of Venetian rule. The martyrdom of Bragadin, while no more horrific than other tales from the Turkish conquests, acted as an additional stimulation for the crusading spirit with which Don John had animated the fleet of the Holy League.

The Turkish fleet which had taken reinforcements for Mustafa's army to Cyprus in the spring, had sailed west for Crete before the fall of Famagusta, and thence to ravage the Ionian; it was anchored off Lepanto in the Gulf of Corinth when the Christian fleet arrived at Corfu at the end of September. It consisted of some 210, perhaps more, full-sized galleys, a few more than the Christians, and about sixty galleots, perhaps not so many, but again more than Don John had. Although the Turkish galleys had followed the trend to increased size and some had as many as thirty oar benches a side, they lacked the protected bow platforms of the Christian craft, and mounted fewer guns (judging by those captured, an average of less than three against the Venetian standard of five) and the Spanish craft had up to seven swivels in addition. There were no Turkish galleasses.

Many of the Turkish commanders were corsair chiefs in the tradition established by Kheir ed Din, whose son Hassan was amongst them, and, in marked contrast to Don John and the patrician commanders of the West, were generally of low birth. The Commander-in-Chief, Muezzinade Ali Pasha, had been a muezzin calling the faithful to prayer when his beautiful voice attracted the attention of the sultan's wife – to whom he owed his subsequent advancement! The second-in-command, Uluch Ali, had started life as an Italian fisherman. He renounced his faith after being captured and chained to the oar bench of a Turkish corsair. At a council called while Don John was leading his fleet south towards Lepanto, most of these experienced sailors were against seeking battle, but Ali had a letter from Selim which ordered him to fight the League fleet. He had this letter read aloud, and encouraged his captains with tales of dissension among the Christians – quite true, as Andrea Doria was taking his usual obstructive line – and made much of the triumphant Turkish record at sea. It was perhaps over-confidence, as much as Selim's instructions and the threat of the executioner's sword hanging over all unsuccessful Ottoman commanders, that prompted the final decision to leave the shelter of the fortress and give battle in the open sea.

So it was that when the leaders of the Christian fleet rounded Point Scropha at the western entrance to the Gulf soon after sunrise on the morning of 7 October, the Turkish sails were sighted in mid-channel some ten miles to the eastward. In the face of this unexpected appearance, the allied command organisation, a committee of the national leaders each of whom under ordinary circumstances needed the authority of his own council of officers, acted with a speed which is testimony to the spirit Don John had created. The Commander-in-Chief simply hailed the Papal and Venetian capitanas on either hand, and receiving their immediate assent, ordered a gun fired and the green flag for battle hoisted to the elevated yard end; then the League standard, bearing the image of Christ crucified, which had been consecrated at Messina, was hoisted for the first time. As sails were furled, yards lowered and the galleys prepared for battle, Don John ordered the spur to be sawn from the bows of his flagship so that it would not interfere when the guns were depressed; the Turkish galleys were generally lower in the water, much lower than his flagship which rowed no less than thirty-five benches of oars, six men to a bench. The other allied commanders followed suit.

Slowly the opposing lines stretched out. Don John in full armour, boarded one of the communication fregatinas and passed from galley to galley shouting encouragement: 'Christianity is at risk today! God will not let those dogs beat us! Both the survivors and the dead will be happy tonight, the former for having fought in this great battle, the others will have their celebration in heaven!'[14]

When at length he returned to his ship, he went forward to view the enemy, then he summoned his pipers and danced a galliard with a young aide who was also in full armour. The courtly upswing of youthful legs and glint of the morning sun on crooked armoured arms made a dazzling sight for the old and hideous gods of war. Afterwards general confession was made throughout the fleet, and priests holding crucifixes aloft, moved forward along the corsiers of the galleys with the commanders exhorting the men to the holy battle. National jealousies were temporarily submerged by 'a single will, a single desire without thought or care for death; all wished to fight for Jesus Christ.'[15]

It was well after nine o'clock by the time the immense lines had formed, facing each other across some four miles or so of lightly ruffled sea. Each line was in three divisions with a reserve in parallel behind. The rows of oar blades from each galley rose, separated by some twelve feet from the blades of their neighbours on either hand, moved forward, down and bit again in slow time. From wing to wing the lines stretched over three and a half miles, snaking as they slid forward, at scarcely one knot in places, to preserve the formation and the strength of the oarsmen. Two of the Venetian galleasses had reached their station ahead of the Christian left wing, but the others struggled, lacking their full complement of oarsmen and were under tow by four galleys each. Two were far behind. The galleons and other sailing ships had not kept up with the fleet.

The centre squadrons on both sides were just over sixty galleys strong, the heaviest massed in the middle on either side of the opposing flagships which directed their course towards each other. The Christian left and the Turkish right, close in to the shoal water under the land, were also equally matched with some fifty-four galleys each, but as Don John had stationed thirty of his galleys astern as reserves, whereas Ali's reserve was made up chiefly of galleots, the Turkish left outnumbered the Christian right by perhaps eighty-seven to fifty-four. To counter this overlap Andrea Doria, who

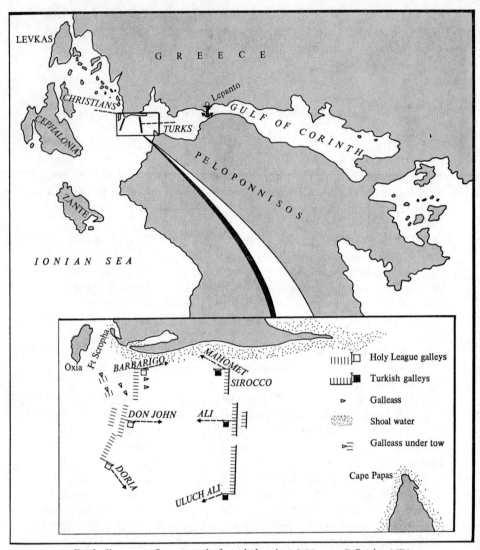

Battle diagram 2: Lepanto – the fleets deploy about 9.00 a.m., 7 October 1571

commanded the Christian right from the extreme flanking position, eased
out away from the centre; the Turkish commander opposing him, Uluch
Ali, conformed, and gaps grew in each line. A similar movement away from
the centre was made by the two inshore squadrons as the lighter Turkish
craft sought to outflank the Christian left by getting into shallower water.
So the separating squadrons closed their opponents. The plash and groan of
the great sweeps, creak of the benches, clink of chains was drowned by
trumpets, pipes and gongs and the beat of massed drums from the Turkish
fleet. The stench from the bilges was overlaid on the carved and gilded poops

by the perfumes of the nobles. Arms and armour glinted in clear sunlight. Cross and crescent flamed on banners, and on the rich purple and red canopies over the poops. In the Turkish craft a patchwork of coloured robes and turbans made a brilliant design over the swing and dip of the oars. It was a dazzling picture and such as the world would never see again, the last and greatest of all the galley actions that had been fought in these waters for more than a thousand years. Those who left a record described the terrible grandeur of the scene as the lines closed and 150,000 men were drawn inexorably towards their fate. *Domino Gloria!*

Action was joined first on the inshore wing, where the Christian galleasses were furthest advanced. Muezzinade Ali had instructed his commanders to ignore these and make for the galleys, so the line of the Turkish right split, the greater part swinging diagonally inshore as it approached them, increasing the stroke as the galleass's bow batteries opened. Muscles of thigh and torso bunched; sweat rose, glistening row upon row of naked men, faces set with apprehension. Ripples under the bows of the craft thrust higher. The tattoo of the drums was rent by cries as the first oars were scattered and hulls splintered by shot; the first galley started to fill and sink; the rest swarmed on in a froth of oars, the formation dissolving, janissaries standing shaking their long bows, yelling savagely above the drum beat. The Venetian commander of the Christian left, Agostin Barbarigo, himself on the extreme left, backed his oars to allow his line to wheel to face the Turks as they headed further into shoal water to outflank him. The inshore galleass backed its port oars to enable its bow batteries to keep in bearing. Clouds of gunsmoke drifted off to starboard. Barbarigo's gunners stood to their pieces, waiting. Above them armoured arquebusiers were massed on the bow platform, waiting. Minutes hung in the bloodcurdling din.

It was well after eleven o'clock by the time the first wave of Turkish craft had worked down inshore of the mainly Venetian galleys on the outside of the Christian left, and the air began to quiver with dense flights of arrows slot-slotting into the leather shields and defensive pavesades, humming off angles of steel armour, thudding into timber, the sounds interspersed with cries from oarsmen transfixed through the back. The Venetian gunners waited while their galleys were turned slowly to port to keep the leading wave of Turks right ahead; as the enemy surged forward in the final moments they touched off their pieces, depressed to aim for the waterline. The clouds of smoke dispersed slowly and the arquebusiers, roaring as savagely as the Turks, raised their pieces and fired a volley, decimating the archers. Massed arrows still fizzed about them as they re-loaded, scores finding a mark and punching straight through the armour; the air darkened with smoke from fireballs and shells.

Shortly afterwards the headmost Turkish galleys collided with Barbarigo's capitana, crowding in between the Christian craft, scattering

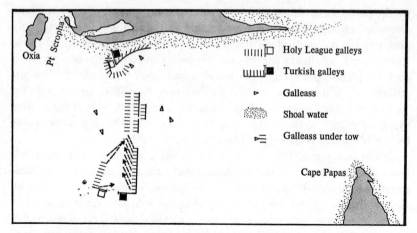

Battle diagram 3: Lepanto – the centres clash about noon, 7 October 1571

the oars and gaining a temporary superiority. As grapnels were flung
to heave the craft together and the clash of pike and halberd, sword and
scimitar began, all formation dissolved; craft from both sides were drawn
to reinforce the engaged galleys and became locked together like so many
jumbled pontoons over which the armoured men scrambled to reinforce
their consorts or take a weakened enemy. The inshore galleass had turned
right around and was making its way back, firing into the rear of the
Turkish division, still rowing to join the fight. The heavier Christian galleys
on the unengaged right flank of Barbarigo's division had also turned and
were steering to outflank those Turkish craft which were coming round
from inshore to the Venetian left. Barbarigo's capitana was the focal point
of the struggle; the Turks were aboard and pouring reinforcements over
from galleys astern. Barbarigo raised his visor to make himself heard above
the savage noise; an arrow pierced his eye and he fell. The galley's captain
took command of the defence, and shortly reinforced by men from another
Christian galley, succeeded in holding the Turks, then driving them from the
deck.

Meanwhile, the Turkish centre had divided to bypass the two galleasses
ahead of the Christian centre, and reforming again as best they could, were
making the final surge to contact, Muezzinade Ali himself aiming for Don
John's huge *real*, largest of all the galleys there with over 400 arquebusiers
besides his entourage of knights and nobles. Here too, the sky was filled
with arrows and the smoke from cannon, swivels and fireballs. Both opposing
Commanders-in-Chief had called up several galleys from the reserve; these
were following close astern ready to throw their troops aboard as soon as
the lines met. Meanwhile a wide gap had opened to the right of the Christian
centre as Andrea Doria steered outwards to avoid being outflanked, at the
same time holding back to give his galleasses a chance to come up from the

rear. As the flagships of the opposing Commanders-in-Chief and their powerful seconds came together with thunderous volleys and locked in combat, about fourteen Venetian galleys on the left of Doria's division, suspecting him of desertion, turned to port of their own accord to go to the support of the centre. As this little group separated, Uluch Ali, commander of the opposing Turkish wing, saw his chance, and swinging his squadron to starboard, increased his striking rate to cut them off. Doria, in his turn, wheeled to port to support them, compelled to pass ahead of the labouring galleasses. The heavy Genoese and Spanish galleys were significantly slower than the Turks though, and compelled by their smaller numbers to preserve a tight line formation, they took longer to perform the wheel. By the time they came up, the deviant galleys had been surrounded, over-whelmed by sheer numbers and taken, and Uluch Ali had passed on to throw his headmost unengaged galleys at a great capitana of the Knights of St John which was posted on the right flank of the Christian centre.

It was now well after noon; the boarding mêlée on the inshore flank had turned into a rout of the Turks after the simultaneous arrival of the right flank of Barbarigo's division from the west, and the inshore galleass bom-barding the rearmost Turkish craft from the east. At the focal point about the locked flagships the heavy armour of the Christian soldiers gave them the edge in close fighting where the deadly Turkish bows were powerless, and they forced and took the flagship; the Turkish admiral fled shorewards wounded, and shortly after the rest of his division broke, also rowing shorewards to try to escape in the shallows; the galleys collided with each other in the confusion so that the panic-stricken men left and scrambled from deck to deck to escape. The Christians fired their artillery into the midst of them, then landed a force to capture those who managed to reach the shore. The victory here was complete, not a single Turkish vessel escaping.

At the decisive point of the battle about the massed flagships and capi-tanas in the middle of the centre divisions, the initial advantage went once again to the Turks. Muezzinade Ali, himself a redoubtable archer, stood at the waist of his vessel with his bow in the midst of his janissaries, inspiring them to prodigies of rapid shooting which opened gaps in the packed ranks of arquebusiers reloading after their initial volley. He had no less than six galleys and galleots feeding men from astern and both sides, and even wedging themselves between Don John and the Venetian capitana, and after the onslaught of arrows, boarders were thrown on to the bows of the Christian flagship. The assault was held by the mast at push of pike, and a counter attack led by Don John himself eventually cleared the deck. Once again arrows hummed. Meanwhile, from both sides, the heavy capitanas had converged on this central struggle. Elsewhere along the line stretching over half a mile each side similar groups of galleys locked together; the commanders of the reserve directed reinforcements where they were needed.

After the first Turkish onslaught had been held and thrown back and their archers' muscles began to tire, the tide of the central battle turned (as it had on the left) in favour of the heavily armoured Christians operating from their higher and better protected platforms. The Turks resisted fiercely, falling in droves, Muezzinade Ali everywhere rallying them and leading in more reinforcements from the quarters as Don John's men swarmed down on the bows of his flagship. Three times the armoured assault reached his mast, three times it was held and driven back. Finally, after more than an hour the Papal capitana to Don John's left, having overcome her own opponent, ranged alongside the Turkish flagship, sweeping the deck with arquebus fire, wounding or killing Ali himself, and establishing an overwhelming Christian superiority at this decisive point. The Turkish decks, red and slippery with blood, were soon overrun, Don John among the boarders. After this, Turkish resistance began to break and their centre dissolved in rout.

Uluch Ali meanwhile succeeded in capturing the Maltese capitana after nearly all aboard her had been killed, but Andrea Doria's line had fallen on his rear by this time and re-taken all his earlier prizes, except for two that were destroyed. The Turkish second-in-command saw the day was lost, and made off westwards between Doria and the centre, urging his oarsmen to strenuous efforts and soon setting sails to a light wind that sprang up from the east; several others from his division and some galleots from the Turkish reserve also fled and succeeded in making their escape. Otherwise it was an annihilation, in terms of ships and men lost one of the very few total naval victories. After the news reached Spain, Philip II's secretary wrote: 'It seems to us a dream, for never was such a naval victory seen or heard of.'[16]

Nearly all the Turkish galleys were lost or captured, perhaps as many as 200 of them – 117 of which were considered worth preserving – together with a number of galleots and smaller craft; some 30,000 of their men were killed, a large proportion probably in the indiscriminate butchery after the battle had been won; a few prisoners were taken, perhaps 4,000, and some 12,000 Christian slaves were set free. Nearly 400 guns were captured. Against this, the allied fleet lost only twelve galleys and some 8,000 men, although it is probable that many more died from their wounds later.

It is difficult to say how much the fire power of the galleasses contributed to the victory. The battle seems to have turned on hand-to-hand fighting in the old manner, and, especially on the left flank, the Turkish arrows appear to have wrought quite as much havoc as the superior weight but much slower fire of the Christian artillery. However the fire of the four galleasses that succeeded in getting into position, although unable entirely to disorganise the Turkish advance, must have contributed to their demoralisation by attacking from the rear after the hand battle had been joined – particularly on the left. In view of the number of Turkish vessels that were sunk or so seriously damaged that they were not worth preserving, it is possible the galleasses played an even more decisive role. Certainly, attempts were made to use them in the same way during the League campaign of the following season, and the Turkish fleet under Uluch Ali manœuvred to refuse battle. They were copied, too, by other Western powers, all of which suggests that their batteries played a significant part in the victory.

On the moral level Lepanto was decisive; it broke the spell of supremacy which the Turks had woven over the whole Mediterranean, and reduced them to the status of mortal men. It also caused serious deficiencies in their supply of trained oarsmen and archers. Oarsmen could be pressed and enslaved, but archers were impossible to replace as quickly since skill with the composite bow went with the nomadic way of life; they were bred rather than trained like gunners or arquebusiers. However, the actual measurable effects of the Christian victory were no different from the effects of the previous defeat at Prevesa. Don John could not continue eastwards into the Turkish zone or attempt to re-take Cyprus because of the lateness of the season; the same considerations would have prevented Muezzinade Ali from devastating any more Venetian outposts with or without the battle, and Selim's grand Vizier remarked that while the Christians had singed their beard, they had cut off one of Venice's arms; both would grow again.[17]

In fulfilment of the boast, by the following spring a fleet of 150 galleys had been built in the dockyards at Constantinople; much of the wood was green, many of the guns ill-cast, but they and some seventy others, mostly galleots, sallied out under Uluch Ali and raided the Venetian outposts again as if Lepanto had never been fought. On the Christian side dissensions erupted as they had after Prevesa. Don John was an engaging character, but spoiled and prickly and the fame he had won did nothing to reduce his arrogance. Quarrels broke out with the Venetians who were just as arrogant. Of more importance, French designs in north Africa forced Philip to hold Don John in the western Mediterranean, and Colonna took over command of a reduced fleet. When Christian and Turk met again, the Christian command agreed to avoid action until they could bring their galleons and other gunned sailing craft into battle as well, but directly they succeeded in combining with the galleasses and lining them up ahead of the galley formation, Uluch Ali avoided action; he attempted to manœuvre so that the midday change in the wind direction would allow him to bypass the heavy ships; the League fleet, seeing his intention, shifted their lines. And so it went; although there was much manœuvring and some long-range artillery skirmishes over the following days, there was no close battle; as earlier, Venetian commanders had discovered, the totally different characteristics of galleons and galleys made it impossible to combine them effectively *and* meet the enemy.

The same year the Pope died. The spirit went out of the League, and Spain and Venice reverted to a consideration of their own real interests in their own spheres. Venice made a separate peace in 1573, as humiliating as that in 1540 after Prevesa, giving up her claim to Cyprus, and paying a large war indemnity to the Turks. The Mediterranean returned to balance, and both great powers at either end turned away, distracted by their territorial concerns, Spain to a revolt in the Netherlands, Turkey towards Persia.

Lepanto was a famous victory, but it had no significance. All it proved was that in combination the major sea power and the major territorial empire of western Europe were more than a match for the hybrid Turk. Western Europe, however, was growing too strong to combine, and its centre of gravity was shifting from the Mediterranean to the Atlantic fringe. The next decisive battle in the middle sea would be fought by Atlantic powers with Atlantic ships.

CHAPTER 4

ATLANTIC WEALTH

Spain's chief military, naval and diplomatic effort after Lepanto went into fighting heretics in the north; her armies campaigned against Netherlands' Protestants and French Protestants, and embarked in huge armadas for campaigns against English Protestants; meanwhile her naval concern was to protect her treasure fleets and colonies in the New World from Protestant privateers, and to keep Protestant smugglers from the area. Religion appears the dominant motif. A far more important link between her enemies was their situation along the Atlantic coastline; they had either grown prosperous from Atlantic trade and smuggling or hoped to do so! What seemed a Spanish offensive against heretics was really a war of imperial defence; the heretics' defence of the Protestant cause was really a commercial offensive against the wealth of Spain. As men thought in religious terms, religion again provided the banner under which both sides fought.

The chain of cause and effect is not so simple, and to follow it is to become lost in a number of different Continental balances and accidents of fortune and personality; these accidents filled in the details of the result, but the overall pattern was determined by the wealth flowing from the New World, increasing the tension between the territorial centres and the oceanic fringes of western Europe. As the tension increased, one after another the coastal provinces broke away from the centre. Different causes were ascribed in each case, and the rebellions were usually led by territorial nobles, yet they drew their strength from the seaports and commercial wealth founded chiefly on trade, smuggling and piracy in the Atlantic system. This was the underlying cause of the revolution; the revolutionary religions of Calvin and Luther were natural bedfellows. Those who have seen the austere Protestant ethic as one of the causes of industrial success have it the wrong way round; it was only those areas which were successful and prosperous which were strong enough to revolt and hold their own against the established Catholic centre in the commercial revolution brought about by the exploitation of the New World.

The first provinces to break away were French. They had provided the first pirates and smugglers off the Azores and in the Caribbean – apart from the Portuguese, already separate. The exploits of the Angos of Dieppe in capturing the Spanish treasure fleet in 1537 have already been mentioned in Chapter 3. As the flow of bullion grew through the 1540s the scale of French privateering, coastal ravaging and illicit trading in the Caribbean also grew; Spanish defence measures provide an indication; in 1543, ships of less than one hundred tons were prohibited from sailing to the Indies. Indies fleets had to be at least ten ships strong, and squadrons of well-armed ships were detached to patrol the Caribbean while the merchantmen were loading. This and the need for patrols from the Spanish coast to the Azores led directly to the adoption of galleons as armed escorts. The chief feature of the galleon was a very much slimmer hull, hence better speed than the vessels known as carracks, which were employed for trade and war by all Western powers. Whether the galleon was evolved in the Atlantic war against privateers or by Venetians out of their great galleasses is a technical argument; the type was bound to appear as a reaction to the sheer sluggish-ness of the carrack, which had an extraordinarily round hull and towering castles. A Portuguese carrack captured by the English in 1592 had a beam of almost 47 feet on a keel length of 100 feet, and drew no less than 31 feet when loaded; she would have needed almost a gale to move her. A large Venetian galleon of mid-century had a beam of only 33 feet on the same keel length.

A Spanish Instruction of 1549, reminding colonial governors that trade with French ships was prohibited, indicates that plunder was not the sole object of French Caribbean voyages; again the Normandy ports of Dieppe, Le Havre and Rouen figure prominently in this illicit trade, taking manu-factures out to the West Indies and Spanish Main, returning with hides, dyewoods, cochineal and other colonial produce. The French were also intruding in the Portuguese sphere in Guinea, hence they were able to add to the volume of negro slaves which were coming illicitly to the Spanish West Indies. By this time the 'legitimate' slave trade was being conducted on a contract basis; in return for a lump-sum payment to the Spanish Treasury, the contractor guaranteed to deliver 4,000 slaves each year for a fixed period; the contract, or *Asiento*, went to the highest bidder, and such were the profits to be made that the bids were very high, 20,000 ducats in 1538.

In the 1550s, as the flow of bullion from the newly-discovered silver mountains in New Spain and Peru reached a value and produced an impres-sion on men's minds which can, perhaps, only be compared with the oil wealth of the Middle East today, the scale of French ravages in the Caribbean mounted with it. Royal ships as well as merchants' vessels with Royal Commissions were sent out in fleets and their commanders, notably François le Clerc, known as Pié de Palo (Pegleg) and Jacques de Sores, created a reign of terror throughout the islands. They sacked and pillaged

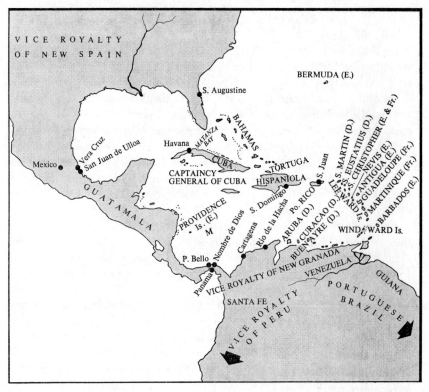

Map 3: The West Indies. The Atlantic fringe settles on the fringe of the Spanish Empire in the New World

not only the small, coastal settlements, but Santiago de Cuba and Havana, the new seat of government and rendezvous for the homeward-bound fleets. It was after this that the Spanish escort commander, Pedro Menendez de Avilés, began a defence system hinging on secure fortifications at the key fleet bases, and small local squadrons of fleet galleons and galleys to protect the coasts. The strongpoints were to be Santo Domingo on the south-west coast of Hispaniola, a fine harbour and first capital of the island, where the out-ward Indies fleets arrived; Nombre de Dios on the Panama Isthmus, where the treasure from Peru and the Pacific came by mule train and river boat; Vera Cruz/San Juan de Ulloa, the port for New Spain; Havana on the north-west coast of Cuba, where homeward-bound shipping collected for the passage through the Florida Channel into the Atlantic; and the coast of Florida where French privateers lurked to pick up stragglers. The system was more or less complete in the 1560s and although the local squadrons were never kept up to strength so that coastal settlements and local commerce were never safe from sea rovers, the main bases and their semi-annual escorted fleets to and from Spain were not at risk from anything less than a major national fleet. For the bullion itself a new class of vessel was built, similar to the Venetian galleass, with lateen sails and oar ports; they were called gallizabras.

By this time France's territorial centre was bankrupt from the wars and could not hold the centrifugal oceanic fringe. The nation disintegrated in civil, ostensibly religious, wars. The Atlantic and Channel regions, which supported the Protestants (Huguenots) in the break-away, continued to send out small squadrons on voyages of plunder and piracy. They were granted commissions as privateers by the Huguenot leader, the Bourbon Prince of Condé, but increasingly their attention and wealth were dissipated in the internal struggle for France itself, while the industries on which much of their illicit trade depended were crippled by continual campaigns. England under Queen Elizabeth I took over the lead in the attempt to relieve Spain of her New World wealth.

England was an undeveloped island. Elizabeth's Tudor ancestors had done their best to stimulate trade and shipping by navigation laws and tariffs, but although sailors from Bristol and the West Country had adventured to Iceland and as far as the Newfoundland Banks in the late fifteenth century – as early as the Portuguese and Bretons – and London merchants sent a few 'defensible' ships of size into the Mediterranean and Baltic, most of her vessels were small fishing boats, coasters, or short-haul Channel or Biscay traders; there were scarcely more than a dozen merchant ships over 200 tons at Elizabeth's accession. By comparison with the Spanish Netherlands or the confederation of Baltic and North German ports of the Hanseatic League she was a minor mercantile power, and they had captured much of her foreign trade. By comparison with the port of Antwerp, which both Spain and Portugal had made their *entrepôt* for north Europe, London was a minor mercantile city. By comparison with France, which had perhaps twelve million people, England was underpopulated with three million or less; by contrast with the developing industrial regions of the Netherlands and northern France she was scarcely more than a primary producer of wool and unfinished cloth.

Henry VIII had built up a formidable, though short-range, navy at the beginning of the century, but the effort had not been sustained; the revenues were not available; Elizabeth in the early years of her reign could rely on an annual income of no more than £250,000, a pittance compared with Philip's revenue. She did however have a valuable and unique resource in a cast-iron cannon industry which Henry VIII had established on the site of deposits of iron ore in the forests of Sussex and Kent. Nearly all the cast cannon which were replacing the earlier built-up pieces as weapons of battery in Western ships and armies were made of bronze because of the difficulties of casting iron of a consistent quality, able to withstand heavy charges of gunpowder. The foreign experts whom Henry had called in had succeeded however in producing workmanlike iron guns; these were not so reliable as bronze pieces and were heavier because of the need to cast the metal thicker, but they were between one-third and one-quarter cheaper than similar weights of bronze ordnance.[1] By Elizabeth's time nine foundries were producing some 500 tons of cast iron guns and balls annually (an average 32-pound cannon was some 10 feet long and weighed just under three tons) and their fame had spread throughout Europe; Elizabeth considered them one of the principal jewels in her Crown.

England's other advantages, which were clear to many men at the time, were her chain of fine, deep natural harbours, estuaries and sheltered anchorages along all her southern coasts, and her position separated from Continental armies by a wide and often stormy moat, yet flanking what was becoming the richest trade route in the world. The growth of Spanish and Portuguese Atlantic and Eastern trade, and the use of Antwerp as their northern outlet had turned the Spanish Netherlands into the wealthiest and most industrially advanced province in Europe. The merchants of the Netherlands were middlemen at the junction of three complementary trade areas; the Mediterranean/Atlantic, the Baltic and the river routes from the south German mining regions around Augsberg and Nürnberg. The timber, flax and naval stores of the Baltic and the copper and tin of South Germany were needed in growing quantities for the ships and gun foundries which the expanding oceanic trades demanded; the products were paid for with Eastern spices, colonial produce and New World bullion. By the 1560s this upward spiral of exchange had turned Antwerp into a city of 100,000 inhabitants, the centre of the most modern and prolific bronze gun-founding and textile industries and heir to Genoa as the financial capital of the Spanish empire.

If the southern English, with their fine harbours strategically placed along the narrowing shipping lanes to Antwerp and the other ports of the Low Countries, with their forests of oak to build ships, cheap iron guns to arm them, and their primitive economy to bestir them to envy had not set about intercepting this ever-expanding stream of wealth, they would have been more than human. This they were not; a great many were pirates, had been for centuries and continued to be so; as a Venetian remarked one hundred years later, 'the English would be a fine and praiseworthy race if they were not so given to robbing the ships of Christian merchants'.[2] They robbed the ships not only of merchandise, but of well-dressed Dons, putting them up for auction at Dover; in the first years of Elizabeth's reign, Spanish gentlemen who looked as though they might be worth a good ransom were fetching as much as £100 apiece.

The piratical centre of the southern counties had shifted by this time from the eastern ports to the West Country and southern Ireland, but chiefly to Devon, Dorset and Cornwall; here it was an industry as interwoven into the fabric of society as that of any Barbary kingdom. Trade, especially the export of tin and woollens, and the import of wines and salt was carried out in parallel from Bristol and the smaller south coast ports, but this was the concern of a few merchant houses. Everyone was implicated in piracy and the companion trade of smuggling from the Lords Lieutenant of the Counties, and the squirearchy who acted as receivers of stolen property or contraband, the merchant families who adventured ships, the yeoman farmers who leased coves, the local port and customs officials whose palms were greased, down to the sailors and fishermen rovers themselves. The proceeds contributed to the vital margin of wealth which helped to make England something more than a primary producer. The piratical centres were linked by family and finance with the merchants of London, with the highest officials of the Royal Navy and hence with the Queen herself, who soon began to adventure Royal ships on the larger expeditions; she above all desperately needed the marginal wealth they promised. She was not perhaps so blatant as the Bey of Algiers and she had other interest groups to hear and charm, as England was still a territorial kingdom with its economic centre in agriculture and wool, yet her diplomacy was not far removed from Barbary.

During the struggle between France and Spain, England under the early Tudors had steered generally within the Spanish orbit, for France was the nearer and more dangerous of the two great territorial nation states of western Europe. But as France disintegrated in civil war and ceased to be a threat, England became free to play another role. How that role was conceived remains locked within the tortuous ambiguity of Elizabeth's correspondence, but it is plain to see how it developed naturally in an attempt to break into Spanish wealth at source in the New World, the focus of envy.

The sequence of events makes it clear that this was commercial aggression which quickly degenerated into state piracy – for want of a word to describe the forcible exchange of wealth for the benefit of the national treasury – which owed nothing to the religious struggles of the time. England had been officially a Protestant country since 1533 when Henry VIII broke from Rome to solve his marriage and male heir problem – and solving thereby a good many pressing financial problems by seizing Church property. Despite this personal and rather accidental heresy imposed from the top, as distinct from the Continental heresies which welled up as a complement to separatist forces within territorial empires, England remained within the Spanish diplomatic and commercial spheres: her merchants traded with Spain and the Atlantic islands, and through Spain with the West Indies, where they had representatives, and Englishmen formed one of the merchant colonies at San Lucar at the mouth of the Guadalquivir leading to Seville, the terminus and commercial hub of the Indies trade. At the dynastic level, Henry VIII's daughter, Mary was married to Philip II of Spain. During this time Spain was continuously at war with her co-religionist Catholic neighbour, France, and French Royal squadrons and privateers – both Catholic and Protestant – ravaged the Spanish Indies. It was only after the collapse of France in the early 1560s that this diplomatic and commercial

1   Vasco da Gama, 'a very disdainful man, very haughty in his speech', whose voyage was the prototype for Western expansion

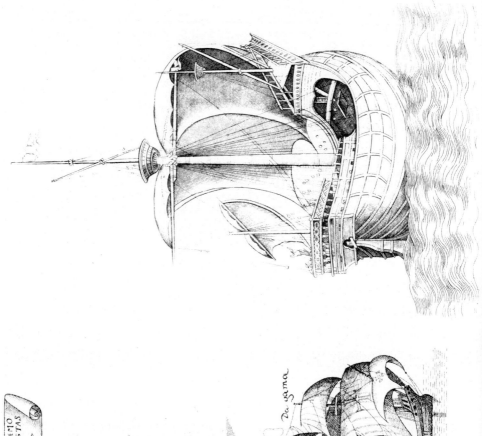

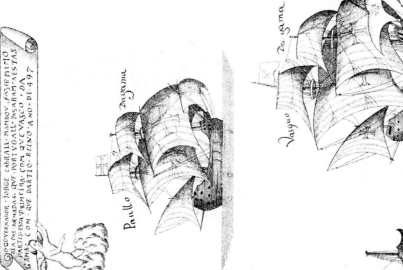

Paullo

Da gama

Vasquo

Da gama

Honario de necula acoelho q is fizerao

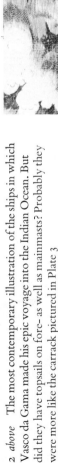

2 *above*   The most contemporary illustration of the ships in which Vasco da Gama made his epic voyage into the Indian Ocean. But did they have topsails on fore– as well as mainmasts? Probably they were more like the carrack pictured in Plate 3

3 *above right*   A contemporary drawing of a carrack of the type in which Columbus sailed to America

4 *below*   An early sixteenth-century lateen-sailed vessel of the caravel type with low, fine lines and square stern. This one has been rigged with a foremast carrying a square sail, and consequently a bowsprit from which to stay the mast. The all-lateen caravel had no such mast or bowsprit

5 *right*   A Dutch merchantman of a similar type to Vasco da Gama's carracks, with rounded stern, high aftercastle, topsails, and all guns at upper-deck level

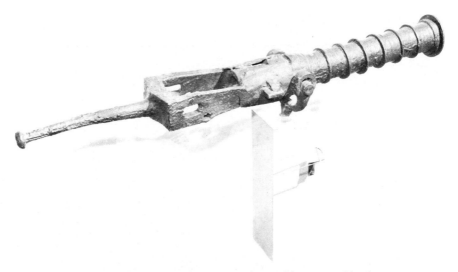

6 A breach-loading, wrought-iron swivel gun of the type used by the Portuguese with devastating success in the Indian Ocean. The chamber is missing from this piece, but the aperture for it can be seen before the aiming bar protruding from the breech end

7 Early wrought-iron, breech-loading bombard on timber bed. Note the rings for making the piece fast to the bed, and the spare chamber in the foreground. This bed, recovered from the English ship *Mary Rose*, which foundered in 1545, was mounted on wheels

8 'The Great' Affonço d'Albuquerque, architect of the Portuguese eastern empire. 'This great captain was a man of middle stature with a long face, the nose somewhat large.... He was of ready words, very authoritative in his commands, and greatly feared yet greatly loved by all'

9 A Venetian galley of the early sixteenth century firing its bow guns as it returns in triumph from an engagement with the Turks. Note the raised spur for boarding, and the as-yet unprotected platform above the bow for cross-bow and arquebusiers

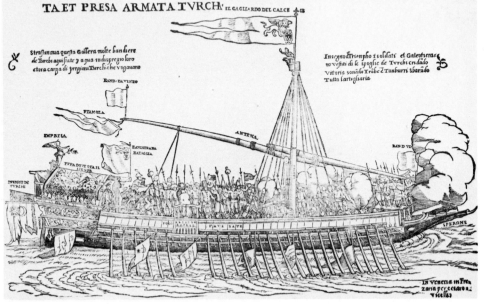

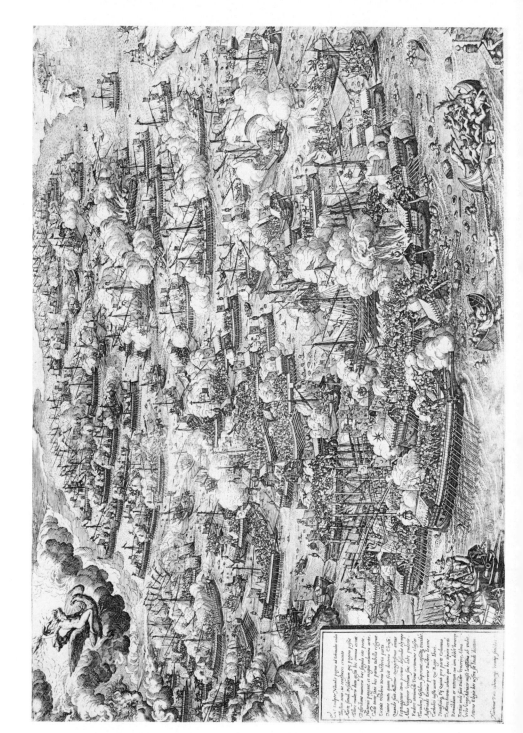

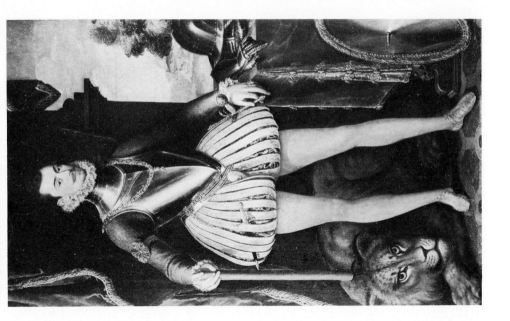

10 *Above* The Battle of Lepanto, a victory for the Christian alliance, which shattered a legend of Turkish invincibility at sea. Note in the centre foreground and right middle-ground the three-masted Christian galleasses doing execution with their great guns in the thick of the battle

11 *right* Don John of Austria, Commander-in-Chief of the Christian fleet at Lepanto

12   Sir John Hawkins, Elizabeth I's great naval reformer, who re-modelled the English navy in time to meet the Spanish invasion armada of 1588

Carol: D: Howard: Comes:
Notingham: Summ^s Angl:
Admiral Georgianæ perisheli:
dis Eques Auratus

13 Howard of Effingham, Commander-in-Chief of the English fleet during the
first Spanish Armada campaign. He was the first in a line of unspectacular, but
eminently successful, English home-fleet commanders who knew their advantage
and held to it

14 *above left*   Outboard loading depicted
by Van de Velde. There is little doubt
that this was the earliest method of
loading long, cast guns on shipboard;
this influenced tactics since ships did not
stay close by an opponent while loading!

15 *below left*   A sixteenth-century,
English iron demi-culverin, eleven feet
in length. Note the absence of any
decoration

16 *above*   Spanish galleons of the type
that fought in the Armada campaign of
1588. Compare the high castles with
those of the 'race-built' type [overleaf]
the English favoured

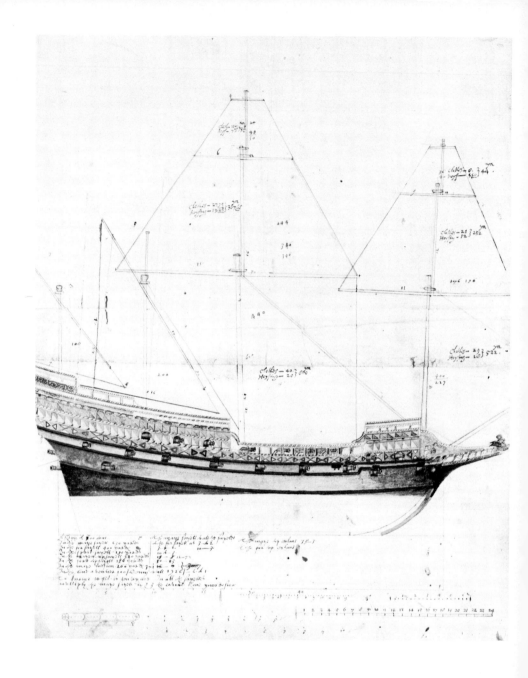

17 Design for a 'race-built' man-of-war, the type favoured by the progressives among Elizabeth I's fighting sailors. Note the topgallant sails above the topsails on fore and main. From Matthew Baker's *Fragments of Ancient English Shipwrightry*

18 *above* Medina Sidonia's re-formed fleet with galleasses and galleons as a powerful rearguard off Portland

19 *right* Contemporary diagram of the action off Portland in the Armada campaign of 1588

20 *above left* Maarten Tromp, Commander-in-Chief of the Dutch fleet in the great battles of the Spanish and first English war, whose victory over the Spanish Armada in the Downs in 1639 heralded the end of Spain's predominance as a world power

21 *below left* *Jupiter*, a typical larger, two-gun decked Dutch warship of the early seventeenth century – a type evolved on the lines of 'race-built' ships of the late sixteenth century

22 *above* Twenty-two-pounder bronze demi-cannon recovered from the Swedish warship *Wasa*, which capsised and sank on her maiden voyage in 1628; the timber carriage and the loading implements are original, but the ropes and tackles and the way they lead are reconstructions. The shape of the ship-board gun carriage changed little, but there were significant improvements in detail in the following century

23 Robert Blake, the epitome of the Puritan soldier, joint Commander of the English fleet in the epic battles of the first Anglo-Dutch war, during which the English navy became a formidably disciplined fighting force employing fleet line of battle as a standard formation for the first time

24 *below* A mêlée during the Battle off the Gabbard, 1653, the first battle fought under the new English line of battle instructions; it is doubtful if many of the engagements of the battle were as close as here depicted!

alignment, cutting right across Catholic/Protestant divisions, also dissolved. This can be seen most clearly in the series of voyages to the Indies by John Hawkins, whose beginnings in 1562 coincided with the break-up of France into warring religious factions. So far as is known these were the first consistent attempts by any Englishmen to trade directly with the Spanish Indies, and break into the monopoly claimed by the Spanish Crown; their ambiguous nature exactly illustrates the changing balance of Europe.

John Hawkins was the second son of William Hawkins, a merchant ship-owner of Plymouth, who had trading connections stretching down the Biscay coast to Seville and the Canary Islands. It is a reasonable assumption that he dabbled in piracy; certainly John's brother, William, appeared before the Privy Council on charges of piracy later. John was brought up in the family business, made several voyages to the Canaries himself, and in 1559 joined in marriage an even more prosperous merchant family, the Gonsons of London. One of the few shipowners operating large, well-armed vessels in the Mediterranean trade, Benjamin Gonson, the father of John's bride, Catherine, was also Treasurer and virtual head of the Royal Navy. His father had been the civil head of Henry VIII's navy. Three years later a syndicate including Benjamin Gonson and William Winter, who held the other two senior posts on the Navy Board, Surveyor and Master of the Ordnance, together with several London financiers, backed Hawkins in his first venture to the Indies. This was also, so far as is known, the inaugural voyage of the English 'triangular' trade, for the essence of the venture was to supply West African slaves to Spanish colonies. Not only were slaves in great demand throughout the New World – by reason of their short life-span as slaves, and the boom economy out there – but it was easy for private traders to undercut prices charged by the monopolist holders of the Spanish *Asiento*. Hawkins had learnt this from his Canary Island contacts.

He sailed in October 1562 with English manufactures, probably mainly cloth, in three small vessels, the largest 120 tons; his total force was not above 100 men 'for feare of sickness and other inconveniencies, whereunto men in long voyages are commonly subject'. Calling first at Tenerife where he sent messages via his local contacts to Hispaniola, he continued on to the west African coast, sailing as far south as Sierra Leone, and collecting negroes on the way. Hakluyt states that he got them into his possession 'partly by the sworde, and partly by other meanes, to the number of 300 at least'.[3] The Portuguese complained that he had taken them from their ships on the coast by means of 'tortures and many blows and torments'[4] to the number of 900, and stolen one of their vessels into the bargain! Exactly what happened will never be known, but he did cross the Atlantic with an extra vessel, which appears to have been a caraval. Arriving in Hispaniola, he avoided Santo Domingo and bartered all his slaves and his English goods at isolated settlements along the north coast of the island, 'gaining at these places such quantitie of merchandise that he not only laded his own three

E

ships with hides, sugar, gingers and some pearls, but freighted also two other hulks with hides and commodities and sent them to Spain.[5] Why he sent them to Spain is a mystery. Perhaps it was on account of a bargain he had struck with the Portuguese in west Africa, who – to clear their own yardarm – accused him of plunder, blows and torments. Perhaps he genuinely thought he would be allowed to open a direct trade with the English merchants in San Lucar. If the latter, he was disappointed, for both vessels and their goods were seized and he was accused by the Spanish authorities of sailing to the Indies without a licence and trading there without a licence in goods not entered at Seville.

Despite the total loss of these two cargoes, the expedition was sufficiently profitable for the Queen and three of her privy councillors, including Sir William Cecil and Lord Robert Dudley (later Earl of Leicester) as well as the Lord Admiral of England, to join Gonson, Winter and other members of the first syndicate in backing a larger expedition. The Queen's contribution was one of the great Royal ships, the 700-ton *Jesus of Lubeck*; she also allowed Hawkins to fly her Royal Standard and call his ships a Royal squadron; besides the *Jesus* there was one 140-ton ship and two very much smaller vessels with a total complement of 170. Hawkins's biographer has suggested that Elizabeth's idea, and that of her courtiers in so obviously supporting another intrusion into the West Indies was to offer the Spanish naval help in ridding the area of French corsairs, hoping to gain in return a contract to supply slaves to the islands. There is no evidence to support the inference, and plenty of indications that the Spanish were making their opposition to any further English intrusion very clear. England meanwhile was moving away from Spain at surprising speed; in October 1562 Elizabeth had concluded a treaty with the Huguenot leader, Condé, and sent a force to occupy Le Havre, not a move calculated to please Philip II, defender of the Catholic faith. In the same year the Huguenots had planted a colony on the coast of Florida as a base for their privateer operations against the Spanish trade and islands, and it is more likely that the English Court aimed at an understanding with these Protestant interlopers than with the Spanish Crown. But like so many aspects of Elizabeth's policy the real motives behind this rather surprising flaunting of the Royal Standard are obscure.

The expedition sailed in October 1564, and this time there are more details of the manner in which the negroes were captured; at one point eighty men in armour failed to catch fleeing natives, at another place they succeeded in taking only ten while losing seven Englishmen in the process. Most of those with whom they finally sailed from the coast were plundered or purchased from the Portuguese. Arriving in the West Indies the following March, they found the local governors had been forewarned of their approach by the Governor at Santo Domingo and instructed not to trade with them. Failing to do any worthwhile business in the islands they sailed to the mainland at Rio de la Hacha, but were met with a similar refusal. Hawkins told the Governor that this was 'an armada of the Queen's Majesty of England', that had been sent on other affairs but had been driven to these parts by contrary winds; he had hoped to find 'such friendship as hee should doe in Spaine, to the contrary whereof hee knewe no reason, in that there was amitie betwixt their princes.'[6] But as they refused to do trade he did not intend to let it be said that, having the force to compel them he had been sent away empty handed; 'he would rather put it in adventure to try whether he or they should have the better, and therefore willed them either to give him licence to trade, or else stand to their own harmes.' They then agreed to trade, but offered only half the price that slaves and merchandise had fetched on the previous voyage; at this Hawkins prepared the ships' boats with falconets, breech-loaders, and a landing party of one hundred armoured men. The townsfolk, who made a brave show of resistance on the shore, fell flat or broke in panic at the first discharge of the boats' ordnance, after which Hawkins dictated his own trade terms. Whether this was all a charade by the townsfolk to convince the authorities that they had been forced to trade at gunpoint must remain a matter of conjecture.

On the way home Hawkins called at the Huguenot colony in Florida, which was in poor shape for want of reliefs and provisions, and offered to return them to Europe. They declined his offer. A few months later they were exterminated by a powerful Spanish force under Menendez, who gave no quarter. Afterwards Menendez set about constructing a powerful fortress, St Augustine, to prevent further incursions in this vital strategic area. Hawkins meanwhile arrived home safely, and when the proceeds were shared out (as was the fashion in most joint stock enterprises of the day) it is believed the backers made sixty per cent profit on their venture.

Despite renewed Spanish protests a third expedition was organised and sailed in 1566 under the command of John Lovell. He made a similar 'triangular' voyage, while Hawkins himself prepared an even larger expedition for the following year. For this, Elizabeth adventured the 300-ton *Minion* as well as the *Jesus,* and the backers again included high officials of the Royal Navy, members of the Privy Council and leading London merchants and financiers; it was one of the typical part-merchant, part-Court joint-stock ventures forced on Elizabeth by her penury; again Hawkins was to fly the Royal Standard and call his ships a Royal squadron. Although originally advertised as a voyage in search of west African gold – probably to mislead the Spanish Ambassador, who reported the preparations and the Court backing – Hawkins, after departing from Plymouth in October 1567, took his usual course to the Portuguese slaving rivers. This time there can be no doubt that he plundered negroes from the Portuguese caravels by force; however, the greater part of the captures were made by taking sides in a war between native kingdoms, and he eventually sailed for the West Indies with some 500 negroes. Despite another Spanish injunction not to deal with the English, he had 'reasonable trade and courteous entertainment' except at Rio de la Hacha, which he again had to force to terms, and Cartagena, which was too strongly defended to attempt. By this time he had a rich cargo of bartered goods as well as gold and silver bullion to the value of at least 3,000 ducats – no treasure haul, but a respectable sum – and with only fifty slaves left unsold, Hawkins set sail for the Florida Channel and home. Passing to the west of Cuba he ran into one of the fearful summer hurricanes of the area, and the *Jesus*, a crazy old high-charged carrack which had almost foundered in a storm on the way out, strained to such an extent that they had to cut her castles down; even then her hull timbers worked independently, admitting such floods of seawater that fish were soon swimming about in the hold. Hawkins was on the point of abandoning her when the weather abated and he was able to run for San Juan de Ulloa to refit. Arriving at the harbour, which was nothing more than an anchorage between the shore and a stony bank scarcely 200 yards long, three feet above water level, Hawkins bluffed his way in after the Spaniards had mistaken his Royal Standard for their own. All would have been well had it not been the time for the arrival of the annual Spanish fleet.

The following morning the *flota* hove in sight, eleven merchantmen and two escorting warships, bearing the incoming Viceroy of New Spain, Don Martin Enriquez. Hawkins was in a quandary; to let the fleet in to the anchorage would enable the Spanish to overcome his smaller force, to keep them out of their own port (the only safe haven in the area) might result in their destruction in the case of bad weather and would in any case be an act of war for which the Queen would be held responsible. Thus far his operations, although forcible, had all been in pursuit of trade; he had not plundered, ransomed, sacked or burned in the manner of French corsairs, and it seems that his instructions did not envisage piracy or open war, certainly not against Philip's representative in New Spain. So he opened negotiations. Eventually it was agreed that the Spanish ships could enter but that the English would hold the stony bank and the guns mounted on it, and no Spaniards would be allowed to land there with any kind of weapon. Ten gentlemen from each side were exchanged as hostages to seal the bargain, and the great fleet worked in; the English vessels warped together for safety, heads to the bank, anchors from astern into the middle of the anchorage in case they should need to haul themselves out quickly.

The precautions were well advised; probably Enriquez never had any intention of adhering to a bargain forced on him by heretics and interlopers. In any case on the third day movements of men and arms among the Spanish ships alerted Hawkins and he had a little time to prepare his own vessels before a trumpet sounded and Spanish soldiers swarmed on to the bank and drove the English from the guns there, following them towards the ships, while others clambered aboard the *Minion* out of a great Spanish vessel that dropped alongside. Hawkins was ready; while the English crews cut the headropes to the bank and hauled heartily on the sternwarps he leaped down on to the *Minion* at the head of an armoured party from the *Jesus* alongside, calling 'God and Saint George! Upon these traitrous villains.' The Spaniards were driven off, and as the English ships warped away they opened fire with their broadside guns; the Spanish replied at point blank. As shot flew thick, Hawkins called to his page for beer, and when it was brought in a silver cup, 'he drinking to all men, willed the gunners to stand by their pieces lustily like men'. He had no sooner put the cup down than it was struck away by a shot, 'which nothing dismayed him, for he ceased not to encourage us, saying "Fear nothing, for God, who hath preserved me from this shot, will also deliver us from these traitors and villains!" '[7]

The *Jesus* had five moderately heavy (18–20 pounder) pieces, five medium and five light guns on the upper deck, a substantial battery for the day; most of the lighter pieces from the castles which had been cut away were struck below in the hold. The *Minion*'s armament is not known, but no doubt she had several 9-pound or 10-pound demi-culverins, the favourite gun in the English service, and a few heavier pieces. Between them they had sufficient weighty ordnance to knock holes in the two Spanish escorts, sinking one and causing the other to burn to the water's edge – this within an hour or so according to Hawkins's own account. However the Spanish guns, particularly those ashore, sank all the smaller English vessels except for the fifty-ton *Judith* – which was commanded by a short, thick-set, ruddy-faced young kinsman of Hawkins named Francis Drake – and so damaged the *Jesus* alow and aloft that it was evident they would not get her out to sea; Hawkins had her placed to shield the *Minion* from the bombardment, planning to transfer to her and slip away under cover of darkness. However, about four o'clock that afternoon, the Spaniards equipped two fireships and as they bore down the crew of the *Minion* panicked and set sail without orders, leaving Hawkins and the survivors from the *Jesus* to jump aboard as best they could, or follow in the ship's boat.

In such an undisciplined way, the *Minion*, with some 200 men aboard, and the small *Judith*, which had drawn out of range earlier, escaped from the general destruction. That night Drake and his thirty or so men parted company for reasons or mischance that will never be known. Hawkins in his account did not refer to Drake by name, writing cryptically that the *Judith* 'the same night forsook us in our misery',[8] it was an inauspicious beginning to the career of a man lauded as the greatest of all Elizabethan sailors. Some days later Hawkins landed about half of the *Minion*'s complement at their own request on the shore of the Gulf of Mexico to fend as best they could, then set about taking the damaged and leaking, ill-provisioned vessel back across the Atlantic. After a desperate voyage during which the few survivors were reduced to eating rats and stewed ox-hide from the cargo he brought her to Mounts Bay, Cornwall, at the end of January 1568. Drake had already arrived home.

The 'treachery' at San Juan de Ulloa was something of a turning point in English relations with Spain, certainly in the popular imagination. Besides the deceit of the Spanish Viceroy, who had told Hawkins that he himself 'in the faith of a Viceroy would be our defence from all villainies',[9] the English prisoners taken in the battle were delivered as heretics to the dreaded Inquisition; two spirited gallants who refused to compromise were burned alive, several others were chained to the oars of Spanish galleys. However, the break with Spain would have occurred with or without the battle; everywhere on the Atlantic fringe events were tending in the same direction.

The most significant event was rebellion in the Spanish Netherlands. Revolts against Spanish rule had been breaking out in these provinces since long before Philip II inherited them. Protestant groups in the burgeoning commercial and industrial towns had called on themselves the most cruel repression; it has been estimated that some 30,000 heretics of one kind or another were roasted over slow fires, burned at the stake, drowned or submitted to other revolting tortures in the time of Philip's father, the Emperor Charles V. This had not endeared Spanish authority to the people, nor had the tax impositions that both Charles V and Philip II placed on this wealthy region to pay for their wars in Italy, the Mediterranean and eastern Europe. Here was the nub of he matter. The burghers who had acquired great wealth through trade and had formed local power groups in the towns were, naturally, opponents of a system which fought its wars at their expense and without their consent. Such was the position in 1564 when Philip II, reacting to religious turmoil throughout northern Europe, issued decrees for an even more rigorous campaign against heretics in the Netherlands. This served to increase the spirit of rebellion; Philip responded by sending the Duke of Alva with an army of Spanish and Italian mercenaries to suppress it by force; instead the atrocities Alva and his troops committed, and the sales tax imposed on the burghers to pay for this foreign garrison on their own soil proved the catalyst for a united popular revolt against Spain. Of the original leaders, two were caught and executed, leaving one, William of Orange, as the focus of resistance.

By 1568, therefore, when Hawkins returned from San Juan de Ulloa the entire coastline of western Europe from Biscay around Brittany and Normandy and up to the Netherlands, had broken out in revolt against the territorial centres of Paris and Madrid. England joined in enthusiastically, not because the revolts were Protestant and she was nominally a Protestant country, not even because her attempts to break into the Spanish monopoly of New World wealth had been so contemptuously dismissed, but chiefly because the victory of either territorial centre posed the greatest danger to her own safety. She threw her weight in with the break-away fringe against the powers of the centre, chiefly against Spain, whose wealth and strength filled every horizon. That Philip ruled autocratically and his instruments suppressed heresy with every refinement of cruelty, and burned English sailors for their faith was enough to provide the spiritual stimulus necessary in any war; Spanish wealth was the material stimulus. As Philip was drawn by the changing territorial balance into supporting the Catholic party in France, the conflict developed along the religious divide.

England did not announce the opening of hostilities; the country was too poor to declare openly and still divided with powerful Catholic nobles and the exiled Mary Queen of Scots as potential instruments of the territorial powers. She continued to aid the Huguenots in France, and later the Orangists in the Netherlands, with both men and money, but her chief contribution was in the sea battle against Spanish trade and communications with their army in the Netherlands. In the year of Hawkins's return several ships freighted with cash that Philip II had obtained on loan from his Genoese bankers to pay Alva's army were chased into the harbours of Devon and Cornwall by Huguenot privateers. The money was seized by the English and a good portion of it sent up to London. Elizabeth appropriated it, maintaining against the impassioned protests of Philip's ambassador that as it had not arrived at its destination it was still Genoese property. She transferred the loan to herself.

The undeclared war followed a pattern that was to become familiar to generations of Englishmen in the formal wars of the following centuries; at first the armies of the territorial powers swept all before them and Elizabeth was forced to prop up beleaguered and isolated centres of resistance with troops and subsidies. Then as the war of attrition at sea whittled away at the margins of territorial strength a slow but inexorable change was worked in the balance. In this case it was Huguenot privateers, Dutch privateers – or 'Sea Beggars', a name they took from a scornful Spanish allusion to the body of Netherlanders who protested at the edicts against Protestants – and English pirates, often commissioned as privateers by one or other of the Continental admirals, who infested the narrow seas. They brought a flow of plunder to the West Country ports, particularly Plymouth where the Hawkins family operated, and Southampton and Dover, where the Sea Beggars established their headquarters. The goods were disposed of through the usual pirate syndicates while Elizabeth made a show of sending Royal ships after sea rovers, and bringing a few notable receivers to trial to placate Spain.

Within a few years trade was almost paralysed, the flow of loot had begun to fall off and protests from her own merchants were added to those from Spain and France as privateering degenerated into indiscriminate pillage. In 1572 therefore she sent a Royal squadron on a rather more serious patrol against pirates in the Channel and cleared Plymouth and Dover of Sea Beggars; as a result they seized Flushing on the island of Walcheren at the mouth of the Scheldt, and imposed an even tighter blockade on Antwerp, finally ruining its trade. Three years later unpaid Spanish troops mutinied and wrote a bloody epitaph to the former financial capital of north Europe.

Meanwhile English sea rovers had taken the lead in plundering the Caribbean and Spanish 'Main'. Elizabeth adventured no Royal ships and the expeditions were small-scale, rather sordid affairs directed against the smaller coastal settlements and local trading vessels; such were the early voyages of Francis Drake. For his third independent command in a Hawkins's ship in 1572 he determined to outflank the Spanish defensive system by plundering the treasure route across the isthmus between Panama and Nombre de Dios. His first attempts were unsuccessful and his force was decimated by yellow fever. The next year fifteen of his surviving men together with a Havre corsair captain, Le Têtu with twenty men and a party of escaped negro slaves known as Cimaroons, who waged guerrilla war against their former Spanish masters, succeeded in surprising a mule train loaded with silver, gold and pearls outside Nombre de Dios. Le Têtu was killed in the skirmish, but Drake and most of the party made it back to their vessels with as much of the booty as they could carry.

Drake was one of the more gifted and daring of the English leaders; the triumph which rewarded his perseverence on the isthmus in the face of daunting discouragements made his name and his fortune. Although he and all his kind were technically pirates, since Elizabeth's devious game did not allow her to recognise them formally, there is no doubt that in reality they were agents of English state policy, acting against the main enemy, Spain. Drake's first remark on returning from his later piratical expedition to the undefended Pacific coast of Spanish America and subsequent epic circumnavigation of the world, was to enquire if Elizabeth were alive and well; such were the dangers of the unofficial game. Fortunately for him Elizabeth was still in control of the fine balances within the country. In response to Spanish protests about his piracy she went through a charade of impounding the considerable loot then knighted him! There can be little doubt that she was the major investor in the voyage.

Small scale as much of the plundering was, it had sufficient cumulative effect to spur the Spanish to more defensive measures. Most interesting was the proposal from Pedro Menendez that the proper place to defend the Caribbean was the English Channel; he planned to seize the Scilly Isles and base a squadron of fifteen to twenty well-armed and weatherly warships there to intercept the English, Dutch and Breton and Norman rovers from the windward position – the prevailing winds being south-westerly – before they reached the Atlantic. It is remarkable how the great strategists of the sailing warship era all proposed 'forward' policies for defence and attack, from Albuquerque, the Huguenot admiral, Coligny, with the Florida attempt, Menendez, and soon Hawkins and Drake. In this instance Menendez's plan was accepted and only an epidemic which swept through the expedition as it was preparing in 1574 prevented the attempt. Menendez himself was one of the victims and the scheme died with him. The fact that it got so far is

an indication that piracy, while unable to molest the treasure fleets themselves or the main fortified bases, and never in this period achieving another
haul like Drake's must have added to England's wealth. English vessels
trading with the Mediterranean were also becoming notorious as pirates,
and taken together with the Channel and Atlantic plundering it adds up to a
significant exchange of marginal resources in which Spain was the loser.
Whether England gained by plunder more than she lost in legitimate trade
is impossible to say. To judge by Elizabeth's policy, which veered back
towards normal trade relations with Spain in the mid 1570s, she gained at
first, but as Spanish defensive measures caused the returns from piracy to
dry up, she became a net loser.

More important than the temporary and marginal increase in English
wealth was the great and permanent damage to Spanish resources caused
by the privateering war. Not only had she lost the trade and revenues from
the richest provinces in the empire, lost the loans from her former financiers
in Antwerp, not only was she forced to send troops and cash to pay them
on a difficult and dangerous overland route across the Continent, but she
had lost in Antwerp and surrounds the most advanced and productive
ordnance manufacturing region in Europe. Although Philip's new general
in the Netherlands, the Duke of Parma, returned the southern provinces,
including Antwerp, to Spanish control in 1578, industry had been ruined by
the combination of sea blockade and land campaign, and skilled gunfounders
had emigrated *en masse*. As the gunfounders in the Spanish–Italian provinces
had not kept pace qualitatively or quantitatively with the developments in
the Netherlands, and as her own foundries established the previous century
at Medina del Campo, Malaga and Barcelona had never been consistently
supported and had small capacity, she began to suffer a shortage of
ordnance and also of gunpowder which reached crisis proportions by the
late 1570s. She sought guns wherever she could, and there is no doubt that
many came from England, despite Elizabeth's prohibitions on arms exports;
by 1587 shiploads of English iron ordnance and ammunition were being
despatched to Spain and her Italian possessions.[10]

The gun crisis was symptomatic of Spain's failure to become an industrial
nation. There were many possible causes; poor internal communications,
government regulation and heavy taxation, inflation caused by a combination
of defensive wars financed by loans, and bullion inflow, making Spanish
costs uncompetitive, the contempt in which trade was held by the territorial
nobility, conversely the success attained by conquest and exploitation of
subject people, and the Royal and bureaucratic absolutism. Except for the
first, these are all inter-related symptoms of the territorial/central-control
ethic. So far as armaments and a fighting navy are concerned a main reason
for the lack of government support for a home-based ordnance industry and
a Royal navy were the resources available elsewhere within the empire.
Before buying armaments or contracting for ships abroad, the Spanish

bureaucracy made meticulous comparative costings between theh ome-made and the empire or mercenary product.[11] These showed the Netherlands or Italian guns cheaper, Italian galleys cheaper, and hence the home industries were not supported. Similarly with the slaving *Asientos*, which were granted to foreigners for cash urgently needed by the Spanish Treasury. In short, while the Spanish government could control the divers productive areas of its empire by force of arms it sought what would now be called cost-effective solutions to its arms and shipbuilding requirements; as it always needed money to defend this vast empire it also sought immediate cash in return for commercial privileges; it thus assured that the most lucrative privileges would be monopolies which private merchants, without the huge capital outlay and the need to observe the regulations stipulated, would be able to undercut. The slaving *Asientos* were the most important example, for slaves were the sixteenth-century equivalent of the fossil fuels which power modern industry. And it was in the 'triangular' trade of manufactured goods to west Africa, negroes to America, slave-produced tropical produce back to Europe that the western European 'Atlantic' economies 'took off', and the seeds of what is known as the 'industrial revolution' were sown. Hence Spain's failure here was profoundly important. Portuguese, French, John Hawkins, later the break-away provinces of the Netherlands, all undercut and intruded into the Spanish monopoly. This was both symptom and cause of her failure; as a contemporary observer wrote, 'Spain supplies herself from other countries with almost all things which are manufactured for common use and which consist in the industry and toil of man.'[12]

It was the very success of the Spanish empire that doomed it; it was not Philip's self-imposed burden as champion of the Catholic faith that drained his Treasury, but the very necessary task of defending the empire which provided the manufactures, wealth, men and armaments without which it could not be defended! The flow of silver from the New World obscured and, at the same time, contributed to this; it dazzled contemporaries, persuading them – not least Philip himself – of the overwhelming resources of Spain; it was the security against which Philip borrowed hugely and ruinously to finance his defensive wars; it was also the focus of envy.

The first sign of this fateful interaction was the loss of the Netherlands' trade, finance and guns, the direct result of the Protestant privateering offensive in the English Channel and approaches. By the late 1570s it was clear to most of Philip's advisors that the key to the Netherlands was control of the English Channel – as Menendez had realised it was also the key to the American colonies. The key to the English Channel was England. It was from this period that Spanish subversion in England was stepped up and plots hatched to overthrow Elizabeth and place Mary Queen of Scots on her throne. When they failed and Elizabeth reluctantly and ambiguously ordered Mary's execution, more expensive expedients became necessary. Detailed plans were prepared for the invasion of England.

In 1577 John Hawkins was appointed Treasurer of Elizabeth's navy. It was a home-waters navy which had served to repel a French threat in the first years of her reign as it had in Henry VIII's time. It was headed by five great ships of up to 1,100 tons, and five medium ships of some 400 tons, all but one of which had towering castles at bow and stern in the contemporary warship style; there were also a dozen lesser craft, but as with all navies of the day it was expected that for major campaigns the core of queen's ships would be supplemented by hired merchantmen. It is possible that Hawkins's appointment was designed to convert this essentially defensive nucleus into an offensive oceanic force – not perhaps in Elizabeth's schemes but in those of her chief minister, Lord Burghley. Certainly this was how Hawkins himself saw it. Ever since his attempts at more-or-less honest trade in the Indies had been blown apart by the guns at San Juan de Ulloa, he had been planning an expedition in force to seize the treasure fleet from the isthmus. It was not a novel idea; French ministers, probably inspired by the Huguenot leader, Coligny, had prepared detailed plans for such an expedition in 1559 just before the French civil wars; countless other Dutch, French, English sailors and statesmen were to hatch similar schemes in the future, for Spanish treasure was not simply the focus of envy, it was accepted as the mainstay of Spain, without which the whole mighty empire would collapse.

Elizabeth had not agreed to Hawkins's early plans for fear the Spanish army would slip across from the Netherlands while a sizeable part of her fleet was at the other side of the Atlantic. Hawkins drew up a similar plan after his appointment as Treasurer, but again it was not approved. This was probably fortunate as it allowed him to devote his energies to reconstructing the navy. The two chief obstacles he had to contend with were extreme shortage of money and extreme conservatism among the long-serving officials of the board. He contrived to overcome both obstacles with an attack on corruption and overspending by the officials. Elizabeth, he wrote, was being 'monstrously overcharged' for repairs and new building:

> in general the Queen has paid for 900 loads of timber where 500
> would have been sufficient . . . the purveyors of timber make great
> profits, for they sell the best of the material for private use and make the
> State pay extremely for the refuse.[13]

No doubt the strictures were justified as Elizabeth's paltry income and the English tradition that taxation was only for exceptional circumstances meant in those days before 'national debt' had been invented, that her officials were underpaid, hence made up their salaries by 'perquisites' and plain graft.

Hawkins made a firm promise to save the Queen £4,000 a year by eliminating fraud; the 'ordinary' expenditure, exclusive of new construction and major repairs, was then £6,000. He made a 'bargain' with Burghley that for a lump-sum payment each year he would provide and renew when necessary all the cables and cordage of the fleet, and he prevailed on the two master shipwrights to accept similar lump-sum payments for grounding all the large vessels at least once every three years, renewing any necessary timbers, masts and spars and paying the workforce. This reduced the 'ordinary' expenditure to a fixed £4,000 a year; saving in major repairs allowed him to keep his promise, and a second 'bargain' was struck on similar lines in 1585.

The stringent economies did not allow any new building, but his ideas for a modern ocean-going fleet were met by cutting down the huge castles of several of the great and medium sized vessels, and lengthening the hulls. This displeased the other board members as much as his exposure of graft. They complained that without the superstructure, or 'commodious fights', these 'majestic ships of the Queen' had been made to look like galleasses; they might even be taken for merchantmen; further it was 'not right that one man should prevail in these matters. All things ought to be done jointly by the board.'[14]

The rancorous continuing dispute between Hawkins and the other high officials – who remained in office despite his exposure of their corrupt practices – was essentially a dispute between two schools of naval thought. The traditional view represented by the board, none of whom had experience outside home waters, demanded extremes of height to inspire awe, to confer the advantage in a close soldiers' action, to give accommodation and protection to the numerous fighting men necessary for such an action, and space to mount literally hundreds of quick-firing swivels. This concept sacrificed speed and manœuvrability because the hull had to be wide and deep to support such great buildings, and the wind acted on the superstructure much as on sails, driving the vessel to leeward, making any change of tack an extraordinarily difficult business. The great weight aloft also strained the ships in rough weather and had to be cut away in gales. Hawkins, who had experienced all these disadvantages with the crazy old *Jesus of Lubeck*, who had always been aware of the dangers of disease among men crowded together in ships for any length of time, and who had experienced at San Juan de Ulloa the devastating effects of cast ordnance on ships' hulls, was representative of what might be called the privateering school. This demanded fast and manœuvrable vessels to cut out stragglers and avoid heavy enemy escorts whose fighting strength was in massed soldiers. As Hawkins was still planning to take the war to the enemy coasts (especially the Caribbean) and the treasure fleets, he also demanded ocean-worthy ships. All these considerations led to the long, low clean lines of the vessels which were nicely described by contemporaries as 'race-built' galleons.

Exactly how or where the type evolved is not clear; the *Foresight* of 1570 is regarded as the first English example; the next was the famous *Revenge*, built for the navy in 1575 before Hawkins's arrival as Treasurer, but perhaps to his ideas. The *Revenge* of 450 tons was the ideal of the modern school. She combined nimbleness, which meant speed and the ability to tack in under quarter of an hour, with the capacity to fire a heavy 'broadside' of guns; her official armament was 2 demi-cannon (32-pounders), 4 cannon periers (short, wide mouthed 24-pounders), 10 culverins (long 18-pounders), 6 demi-culverins (long 9-pounders), 10 sakers (long 5-pounders) and 14 lesser pieces, chiefly the older type of breechloader. The variety of types and sizes must have been the result of attempting to mount as heavy a battery as possible in what was a very small hull. It was not to compromise between long- and short-range guns, a theory that has bedevilled all discussion of sixteenth-century naval warfare. There was no need for long-range guns because of their inaccuracy and because of the impossibility of laying them in a pitching and rolling ship with sufficient precision to make it worth while to fire at anything outside about 500 yards; even at that range it was throwing most of the shot straight into the sea. 'Long range' is not a useful concept and although the whole question is still obscure, it is more likely that the culverin or long gun was chosen either for its assumed greater penetration power or because casting iron guns of great length produced better results; the breech end where the explosion took place was always the lower end in a vertical casting, hence cooled under pressure and this was the reason for casting long bronze guns;[15] perhaps it was also one of the secrets of the English iron gunfounders. They did make short pieces, but these were fired with far smaller charges. The reason for long guns remains an open question.

The broadside of the *Revenge* was not heavy by later standards, yet in battering pieces it was 100 per cent heavier than the broadside of the traditional *Jesus of Lubeck*. Moreover her greater manœuvrability gave her a 200 per cent advantage; this was because the tactics of the 'privateer' school involved bearing down on the enemy, firing one side, tacking or, in the contemporary expression, 'winding' and bearing down again and firing the other side. Although this took a great deal of time it took less time than re-loading, for the guns were fixed in action, not allowed to recoil, and loading was an awkward business with the loading numbers straddling the barrels *outside* the gunports. This perhaps explains why the old-fashioned pieces with detachable chambers were retained alongside the far more powerful cast guns; they were a quick-firing secondary armament for close work.

The third major reform was a reduction in the manning scale. Hitherto it had been one man to one and one-third tons; Hawkins reduced it to one man to every two tons, and at the same time prevailed on Burghley to sanction a 50 per cent increase in sailors' pay, to ten shillings a month; this exactly cancelled out any savings from the decreased manning scales, but meant that prime seamen could be attracted and would serve in less

crowded, thus healthier, conditions. It also meant that ships could be victualled for longer periods, a major consideration for Hawkins. Like the
cutting away of the great castles, this change signified a departure from
the traditional boarding tactics in which superiority of numbers told. It was
a clear indication that Hawkins and his school had adopted stand-off gunnery
as the basic naval tactic.

That this was an English invention dating back to Henry VIII's time is
one of many myths resulting from the undue influence of British naval
historical writing. We have seen that Pedro Cabral's instructions of 1500
ordered stand-off tactics, and da Gama and Vicente Sodre practised them
in 1502 as to the manner born; Venetian commanders were trying to use
them in combined galley/galleon actions at the same time. They probably
came in with the great guns themselves at least half a century earlier. But
what emerges from the descriptions of Atlantic privateer warfare in the
first three-quarters of the sixteenth century is that both boarding and stand-
off tactics were practised by every Atlantic maritime power as occasion
served. As a generalisation, vessels used stand-off tactics when in inferior
force; closing and boarding tactics when in superior force. In some actions
between Portuguese caravals and English or French interlopers on the
Guinea coast both sides used stand-off tactics in line ahead. Hawkins's
achievement was to take these much earlier developments to their logical
conclusion by creating a fleet *designed* for stand-off artillery tactics; in doing
so he gave Elizabeth the finest fighting navy in the world for a brief period.
He did not go over entirely to the new type however; the three largest
ships were left as they were in all their majesty. Whether this was a deliberate decision to keep a core of heavy ships which could hold their own against
anything the Spaniards attempted in close combat, or whether it was a
compromise with the rest of the board is not clear.

English planning against the Spanish invasion preparations started earlier
and was more thorough than has been generally realised.[16] The existence
of Philip's 'Enterprise of England' was revealed to the English first in May
1582 through letters found hidden in a looking-glass belonging to a Spanish
agent on his way to Scotland. Burghley immediately turned to the Navy, the
only possible defence against Continental armies, instructing its executive
head, the Lord Admiral, to ascertain the number and size of the country's
merchant fleet.[17] The following year lords lieutenants of the counties and
mayors of towns were instructed to carry out a census of the seafaring population; this revealed the home towns of 1,484 masters, 11,515 mariners, 2,999
fishermen, and 957 Thames watermen; taken together with the list of merchant
ships and their tonnage it gave the naval administration the information
they needed to mobilise the maritime resources of the country. In 1584
Burghley drew up a memorial outlining the probable Spanish strategy and
plans for the English naval response, and in 1585, as Spanish troops seemed
set to subdue the entire Netherlands – after which it would be England's

turn – a large programme of new construction was set in hand which, with purchase, added sixteen new vessels to the fleet in the next three years. The most important of these were the 'race-built' galleons *Ark Royal* (bought from Sir Walter Raleigh), *Vanguard* and *Rainbow*, built on the lines of the *Revenge*. By the time the 'Enterprise of England' was ready the Royal Navy had eighteen galleons from 1,100 to 300 tons, seven lesser galleons of 100 tons or so and eighteen ocean-going pinnaces for recon-naissance and supplies. Detailed plans had been drawn up for adding twenty-two 'defensible' merchantmen, chiefly powerful vessels of the Mediterranean merchants.

For a comparison between this force and the Spanish, here is a statement from a contemporary sailor, Sir Arthur Gorgas, who served in the subsequent armada campaign. After granting to the Spanish navy 'hugeness and numbers of their vessels as for multitudes of sailors and mariners' together with plentiful supplies of weapons, victuals and treasure, 'the very sinews and life of armies', he elaborated the English advantages:

> namely for our swiftness in outsailing them, our nimbleness in getting
> into the weather of them, our little draft of water in comparison to
> theirs, our stout bearing up of our sides in all huge winds, when theirs
> must stoop to their great disadvantage many ways, our yawness in
> staying well and casting about twice for their once and so discharging
> our broadsides of ordnance double for their single, we carry as good
> and great artillery as they do and having far better gunners, our
> knowledge and pilotage of our own coasts, channels, sands, harbours
> and soundings being far beyond theirs with divers other advantages. . . .
> I say setting the one against the other [we] are more powerful to
> annoy them and guard our coasts then they of force to offend and invade
> us.[18]

While English naval defences were prepared, English troops and funds to mercenaries were sent to the Netherlands to support the hard-pressed resistance, and Drake was loosed in search of Spanish treasure to pay for this costly intervention. Drake and Hawkins, supported by Burghley and other ministers, had been urging an offensive strategy for some time. Their ideas had centred on the Atlantic islands. The Portuguese king had died in 1580 without heir, and Philip's troops had marched into the country, incorporating it in the Spanish empire. The English advocates of a forward policy saw this as a perfect opportunity to ally with the Pretender to the Portuguese Crown, Dom Antonio, and take the islands in the Azores where resistance to Spain was strong. With these in their possession the treasure fleets and indeed all West and East Indian shipping would be at their mercy. It was a bold and brilliant plan, but Elizabeth was as unwilling as ever to commit herself so unambiguously to war with Philip. It was left to a soldier of fortune, Philip Strozzi, to lead a mainly French fleet, accompanied by several English ships – including medium-sized Royal warships – to make the attempt in the summer of 1582. The Spanish veteran, the Marqués of Santa Cruz, who had commanded the Reserve at Lepanto, was sent after Strozzi's expedition with some twenty-eight ships, and sighted the numerically far stronger French fleet off St Michaels in the Azores on 22 July. The resulting battle was the first fleet action between broadside sailing galleons in history – a full-scale rehearsal for the armada campaign. Unfortunately the vague accounts which have survived make it impossible to be certain about the tactics; what seems to have happened is that after three days of manœuvring in fickle winds and calms during which broadsides were discharged outside effective range, the two sides closed in a traditional boarding mêlée, and Strozzi entered and took a great Spanish galleon, but was in his turn boarded by Santa Cruz's flagship and forced to yield. Strozzi's Vice-Admiral, instead of supporting his chief, took his squadron off – some said he had been corrupted by Philip II – after which the rest of the French fleet also broke and ran, leaving Santa Cruz in possession. Several of the French vessels were crippled aloft and two, probably smaller ones, sunk by gunfire. Walter Raleigh, a leading member of the offensive school of English naval warfare, commented afterwards, 'to clap ships together without consideration belongs rather to a madman than a man of war. For by such ignorant bravery was Peter Strossie lost at the Azores.'[19]

Over the next two years the leading spirits in the English 'forward' group were thick with schemes, Raleigh for founding an English colony in Virginia on the flank of the Spanish Indies route, Hawkins for organising a combined English, Huguenot and Sea Beggars privateering offensive under the flag of Dom Antonio, aimed both at treasure and fomenting revolt in the Portuguese Atlantic colonies, Drake for an expedition in force to the East Indies. In 1585 when the danger of the Netherlands falling to the Duke of Parma loomed over all other considerations, Drake was despatched instead on a nearer and more certain mission into the Atlantic. The expedition, over twenty ships strong, was a joint-stock venture with the queen contributing a sixth part of the capital and two Royal ships. London merchants, courtiers, Drake, Hawkins made up the rest of the typically state/private syndicate. In the event Drake missed the treasure fleets; after some pillage on the Spanish coast and the Cape Verde Islands, he made across to the Caribbean, sacked the former capital, Santo Domingo, and burned it building by building until he had extorted sufficient ransom. Afterwards he applied the same treatment to Cartagena, gaining a far larger ransom, then on the return he called at Raleigh's infant Virginia settlement, which he found suffering from acute shortages, and took the colonists home. Although the syndicate collected 75 per cent profit on their outlay, it was a disappointing return from a great expedition on which many hopes had been placed.

It was, however, the final goad for Philip II. The Spanish merchant community, frightened by the possibility of the English cutting their silver lifeline on which the whole imperial economy depended, already suffering from the loss of their Netherlands trade, added their voice to the military men who had long seen England as the key to recovery of the Netherlands. Philip was stirred into translating the somewhat vague plans for the 'Enterprise of England' into detailed instructions.

It was an enormous, hugely costly, logistically daunting effort that he had to dovetail. The first requirement was to defeat or neutralise the English fleet with a superior fleet; without this an army, even if it could be landed, would be cut off. The other essential requirement was for the fleet to rendezvous with the Duke of Parma's army in the Netherlands at a deep-water port where the guns could protect the invasion barges Parma would need to gather; as yet there was no such deep water haven in Spanish control. The ports of Flanders were beset by shoals which prevented an ocean-going fleet coming in close, and they and the Scheldt, the ideal embarkation point, were under blockade by the shallow draft armed 'flyboats' of the Sea Beggars. Here as modern historians have pointed out, was the fatal flaw in the invasion plan. Parma's barges could not get out because of the flyboats and a fleet powerful enough to defeat, or contain, the English navy could not get in to cover them because of the sandbanks off that dangerous coast. It is incredible that Philip, who drew ships, men and money for the enterprise from all over his Mediterranean and Atlantic empire, should have overlooked the critical importance of this small area in the soundings off Calais and Nieuport.

In 1587, while the ships, guns, ammunition, supplies and men for the great armada were being assembled at Lisbon and other ports all around the Iberian peninsula, Drake was sent out again with instructions to

> impeach the joining together of the King of Spain's fleet out of their several ports, to keep victuals from them, to follow them in case they should come forward towards England or Ireland . . . as also to set upon those as should either come out of the east or west Indies or go out of Spain thither.[20]

In short, he was to mount a military and commercial blockade of the Spanish coast. It was a triumph of the party represented by Hawkins and Drake over the defensive mentality of the Queen. That it was sound in conception is proved by the whole course of British naval history, especially in the eighteenth and early nineteenth centuries. Whether the Queen had the resources to carry out the policy effectively is another story. She provided only four of the seventeen sizeable ships in the expedition which was the usual state/private joint-stock syndicate, hence in any conflict between state policy and private profit the latter was likely to prevail. As blockade was dull and frequently unrewarding work it was impossible to carry it out for long on a privateering basis. Despite this drawback inherent in the very small revenues of England and the need to spend heavily on the military effort in the Netherlands, Drake, at the very top of his form, succeeded in disrupting the Spanish preparations for that year. The highlight of the expedition was at Cadiz. Having learnt of a concentration of merchant and supply ships there he headed for the port and, flouting all military convention, sailed straight into the harbour without reconnaissance or plan or even discussion at the statutory council of war; he simply informed the captains that he intended an immediate attack without waiting for the laggards to catch up. Complete success justified him. A squadron of six galleys which came up to contest his entry was forced to give way, and he was soon plundering the defenceless merchantmen and supply ships to revictual his own fleet, after which he burnt them, leaving a few only for prizes. The following day the wind dropped right away and the galleys came out from the inner harbour, where they had retreated. Conditions were ideal for them, but again they were forced to retreat from the English broadsides. 'We have now tried by experience these galleys' fight', Drake wrote, 'and I assure you that these Her Majesty's four ships will make no account of 20 of them.'[21]

Meanwhile the town of Cadiz was filling with troops and when the wind came that night Drake sailed out. He had learnt of the wide dispersion of the different units of the Spanish forces, many still at Mediterranean ports, and he set course for Cape St Vincent which these separated squadrons would have to round if they were to join the main force at Lisbon. 'Our interest is [God willing] to impeach the fleet which is come out of the Straits and divers other places before it join with the King's forces.'[22] There was a sheltered bay under Cape St Vincent, and here Drake brought his fleet and prizes, afterwards landing troops and taking the forts overlooking the anchorage so that he had a secure base for the blockade. It was faultless strategy. While his squadron remained there, intercepting a stream of fishermen and coasters carrying individually insignificant but, nevertheless, vital materials for the armada, Philip had all ship movements cease, and ordered Santa Cruz to prepare a squadron to drive the English off.

At the height of his success, with the armada preparations paralysed, and the whole coast ringing with his name, Drake sailed for the Azores, on the way parting company with many of the merchant ships. There is no evidence to explain this sudden abandonment of the coast; it may be that disease, known to have struck his crews, was spreading, or he may have heard rumours of a returning Indies fleet. The blockade work, though extremely damaging to Spain, was making no one's fortune. Only the facts remain; he made for the Azores, captured a great Portuguese carrack laden with eastern merchandise and was back in Plymouth with her before the end of June, a week short of three months from his departure. Sale of the cargo from the carrack fetched £114,000 and the Queen took a one-third share. Perhaps more important for the future were notes found aboard revealing many secrets of the Portuguese route to the East. Meanwhile Santa Cruz had followed Drake to the islands with a squadron of warships, and by the time he returned to Lisbon it was too late in the season to complete the armada for England.

The following year, 1588, Hawkins and Drake were again pressing for a forward policy on the enemy coast. Hawkins, who marshalled his ideas and expressed them with a clarity foreign to Drake's hasty, intuitive temperament, proposed year-round patrols between Spain and the Azores conducted exclusively by Royal ships; with three squadrons, each of six galleons and six pinnaces, each serving four months in rotation, a continuous watch could be kept for only £2,730 a month in wages and victuals. 'It will be a very sad and unlucky month that they will not bring in treble that charge, for they can see nothing but it can hardly escape them.'[23] He proposed that the bill should be met by private investment.

Blockade was not, of course, a novel strategy; it was inherent in the Mediterranean system and in the Portuguese campaigns for controlling the Indian seas; but continuous blockade all the year round was an ambitious extension of the idea that was not fully realised until the eighteenth century, and it may be that Hawkins was some way ahead of his time and England's resources. He had correctly diagnosed the weakness of the combined state/private venture, hence his idea of warships only under single control; he had correctly diagnosed Spain's dependence on American treasure – 'If we might strike once, our peace were made with honour, safety and profit'[24] – and he himself proved later that he could keep a squadron at sea for longer than four months without being crippled by disease; indeed his whole policy with the navy had been directed to that end. It is also true that he intended the blockade as a stroke to bring Spain to her knees in short time at less expense than the Continental armies and subsidies which were draining the Treasury and putting Elizabeth into debt: Flanders had cost nearly £600,000, of which she had paid less than £150,000.[25] Hawkins can be called one of the first of the English 'Blue Water' strategists. But whether the Royal Navy of the day could have maintained such a continuous effort through the north Atlantic winter without bases and within the Spanish and Portuguese sphere for longer than Philip could have survived without his treasure and East and West Indies and Brazilian trade is a large question. The level of Spanish expenditure is suggestive though. In round figures Philip was spending half-a-million ducats a month on his Netherlands army and his armada preparations.[26] This was almost a hundred times the cost of Hawkins's proposed squadron, and rather more than Elizabeth's ordinary *annual* income; more to the point it was in annual terms twice the Crown share of silver mined in New Spain and Peru; equally important, the loans with which Philip covered his huge expenses were secured on the certainty of the silver arriving; if the fleets were delayed or even rendered uncertain crisis must ensue. Hawkins's plan was solidly based. Yet the minimal damage which the English fleet managed to inflict on the armada in its subsequent stately progression up the English Channel provokes questions about the likely effect of the small squadrons he proposed.

It was Drake's less-reasoned assertions that eventually prevailed. Royal and merchant ships had been concentrated in Plymouth through the winter of 1587–8, and Drake begged to be given another opportunity to use them to impeach the Spanish preparations on their own coast. 'Under God's protection the advantage and gain of time and place will be the only and chief means for our good,'[27] he wrote. Such cryptic aphorisms could have meant little to Elizabeth. A fortnight later he repeated, 'The advantage of time and place in all martial affairs is half a victory, which being lost all is irrecoverable.'[28] Again this did not solve the practical problem of where the advantage was to be had. He did however convince the Lord Admiral, Lord Howard of Effingham, whom Elizabeth had placed in overall command of the English naval defences the previous year.

Howard was a courtier and a diplomat, strong, grave and prudent; not sufficiently dashing to win Elizabeth's heart, he had nevertheless earned her trust by staunch service, and in this vital campaign he was to prove her choice sound. He had taken up his task enthusiastically, personally examining every ship in the fleet 'in any place where any man may creep',[29] an inspection which convinced him of Hawkins's faithful work. 'I protest before God, and as my soul shall answer for it, that I think there never were in any place in the world worthier ships than these are.' And finally convinced by Drake, Hawkins, Martin Frobisher and other experienced captains that the Spanish coast was the proper place to defeat the armada, he attempted to take the force out on several occasions during the early summer of 1588. Each time he was frustrated; lack of victuals, reports that the armada had sailed, Elizabeth's sudden changes of heart, gales and contrary winds all played their part.

On the last occasion in July, the winds which forced him back to Plymouth wafted the armada northwards; it was sighted off the Lizard at the entrance to the English Channel by a patrolling pinnace on the 29th – a formidable force, by far the largest ever seen in northern waters. The core of fighting strength was a Portuguese squadron of ten large galleons, a Castilian squadron of ten rather smaller Indies escort galleons, four large merchant ships, and a Neapolitan squadron of four galleasses. Besides this first line were four other squadrons each with ten large, armed merchant galleons. Carrying the provisions, siege and sapping equipment, carts and wagons for land operations were twenty-three lightly armed merchantmen, and there were some thirty-five light oared and sailing craft for scouting and despatches; four galleys which had started with the fleet had been scattered by storms and none took a part in the campaign. In all there were some 19,000 soldiers and noble adventurers in the ships, with 8,000 sailors and 1,200 slaves on the oars.

The Commander-in-Chief was the Duke of Medina Sidonia. Philip II had appointed him on the death of the veteran Santa Cruz in February of that year. The duke was head of one of the wealthiest and most distinguished old Spanish families. His seat was at San Lucar, and he had consequently close connections with the Indies merchants and shipping; by virtue of his station and vast estates, from which he could raise 10,000 armed men, he was military commander of western Andalusia. He had been prominent in the campaign to take the Portuguese Crown in 1580, and had been marked by Philip as loyal and able. Since 1586 he had been intimately concerned with the armada preparations, and he was overseeing the fitting-out of warships of the Indies guard when he received a letter saying that Santa Cruz was dying and the king had 'fixed his eyes' on him to succeed to the command. His immediate reaction is well known. He wrote back pleading inexperience and unfitness for so important an enterprise, asserting that he must give a bad account of himself, 'being guided by the experience and opinion of others, knowing neither what is right nor what is wrong, nor which of my advisors might wish to deceive or displace me'.[30] His portraits show a sensitive, introspective face with melancholy eyes, according well with the tone of this celebrated letter.

Few of his doubts were shared by his contemporaries; his lack of sea experience was held as a handicap, but there were so many experienced officers serving in the expedition it was outweighed by his proved ability as an administrator and diplomat. The Venetian ambassador reported, 'he has excellent qualities and is generally beloved. He is not only prudent and brave, but of a nature of extreme goodness and benignity'.[31] The Duke of Parma, who was to co-ordinate with him, wrote to Philip that he had made a good choice.[32] On the evidence of the campaign itself Philip could scarcely have made a better one. The duke was not an exciting commander, but he was eminently safe and sound; these were the qualities required. The inexperience he pleaded forced him to delegate and listen to all shades of experienced opinion. His lack of ambition and quiet diplomatic nature were ideal for handling the haughty squadron commanders, and Parma himself who was not noted for humility. His position as first grandee of Spain gave him unquestioned authority while ensuring that there would be no sense of grievance among the serving officers passed over for supreme command.

When he took over at Lisbon in mid-March with instructions from Philip to sail as soon as possible, the expedition was in disorder; the men had not been paid, there were little more than half the required soldiers, and arms and ammunition, particularly heavy guns, were in short supply. It was as an energetic administrator that he made his mark, and within two months the organisation, signals and instructions for sailing and battle had been prepared with superbly professional thoroughness.

All comparisons of the strength of the Spanish and English fleets in the ensuing campaign hinge on the weight of ordnance each side mounted.

There are no complete lists for either fleet and all estimates are based on guns known to have been carried by certain ships or squadrons; all rightly concentrate on the fighting cores of the two fleets. The most recent scholarship based on archival evidence of more than three-quarters of the total Spanish armament suggests that the Spanish first-line ships were inferior to the English first-line ships by an average of 182 to 234 pounds weight of shot.[33] There were of course wide variations between individual ships; the Spanish flagships each probably threw nearly 400 pounds total weight of shot. In general the Spanish had rather more of the very heavy cannon and demi-cannon types throwing anything up to a 50-pound ball, and many more of the short, wide perier type, but in long culverins and demi-culverins the English seem to have had a clear advantage; taking all guns throwing a 15-pound ball or over, the English had an advantage of 185 to 119. The greater manœuvrability of the English ships probably doubled this advantage. Of far greater significance however is the weakness of both fleets; of the 2,431 guns in the Spanish fleet only about 160 were of a weight that would have counted in a late seventeenth- or eighteenth-century fleet action, and the English had scarcely one hundred more. Put another way, three standard eighteenth-century seventy-four-gun ships of the line would have been more than a match for the whole Spanish fleet. This is sufficient to explain the small damage in the first rounds of the contest.

As for the characteristics of the opposing ships, all accounts agree that the Spanish galleons were 'very stately built, and so high that they resembled great castles, most fit to defend themselves and withstand any assault',[34] and because of this, far inferior to the English ships in windward performance and manœuvrability. There were exceptions on both sides. The great English ships, *Triumph* and *White Bear* were as lofty as the Spanish galleons, while the Spanish warships of the Indies guard were smaller than the race-built *Revenge*, but in general there is no doubt about the marked difference in performance, nor about the tactics that called forth these differences. Seldom, indeed, have two fleets entered a campaign with a clearer idea of how their opponents intended to fight. Philip's instructions to Sidonia stated that the enemy would fight at long range 'to get advantage of his artillery and artificial fires; you must close and grapple, taking them in your hand'.[35] How he was to close and grapple with his unwieldy galleons was not explained. At least one of his squadron commanders believed that it would be by aid of a miracle. 'It is very simple', he said to a representative from the Pope, 'It is well known that we fight in God's cause. So when we meet the English, God will surely arrange it so that we can grapple and board them.'[36] He believed that unless God helped in that way the English would stand aloof and knock them to pieces with their culverins. This is exactly what the Hawkins school envisaged.

The strategic aims of both sides were equally clear: Sidonia's instructions were to proceed to the English Channel to join Parma off the Netherlands coast, thence to escort his army to north Kent or the Thames estuary; he was to ignore the English if they appeared, fighting only if they followed him, as they probably would; he was on no account to seek battle before joining Parma, but afterwards if the English contested his crossing he might 'gain the wind of them and give battle. . . . After victory do not let the fleet break up in pursuit, but keep it together, and do not land troops until sure of victory.'[37] The English guessed the general plan because Parma had been collecting and building small craft to convey his army, horses and equipment across the Channel, and had employed thousands to construct a canal system between the Flemish ports in his possession and the River Scheldt above Antwerp. He sought to conceal the design by spreading rumours that the preparations were against Walcheren, meanwhile setting up an elaborate charade of peace negotiations with Elizabeth. He succeeded in beguiling several Englishmen, but in the important councils there were few doubts about his real purpose. While the main English force under Howard was concentrated in the west against the armada, a flotilla of thirteen smaller Royal ships and some twenty-three coasting merchantmen under Lord Henry Seymour patrolled the narrows between Dover and Calais against a sudden descent by Parma. The Dutch Sea Beggars contributed some thirty vessels to this squadron, and with the rest of their force under Justin of Nassau, kept a close watch on all Parma's embarkation ports. It was these flotillas of small craft which held the key to the Channel crossing. Unless the armada could defeat or contain them, the enterprise was doomed.

Such was the position when – as legend has it – Captain Flemyng of the *Golden Hind* pinnace came hot-foot with his sighting of the Spanish fleet to Drake playing bowls on Plymouth Hoe in the afternoon of 29 July. The tide was flooding into the Sound, the wind was south-west; impossible to get the fleet out until the ebb started running that evening. 'Time to finish our game,' said Drake, 'and beat the Spaniards too!' It is a nice story; it may be true. Drake had been appointed Vice Admiral of the English fleet; he was the professional on whom Howard relied, and this was his advice. It has the authentic swagger.

The appearance of the armada was a relief. The English fleet had suffered from inaction, sickness, lack of pay for the men, and in the high command frustration and uncertainty; now there was a quickening of the blood. That evening Howard in the *Ark Royal*, Drake in the *Revenge*, John Hawkins in the *Victory*, Martin Frobisher in the *Triumph* started working out of the Sound, followed by some sixty others, many too small to be of any fighting value. The fighting core was composed of sixteen medium-to-large Royal ships and twenty or so large merchantmen.

The following day the fleet was still straggling out, the leaders anchoring off the entrance to prevent being swept up Channel by the tide while Medina Sidonia made a stately progress along the Cornish coast towards them; he anchored for the night some thirty miles short of Plymouth, while

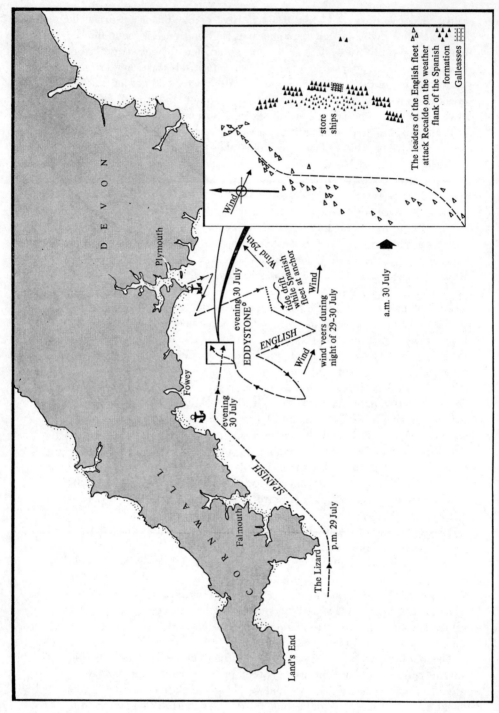

Battle diagram 4: The Armada campaign — opening action, 30 July 1588

Howard weighed and worked out to seaward as the tide turned, beating towards the Eddystone rock. That night the wind veered into the west-north-west, and Howard was able to beat down channel and gain the coveted weather gage. Next morning, Sunday 31 July, Medina Sidonia's lookouts saw through the early haze the English main body in the south-west and in the other direction a smaller group working westwards along the coast from Plymouth.

The first action was joined at nine that morning. Howard led across the Spanish rear, firing from a distance. The armada had weighed and was moving easterly towards the Eddystone, formed in a huge crescent several miles across with the main battle squadrons in the centre, and two squadrons each side forming the wings trailing and protecting the store ships. The flagships of the wing squadrons were stationed at the extremities as in galley tactics to protect the flanks. It was the southern wing that Howard's ships fired at first, but it was the northermost flagship, that of John Martinez de Recalde, that took the brunt of the English attack later; his was the windward position, and a group of some eight English led by Drake, Hawkins and Frobisher, bore down firing their broadsides in succession, after a space tacking and coming back to fire their other side – that at least is the likely mode, there are no detailed accounts. They succeeded in damaging Recalde's spars and rigging, killing seven and wounding thirty-one of his men and forcing him to bear up for them, but nothing significant followed. The Spanish maintained their formidable formation, barely moving before the wind, inviting the English to close; the English kept their distance. As Howard wrote that night, 'We durst not adventure to put in among them, their fleet being so strong'.[38] A volunteer in the *Mary Rose* expressed the same sentiment: 'the majesty of the enemy's fleet, the good order they held and the private consideration of our wants did cause, in my opinion, our first onset to be more coldly done than became the value of our nation.'[39] When after four hours of largely ineffective long-range fire, Howard called off the attack, throwing out the flag for a council, Medina Sidonia tacked and tried vainly to regain the weather gage. He had no chance, and during the manoeuvring the wind got up and the Andalusian flagship, *Nuestra Señora del Rosario* collided heavily with another of her squadron and lost her bowsprit and head gear; at about the same time a powder barrel exploded in the stern of the Guipuzcoan squadron flagship, *San Salvador*, blowing out her poop, wrecking the steering and starting fires. The vessel was promptly taken in tow, and the fires extinguished, and by evening the armada had reformed and was continuing its disciplined progress up Channel, with the English following behind.

The first round had gone to Medina Sidonia. That night Drake, who had been appointed by Howard to lead the English fleet, saw a large straggler; he extinguished his stern light and steered for her explaining afterwards that he feared the enemy were doubling back to gain the weather gage. She turned out to be the crippled *Rosario*, flagship of Pedro de Valdéz. 'Tell him I am Francis Drake,' he called, 'and my matches are burning!' Valdéz surrendered without a struggle, honoured to submit to a captain of such renown. Drake sent the valuable prize into Dartmouth and set sail to catch up with the English fleet which had been thrown into confusion by lack of his guiding light. Howard, with two of the large Royal ships, had followed a Spanish lantern instead and found himself almost within the Spanish formation at first light; the rest of his ships were scattered far behind, several out of sight altogether. Howard seems to have had little difficulty in extracting himself, but most of the day was spent gathering the fleet. One more prize was picked up, the severely damaged *San Salvador*, which had been taking in water during the night, and was later abandoned.

Medina Sidonia now re-formed his fleet with the two wings as rearguard and strengthened by four powerful galleons from the Portuguese squadron and three galleasses under the overall direction of a spirited young soldier, Alonso de Leyva, whom Philip had appointed second-in-command of the expedition; he himself stayed with the rest of the main battle squadron in the van, enclosing the storeships. At the same time, not satisfied with the conduct of several of the captains in the previous day's skirmishes, he sent Regimental Sergeant-Majors through the fleet in despatch boats with written orders empowering them summarily to hang any captain who strayed from his new station. So in a tight, wedge-shaped formation the fleet drifted eastwards under the lightest of airs, which faded away altogether as they came up to Portland that night.

The following morning, still off Portland, the wind came up from the north-east giving Sidonia the weather gage. Howard steered north-westerly for the bay to the west of Portland, then realising that this would not regain the wind and would allow the Spaniards to work in to Weymouth, altered south-easterly, drawing towards the enemy again; immediately ships of the new powerful rearguard steered towards him; the English greeted them with a hot fire as the range shortened, but kept bearing away, never allowing the galleons inside 150 yards or perhaps more, eventually leaving them astern. Meanwhile, a separate mêlée was taking place to the northward close in to the spur of Portland; Martin Frobisher in the huge *Triumph*, together with five merchantmen, had been spotted in that direction long before the main action was joined, and Medina Sidonia had ordered the galleasses to cut them out; others of the Spanish rearguard had also steered towards the isolated group, attempting to close and board, and some of the English main body were working up to their relief. Frobisher's gunners succeeded in shattering the oars of the galleasses, forcing them to hoist sail, and he bore away from the galleons towards the relieving English (that, at least, is the probable interpretation of the course of the mêlée) and succeeded in extracting himself, without great loss, some time in the late morning. The wind meanwhile was veering towards the east, and it continued round

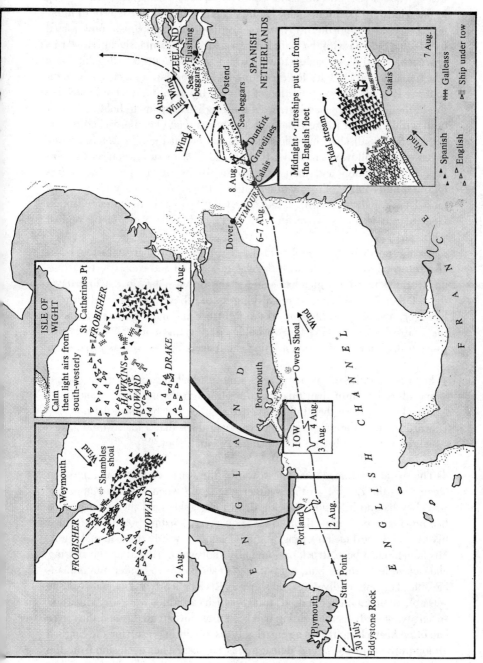

Battle diagram 5: The Armada campaign, 30 July – 9 August 1588

through south-east into the south-south-west, thus putting Howard's group in the windward position again. He immediately led north-easterly to interpose between the northern groups of English and the Spanish, now joined by Medina Sidonia with the main battle squadrons. Sidonia, seeing Howard's approach, stood close-hauled towards him in his 1,000-ton flagship, *San Martin*, and then lay with lowered topsails inviting him to a close boarding contest. Howard had no intention of playing his game; after the ineffective fire of the first day, he had instructed the English captains to hold their shot until within musket range – perhaps 120 yards – and he approached to this distance before discharging his starboard battery at the *San Martin*. Some seven others followed and gave their broadsides in succession as the *Ark* bore away, tacking and then returned with the other side. The others followed him round, joined by other English ships, several very small, which tacked back and forth until it seemed to the Spaniards that their Captain General was beset by some fifty sail of English. The *San Martin* replied with spirit.

To the north of this smoke-shrouded group, Frobisher and others had also returned to the attack with the change of wind and were concentrating on Recalde's flagship which had suffered the heaviest fire in the first day's fight. Other Spanish ships were working up to relieve both isolated targets, however, and after an hour or so the fight became more general. Some of the English seem to have grown bolder during this bout, approaching at times to half musket shot and inviting small arms fire as well as great shot.

> For the time there was never seen a more terrible value of great shot, and more hot fight than this was; for although the musketeers and arquebusiers were then infinite, yet could they not be discerned nor heard for that the great ordnance came so thick that a man would have judged it to have been a hot skirmish of small shot.[40]

The wind continued veering towards the west during the afternoon confirming the English in the weather gage, and when it became apparent that they had no intention of being drawn alongside, and the Spanish ships had no chance of forcing them to close quarters, Medina Sidonia re-formed his fleet and continued his progress up-Channel towards the Isle of Wight. His flagship had been struck by some fifty shot which had cut up the rigging and caused leaks in the hull, but nothing so serious as to render him unmanageable. The only really damaged ship was Recalde's *Santa Ana*, and even she was able to maintain her station; total Spanish casualties were fifty killed and seventy wounded. As the fighting had been intermittent all day and the range had often been close, it was a remarkably disappointing result for the English although their own loss and damage was far less. The conclusion from the scant detail available and from Howard's action the following day in dividing the English fleet into four separate squadrons under himself, Drake, Hawkins and Frobisher, is that the unorganised, undisciplined English lesser ships with their very few light guns actually impeded Howard and the Royal ships. It is also probable that many captains held back at far too great a range to hit, let alone damage, and it is certain that comparatively very few of the English guns threw a large enough shot to break through the massive sides, or even the masts, of the larger galleons.

The following day, Wednesday 3 August, the English spent much time replenishing their powder and shot from small craft, but a portion of the fleet attacked a large Spanish storeship which sailed badly and had dropped astern of station. Once again Recalde was prominent in the defence, and his *Santa Ana* received her third serious concentration of fire. The cumulative damage caused her to part from the fleet later, and she was afterwards wrecked on the French coast, the first loss of the campaign attributable to English gunnery.

The wind fell during the night while the armada drifted south-west of the Isle of Wight, the English close astern; Thursday dawned a flat calm. Now occurred the turning point of the campaign. Medina Sidonia had instructions to use the Isle of Wight if necessary while concerting his plans with Parma, for its eastern and northern waters offered ideal sheltered anchorages before the crossing to the dangerously exposed Flemish coast. Unfortunately the details of the fighting off the island are obscure.

The action was opened by Hawkins having the *Victory* towed by boats towards two galleons isolated in the calm; de Leyva responded by having his flagship towed to the rescue; the galleasses also rowed up, and on the English side, Howard's *Ark Royal* and the *Golden Lion* towed to join Hawkins. During the ensuing artillery duel the wind rose, probably from a southerly or south-westerly quarter, allowing more Spanish to work up into the action which grew as hot as that off Portland. Meanwhile Frobisher's squadron, again stationed on the northernmost flank, also got into action, Frobisher himself so enthusiastically that a group of galleons and a galleass were able to cut him off. To extricate himself Frobisher had eleven boats at bow and stern, which turned his great ship to bring his broadsides to bear, and in the intervals towed him towards others of his squadron making towards him. With their aid, and a freshening breeze which allowed him to cast off the boats, he pulled clear of the Spaniards and soon outdistancing them regained the weather gage – a feat which the Spanish remarked as a marvel. An enormous amount of shot was expended during these and other separated actions, but again with little serious ship damage. A gunner in one of the English ships lamented later, 'what was the cause of so much powder and shot spent, and so long time in fight, and in comparison thereof so little harm?'[41] The Spanish who were firing more deliberately – no doubt to husband their ammunition – had even less cause for congratulation if the English casualty figures (just two!) can be believed. They themselves lost another fifty killed and seventy wounded.

After Frobisher had extricated himself and the isolated ships attacked by Hawkins had been towed back into the Spanish formation Medina Sidonia re-formed his fleet and resumed his course up-Channel. What caused this fateful decision is not clear. Probably it would have been unwise to attempt bringing the whole great fleet to anchor in unfamiliar shoal water while the English ships were close at hand to harass him, and free to draw fresh supplies of powder and shot from home ports while some of his own strongest ships were running dangerously short. Moreover the water in the casks was already foul and some provisions low; these factors would have inclined him to press on towards the junction with Parma; the English pinnaces and light craft which were being reinforced all the time by small vessels from the south coast ports would have rendered any landings for fresh water and provisions a hazardous and costly operation. Here is the professional, Sir Arthur Gorgas, again:

[to invade] they must draw as near the shore as their vessels will permit them and needs cast anchor while their long boats, pinnaces, skiffs and frigates lie by their side to take in their soldiers that they must convey to gain a good landing place. But while they are performing this they will no doubt as near as they can protect those that lie at anchor with a great part of their best shipping under sail, which they will find to be a very difficult and dangerous piece of work while our navy is in force and unrepulsed if we do well discharge our part in pressing on them at the instant. For their great vessels which no doubt carry a great part of their munitions and victuals must lie at anchor in the sea where their boats and pinnaces will find it a long and tough row to convey all these to the shore, and especially we first troubling them with our great ships and having pinnaces and frigates that carry ordnance and musketry besides to chase and intercept them when they are parted from the shipsides.'[42]

There was also the moral factor: all Spanish accounts, including Medina Sidonia's, refer to the extraordinary manœuvrability of the English ships; in four days of fighting they had defied all attempts to bring them to close quarters, meanwhile keeping the Spaniards under a cumulatively morale-sapping hail of shot which had killed or wounded over 400 thus far. Medina Sidonia's report to Philip refers constantly to his inability to get to 'hand-stroke' with the enemy, 'their ships being very nimble and of such good steerage as they did with them whatsoever they desired'.[43] Other Spanish accounts describe the English ships 'as responsive as well-trained horses'. The repeated demonstrations of the impossibility of dictating the tactics, even with the weather gage, must have had a powerful effect on the Spanish Commander-in-Chief and his professional advisors. It is significant that on the day after the Isle of Wight battle, he sent off a request to Parma for forty 'flyboats', which would be able to close with the English; 'our ships being very heavy in comparison with the lightness of those of our enemy, it is impossible to come to handstroke with them'.[44] Above all, perhaps, there were Philip's orders, 'Do not land troops until sure of victory'. Meanwhile the wind was fair for a course up-Channel; why delay for the uncertainties of a landing or an anchorage at which any change of wind might give the advantage to the enemy?

Whatever the reasons, the rightness of the decision to carry on turned entirely on the state of readiness of the army of the Netherlands; of this he had received no word, although he had sent several messages to Parma advising him of the armada's arrival in the Channel – the latest requesting powder and shot. If the army were not ready, or if it could not be carried to sea to join him, the armada was doomed sooner or later to be dispersed by bad weather and probably wrecked on the shoals; there were no safe havens once it passed the Straits of Dover. In fact Parma was not ready, and by sailing to join him the expedition sailed to certain disaster. This was Medina Sidonia's fate, hardly his fault; so far his handling of the expedition had been firm and correct and he had set an outstanding example in defence. The only possible doubts concern his departure from the Isle of Wight, and the scant evidence available suggests that he had little option; it may be significant that the next day Howard honoured John Hawkins, Frobisher and others who had been in the hottest action by knighting them on the quarterdeck of the *Ark Royal*. Howard was still intensely anxious about the little effect all the days' fighting appeared to have had on the awesome Spanish formation, and worried about shortage of ammunition, but it may have been done in recognition of a victory in preventing a Spanish landing on the Isle of Wight.

The armada, preserving formation, continued its deliberate course up-Channel through the next two days until, on the advice of the pilots not to venture into the tidal streams off the Flemish shoals, Medina Sidonia came to anchor off Calais in the late afternoon of Saturday 6 August. Howard, who had used the time to replenish the English ammunition, brought to upwind of him. He was soon joined by Lord Henry Seymour's patrolling squadron, and the following morning a council was held at which it was decided to use fireships; suitable craft, faggots and pitch were requested from Dover. The same morning Medina Sidonia gained his first news that Parma was not ready and so far as his own messenger could see, would not be ready within a fortnight. The Spanish Commander-in-Chief must have had intimations of disaster as he arranged for the fleet to water and provision.

Howard, meanwhile, acting in the spirit of Drake's *mot* that the advantage of time and place was half a victory; 'which being lost all is irrecoverable', resolved not to await the fireships from Dover, but to prepare them from among the small craft with the fleet. The Spaniards noticed the activity, soon convincing themselves that they were not simply fireships but explosive vessels being prepared, for it was rumoured that an Italian engineer who had devised floating bombs of this kind was in England in Elizabeth's pay. Medina Sidonia took the standard precautions, setting a patrol of oared craft equipped with grapnels to tow the infernal machines away from the fleet, and instructing all ships to have their boats ready to grapple any that might escape the screen. Should the enemy vessels nevertheless get through, the ships were to slip cables, buoyed for later recovery, and stand out to sea until the danger was past, then return. The evolution was not so simple in the dark with a rising wind and the tide ripping through the off-lying shoals, and when eight lighted ships emerged from the English fleet on the flood stream after midnight, flames snaking up the shrouds, glowing through the spread canvas, loaded guns going off as the heat fired their charges, and scattering the vessels of the grappling screen, the galleons cut their cables, loosed their sails in haste and ran. Although the *San Martin* and others of the Portuguese squadron made admirably controlled short boards out to sea and back to a position not far removed from the original anchorage, many were not so well prepared with spare anchors, or stood too far out and were carried east by the strengthening flood. It was the end of the formidable order the armada had preserved.

At dawn the following morning, Monday 8 August, Medina Sidonia weighed with the handful of Portuguese ships still with him and steered easterly before a freshening west or north-west wind to collect his dispersed fleet, while the English, now some 140 sail strong, hoisted battle ensigns and chased, for the first time scenting victory. Howard himself, who was to have led the assault was diverted by the sight of a great galleass isolated close in to the shore under Calais Castle, and steered for her; she was the flagship of the galleasses and had disabled her rudder in the scramble the previous night. Seeing the English admiral and consorts bearing down the galleass commander beached her. Boats put out from the English ships and there was a sharp musketry duel at close range until a shot killed the Spanish commander, and resistance collapsed. Entering her, the English found four large cannon, eight demi-cannon (32-pounders) and a dozen culverin and demi-culverin, together with numerous smaller long guns, all of brass. They also found that although she had been struck by numerous English shot, not one had penetrated the heavy timbers below her oar ports. She was undoubtedly one of the most formidable vessels in the Spanish force, and she and her three consorts were the only ships capable of aiding Parma's landing craft in the shallows off the Flemish coast; it is not too surprising therefore that Howard allowed himself to be distracted from pursuit of the main enemy force. Some of the 'rude English' who captured her, finding no treasure aboard, set upon Frenchmen who had come down to the beach in crowds to watch the fray, 'taking away their rings and jewels as if from enemies',[45] whereupon the commander of the Castle opened fire and drove them off.

Drake, Seymour, Hawkins and the rest had meanwhile chased and attacked Medina Sidonia and his accompanying galleons, all of whom put up a stout resistance. The *Revenge* was pierced a number of times but not forced out of the chase, and Hawkins wrote afterwards 'our ships, God be thanked, have received little hurt'.[46] Howard caught them up later in the day off Gravelines halfway between Calais and Dunkirk; by this time some of the galleons which had borne the brunt of the continuous harassing action were running out of shot and the English were pressing in closer and wreaking serious damage. The details of the fighting are not recorded, but it seems certain that at least two warships of the Portuguese squadron and one other great galleon were so riddled they sank later, while another Portuguese galleon, disabled and separated, fell an easy prey to the Sea Beggars. Howard reported three sunk and four so shot through they were forced to steer for the shore. Many others were dangerously leaky and weak aloft. The *San Martin*, always leading to the rescue of those disabled and isolated ships on which the British concentrated, received over one hundred shot during the day and was taking in quantities of water until her divers went over and stopped the holes, reducing the leaks to manageable proportions. She lost only twelve killed and twenty wounded however, which does not suggest that the English came to really close quarters with her – nor do the English casualties of less than one hundred in the whole week's fighting, surely an incredible figure, support the view of really close work. Yet one of the Queen's captains, Sir William Wynter, wrote that he never discharged his pieces outside arquebus range 'and most times within speech of one another'.[47] All that can be said with certainty is that the English guns did succeed in shattering many of the large enemy warships, while Medina Sidonia succeeded in gathering most of his flock and shepherding them northwards into deep water. Late in the day the weather took a hand. The wind gusted up with squalls of rain, veering towards the north-west, driving the fleet back towards the shoals off the coast. By Tuesday morning the situation was critical; the *San Martin* herself was sounding six fathoms, and the short scend of the waves was murky with stirred sand. At the last moment when it seemed that the whole armada must be driven on the banks and lost, God sent the miracle the Spaniards had always needed; the wind backed quickly towards the south; the yards were braced round; the fleet sailed free.

The wind held in the south for the next few days, leaving Medina Sidonia no options but to seek shelter and provisions and probably winter in some Scandinavian port, or make the passage back to Spain northabout around Scotland. He chose the latter course. Howard, with the English ammunition again exhausted in the recent fighting, escorted him 'with a brag countenance and gave him chase as tho' we wanted nothing until he had cleared our own coast and some part of Scotland of them'.[48] Meanwhile he sent Seymour back to the Straits to watch against a descent by Parma while the main fleet was absent. It was some time before he realised that the Spanish threat had been pricked.

Medina Sidonia was defeated by a combination of weather, the superb fleet John Hawkins had fashioned, and English persistence and skill in stand-off artillery tactics. Parma was prevented from sending any of the 'flyboats' he asked for, just as he was prevented from joining with his army by the close blockade of the Scheldt and his entire Flemish coastline by the Sea Beggars under Justin of Nassau – and beyond them Lord Henry Seymour's powerful squadron in the Straits. Without a secure deep-water port for the junction of the two arms of the Spanish expedition Philip's 'Enterprise of England' was quite simply impossible; even if such a base had been secured, the passage of the army in the face of such unbeaten, impossibly elusive English and Dutch warships would have been a rash operation.

Medina Sidonia attempted as firm a control during the long, return voyage as he had on the passage up-Channel, with the result that a large proportion of the surviving ships eventually arrived home – among them forty of the original sixty-four fighting galleons. Most of the losses occurred amongst those ships which disobeyed instructions by seeking succour on the coast of Ireland; at least seven galleons and several storeships were wrecked in this way, and their crews slaughtered in cold blood to the orders of the English Lord Deputy, who considered his own forces too weak to risk any Spaniards alive in that troubled land. But the greatest losses in men the armada suffered were from the natural scourges which always accounted for many more deaths than battle – scurvy, typhus, dysentery, starvation and lack of water. Many of those ships that returned had scarcely enough hands to work them into harbour.

The English fleet suffered similarly even though the ships were less crowded and never more than fifty miles from their own shores. 'Not more than three score',[49] or by another computation 'less than 100 were' lost to enemy shot, but by the middle of August Howard, back at Margate with the ships, was writing 'sickness and mortality begin wonderfully to grow amongst us; and it is a most pitiful sight; it would grieve any man's heart to see them that have served so valiantly to die so miserably.'[50] Part of the trouble was lack of money to pay the men, part lack of organisation to cope with such an unprecedented mobilisation; over 15,000 men served in the English ships during the campaign. The most recent scholarship is far less critical of the administration than has been fashionable.[51] The heart-rending scenes of starving sailors begging for their wages, which undoubtedly did occur, have tended to obscure the quality of pre-planning and effort that succeeded in keeping the whole English fleet and over a hundred reserves and auxiliaries victualled and supplied with powder and shot for the best part of a year.

The defeat of the armada was a defensive triumph for the English, but its chief importance was in preventing Spain regaining control of the Netherlands and northern trade. England, drained by the campaign and by her expenses on land in the Netherlands, lacked the resources to follow up with a successful offensive. This was demonstrated clearly the following year when instead of mounting a state expedition to destroy the surviving galleons the old device of a state/private joint-stock company was used, this time further complicated by the inclusion of a Dutch squadron; the resulting expedition under the combined leadership of Drake and a soldier, Sir John Norris, was some 150 sail strong, but only seven of these were queen's ships. Its aims could not be faulted. It was first to destroy the galleons which represented almost the whole of Spain's oceanic navy as they lay defenceless in the Biscay ports of Santander and San Sebastian, second to take Lisbon if it seemed that the Portuguese could be stirred to revolt in favour of the Pretender Dom Antonio, third to make for the Azores with a similar intent. If they could have been realised these designs must have crippled Spain. The instrument was not strong enough though. Drake, no less than the merchant venturers who had provided the bulk of his fleet, was a privateer at heart; the great galleons were left unmolested, the attack on Lisbon broke on failures in supply, lack of co-operation between the ships and Norris's army, and resolute defence by the Spanish governor; finally a gale scattered the fleet off the Azores. It was a costly disaster comparable to the failure of Philip's armada and accompanied by similar appalling losses to scurvy and disease. Drake spent the next years in disgrace.

Hawkins was still pressing his plan for a year-round blockade on the Spanish coast and islands by Royal squadrons, but although he and Frobisher were allowed to sail on this service simultaneously – Hawkins proving that he could keep his own ship's company healthy during a five months' cruise, a considerable feat which was seldom repeated until the mid-eighteenth century – the effort was not sustained. And directly the English left the coast the Indies fleets sailed. Philip's silver revenues increased, and he set in hand a great building programme for warships of 1,000 tons each, and strengthened the West Indies defensive system. Within a few years Hawkins's plan was out of date; the advantage of time and place had been irrecoverably lost; against the new Spanish oceanic navy, the English had no hope of gaining more than a few isolated successes. The lesson was suggested by the failure of a squadron under Lord Thomas Howard at Flores in the Azores in 1591; this was the occasion in which the *Revenge* under Sir Richard Grenville was battered and finally captured after a lone fight against some fifteen of the new Spanish warships in succession. She was the first ship of Hawkins's remodelled oceanic navy to be lost by any cause. Her guns did however account for four of the enemy ships in this epic contest.

In 1595 the end came for Drake and Hawkins when they sailed for the Caribbean on yet another state/private joint-stock venture. The original aims were to land a force of soldiers on the isthmus and march across to capture Panama, long the dream of treasure seekers. At the last moment a small Spanish squadron made a raid on the Cornish coast and Elizabeth, in a defensive fever because of Spanish forces aiding the Catholics in Brittany, refused to let the expedition leave. Later, reports came in of a storm-damaged galleon lying in San Juan de Puerto Rico, and she eventually allowed her ageing rovers to sail to cut out the galleon and return immediately. Things went wrong from the start; Hawkins and Drake were incompatible as leaders, one a careful pre-planner, the other an ever-optimistic opportunist. The expedition sailed in division, made an ill-judged and profitless attack on the Canaries, thus alerting the Spanish, and failed to force San Juan. Hawkins, then sixty-three, took ill and died just before the attack; subsequently Drake reverted to the original aim of capturing Panama, and landed soldiers at Nombre de Dios to march overland. The party was soon forced back to the ships, and afterwards Drake himself died. It was a tragic end for the two leading spirits in the Elizabethan assault on Spain, but it was not inappropriate; it typified England's failure to advance from an undisciplined private warfare which was little more than piracy sanctioned by the state. This was a failure only of means. Hawkins and others had shown themselves capable of sound strategic conceptions; Hawkins had proved he could organise a fleet capable of carrying them out; what no Englishman could produce was the money to make the strategy effective; England was still too sparsely populated and commercially underdeveloped. While Spain drew increasing wealth from the New World silver mines and a rapidly expanding Portuguese Atlantic trading economy, and built up an oceanic navy, Elizabeth continued to pour most of the pittance she could scrape together into support for French and Dutch Protestants fighting Spanish armies on the Continent of Europe; the share allocated to the Royal Navy fell by one-third to little over £4,000 a year.[52]

When Philip despatched two more huge armadas against England in 1596 and 1597 it was Providence in the shape of timely gales and not the Royal Navy that scattered them. When his successor sent out another expedition in 1601 to support a rebellion in Ireland it was again scattered by a storm, but a portion reached Kinsale unmolested by English ships, and landed troops. Fortunately for the English the effort was too late and in the wrong place, and with their far shorter communications they were able to contain and finally expel the small Spanish force from Ireland.

Elizabeth was criticised by 'Blue Water' strategists then, and has been ever since, for dissipating some four and a half millions on Continental land involvements which gained her nothing but debts, while spending only one million on her potentially decisive navy over the same period: between 1585 and the end of her reign in 1603. Bacon's famous dictum: 'He that commands the sea is at liberty and may take as much and as little of the Warre as he will'[53] has been quoted to emphasise Elizabeth's mistake and point up the peculiarly defensive/offensive qualities of naval power. However, the latest study of the Royal Navy by Paul Kennedy comes firmly down on Elizabeth's side:

> The Queen could perceive, if Hawkins and his peers could not, the true relationship between the Continental and maritime-imperial factors: that if they abandoned their allies, turned their backs upon western Europe and allowed it to be dominated by one hostile power, then their small island would be unable to build and man a fleet sufficient to hold off the accumulated strength of such an enemy.[54]

The Spanish empire was still the colossus bestriding the world, and England, for all the initial promise of the Elizabethan privateers after a share of her fabled wealth, was by comparison a pigmy, bound to seek safety in alliances. She had been fortunate to preserve her independence – for which, not for the first or last time, she had to thank her stormy moat. Nevertheless over the years of the Spanish war, which lasted until Elizabeth's death in 1603, her navy and privateering interests made a vital contribution to the success of the oceanic/commercial fringe against the great territorial centres.

CHAPTER 5

THE DUTCH EMPIRE OF THE OCEANS

Of all the Atlantic fringe, the provinces that gained most from the break with the territorial centres were the northern Netherlands. They enjoyed a depth of natural defence in the web of river and marsh of the Rhine/Waal/ Maas delta, and had used it skilfully to halt the Spanish armies, meanwhile taking the offensive at sea. Parma must have overcome them in time, but he had been diverted, first by the 'Enterprise of England', the key to neutralising the Protestant control of the Channel, later by turning to support the Catholics in France. These and the cumulative effect of harassment by sea saved the seven 'United Provinces' of the north Netherlands from being overrun. While the promise of Elizabethan England faded for lack of finance, then dissolved in the same kind of internal strife which was rendering France impotent, they burst forth as the most triumphant sea power since Venice, the first to encompass the world. They did it by taking over from Antwerp and the southern Netherlands the middleman position between the growing Atlantic trading system, north Europe and the Baltic, which supplied the Atlantic nations with most of their naval necessities. Hence what appears as a phenomenally rapid rise, after a defence that hung desperately in the balance, was more of a transfer of power, financial, commercial and industrial from Spanish Antwerp to the ports of Zeeland and Holland, principally Amsterdam.

There are many similarities between Amsterdam and Venice, not least their position at the edge of lagoons and sandbanks – in the case of Amsterdam the Zuider Zee – at the end of great rivers giving access to rich and extensive hinterlands. In both cases it was easier to travel by boat than on land, and far easier to transport goods that way. Both peoples started their spectacular naval careers as river boatmen and fishermen, graduating to short-sea carriers of necessary bulk goods, salt, fish, timber, grain. Both subsequently laid the foundation of their wealth as specialist carriers and middlemen – and pirates as occasion served – between the most prosperous trading cities of their time, developing formidable war fleets and overseas bases to defend and extend their own spheres. Both growing as natural sea powers with few landward distractions – indeed their cities were both built on piles intersected by canals – developed similar forms of society and government in which power was diffused. Neither were political democracies, yet in their rising phase, partnerships were the characteristic form for all enterprises, spreading risk and profit and giving each man, down to the deckhands of fishing boats, a stake and a voice in his living. This is not surprising as partnership was the traditional form of shipowning everywhere and had been for centuries. A wage-earning class grew as wealth accumulated in some hands, but merchants, industrialists, shipowners, shipbuilders and masters continued to organise their operations by group partnership and maintained a fiercely individualistic tradition.

Political power, meanwhile, became concentrated in the hands of the wealthiest merchant families; in both examples these grew into a hereditary ruling class – nobles in Venice, regents in Amsterdam and other cities and towns of the Netherlands – and it became increasingly difficult for self-made men to break in as the states approached their zenith. In both cases this merchant oligarchy elected from amongst itself the officials and committee members who controlled all local and state affairs; these served for short terms, although re-election was common. There was also a long-term head of state, in Venice's case the doge elected for life after a series of ballots of tortuous ingenuity, in the Netherlands the Stadtholder, a hereditary prince of the House of Orange. In both cases the power of the titular head was severely limited; he could act only with the consent of the ruling committees, yet provided he achieved consent he had great influence and was an effective executive chief.

Both societies were thus at the same time both highly individualistic and highly distrustful of individual power, seeking to curb its growth by every device. In the United Provinces of the Netherlands the checks went so far they made it virtually impossible in principle to agree joint action which conflicted with the interests of one or other state. Each of the seven was sovereign, sending delegations elected in the main from the Regents of its towns to the States General at The Hague. Each delegation went with instructions on the line it should take on national issues, and votes to be carried had to be unanimous; no state was bound to any resolution unless its own delegation had voted in favour. There was no national revenue; each state collected its own taxes and contributed to national effort on a quota basis. Nor were there truly national armed forces since each state maintained and paid regiments, and until 1597, there was no regular navy; when the need for organised fleets became pressing the States General attempted to set up co-ordinating machinery between the local Admiralties which had grown up in each of the five main shipping areas; the attempt failed in many respects; each provincial Board continued to build, maintain, officer, man, supply its own warships, collect its own dues, cling jealously to its own autonomy.

Such in essence was the classic merchants' confederation, abhorring central authority, the tax burdens it laid on trade, the market distortions it created with regulations, tariffs, grants of monopoly rights, the inefficiency and corruption it bred, and the dangers of personal rule and opportunist alliances and wars that would ruin trade. There were landed interests looking to the House of Orange who took an opposite view, but real power flowed from the wealth of the merchants of the seaports; their aim, as it had been the aim of Venetian merchants, was simply profit from the extension of trade to the widest possible markets. For this they believed they needed absolute freedom from interference; this belief was reflected in the constitution and in foreign policy as it was reflected in the society itself. Elsewhere in Europe religious bigotry and intolerance reached frightful proportions; in the United Provinces there were no restrictions on race or religion; each man was welcomed for whatever skills he brought. As with Venice the merchant ethic was expressed in tolerance and rational and humane ideals, which made a great impression on contemporaries – not least for their practical effect. The Fourth Earl of Shaftesbury urged Englishmen to follow Dutch religious toleration in order to keep skilled workers whom persecution might drive away, and at the same time attract others from less enlightened countries.[1]

Naturally Dutch practice fell short of the ideals. Profit was the motive, and as the towns and cities grew in wealth and industry, attracting migrant workers from the countryside and neighbouring states, all the abuses associated with the exploitation of a mass market in human labour flourished. Wages were kept low, men, women and children were worked harshly for long hours in squalid conditions, thrown out of employment in recession. The sailors on whom the whole system rested were a particularly brutalised class – probably no more than those of any other country – but the savage punishments to which they were subject, the under-manning and short rations apparently common in Dutch ships, the enormous losses to disease, were hard human realities beneath the civilised abstractions of the Republic's liberal thinkers. So too was the slave trade, which came to play a major role in the overseas expansion. At bottom this epitome of a sea power was not very different from a territorial power, nor could it be, for both systems had to exploit human labour and fighting strength to gain their ends. The real differences were higher in the social order. The most striking difference of all, objective and measurable, was success; this apparently loose federation of provinces with no more than one and a half rising to two million inhabitants crowded into a waterlogged corner of Europe beat the Spanish Empire practically off the seas, in the process growing so powerful that it became itself the focus of envy.

The foundations for Dutch success were laid long before the break with Spain. They were fishing (principally in the North Sea, where they swept in vast seasonal fleets after herring), the export of salted and smoked fish, and the carrying trade between the Baltic and north Europe. Grain from the southern Baltic ports was and remained so important to Amsterdam it was referred to as the 'mother trade'; Baltic timber was equally vital since the Netherlands had practically no timber of their own for shipbuilding; Amsterdam had engrossed this trade and promoted a vast re-export business in masts, planks and timber by-products: pitch, tar and turpentine. The fishery aided the Baltic bulk trades as its products provided outward cargoes. It has been estimated that the herring catch alone may have been worth two million guilders annually, or the equivalent of England's staple, woollens. Other freights and industries were grafted in to this solid framework, particularly textiles and textile finishing, and in the early sixteenth century, bronze ordnance. As Antwerp flourished as the northern *entrepôt* for Spanish and Portuguese colonial and eastern products, the whole system was stimulated by bullion and demand for sugar, spices and ordnance. In 1551, 800,000 ducats' worth of silver from Peru was minted at Antwerp at a profit of 15 per cent in exchange for artillery and gunpowder exports to Spain.[2]

The wealth accruing allowed Netherlands' shipping by mid-century to take over from the Hanseatic League of German and Baltic ports as chief carriers for all Baltic products to northern and western Europe. A range of industries had grown up to supply the wide market served and the Netherlands had become not only the wealthiest but the most industrially advanced region of Europe. As a symptom of maturity came the revolts against Spanish rule. The resulting fighting over the southern provinces, and the religious persecution ruined industry, as the blockade of the Scheldt by the 'Sea Beggars' and then the Spanish sack ruined Antwerp. Amsterdam began to fill the vacuum. It was not so good a port; the approaches through shoals at the entrance to the Zuider Zee, and the sandbanks within were more hazardous than a deep-sea voyage, and the harbour itself was so shallow goods had to be transported to lighters. None the less its shipping had been important before the revolt, and after the blockade of the Scheldt it expanded steadily, entering the Mediterranean with grain and stockfish, loading Greek wines and raisins and exotic wares from the Levant; undercutting Venetian ships in the Adriatic itself! When in 1584 Philip II, in an effort to bring the Provinces to heel, prohibited them from trade with Spain – a trade that had continued despite the war because it suited both sides – they simply increased their illicit trading in the Spanish Atlantic system.

These movements were unplanned, the result of initiatives by individual merchants and groups; they succeeded for a variety of reasons; most important perhaps was cheaper shipbuilding. Their lack of home-grown timber had forced them to establish a large-scale timber industry employing specialised ships and wind-driven saw-mills; the demand for ships had led to similar specialisation in construction methods and types, and they were able to build at half the cost per ton of English ships. Much of this difference was accounted for by the simplicity and lightness of construction of the standard bulk carriers they developed, the 'fluyt' and the shallower and broader 'catt'. In contrast to the English long-sea ships which were built with all the strength and sailing and manœuvring qualities of warships, and were almost as heavily armed to beat off the pirates infesting Atlantic and especially Mediterranean routes, the 'fluyts' with which the Dutch penetrated the bulk trades were light, low-performance craft, narrow, flat-bottomed, round-sterned, exceedingly bluff-bowed with the minimum concessions to underwater 'lines' so that their long holds were as nearly rectangular as possible. They were little more than tall, ocean-going barges, slow because speed was of little account, and lightly armed, if at all – seeking safety where necessary by convoy. Tradition dates the development of the 'fluyt' to the port of Hoorn in the 1590s, but it is evident from mid-century illustrations that Dutch design was moving towards the type far earlier. They carried less sail than comparable English – or for that matter Dutch – 'defensible' ships, and much attention was paid to mechanical handling gear, hence they were manned with half the hands of other vessels of their tonnage. These advantages, together with Dutch predominance in the Baltic trades which assured them outward cargoes, gave them a decisive edge over competitors, especially the huge bulk carriers of the Mediterranean city states, Genoa, Venice and Venice's latest competitor, Ragusa. During the last quarter of the sixteenth century these large ships were replaced by the low-cost Dutchmen and locally built copies of the type; Venice despite a spate of navigation laws to protect her own shipping, and subsidies to encourage building large ships, declined as a carrier. Meanwhile her great merchant galleys, already long past their heyday because of excessive operating costs, had succumbed to the competition of northern 'defensible' ships. Here, the English may have had the edge if the following letter from the Venetian ambassador in England to the doge and Senate in 1618 is a reliable guide. He had engaged five English vessels:

> Some Flemish ships were offered me at a much cheaper rate, and also
> of heavier tonnage; but the English being held in infinitely greater
> account by reason of the strength of their build, the quality of their
> guns, and their crews, which yet more excel other nations in battle, I
> did not choose to part with them.[3]

As for the Atlantic oceanic system, Spanish industry could not supply the goods the colonists needed, and Spanish shipping was generally uncompetitive and inflexible, burdened by regulations and protection dues, besides being diverted frequently for Philip's wars. France was locked in civil strife; England lacked the financial or industrial resources to be a serious competitor – despite the individual excellence of a very few large ships. So Dutch shipping filled every sea; Dutch pilots became pre-eminent and the charts and systematised sailing directions of the Dutchman Lucas Janszoon Wagenaer became standard works for every educated shipmaster.

By the 1580s Amsterdam had taken over as the north European *entrepôt* for international trade; in 1585 weekly commodity prices were published there for the first time. In the same year Parma entered Antwerp; as part of his campaign for religious purity he gave Protestants two years' grace to pack up and leave the city. The resulting exodus of capital and financial, commercial and industrial expertise benefited all the United Provinces, but chiefly Amsterdam, which entered a period of extraordinarily rapid growth. There were other factors behind this flowering, chiefly perhaps the development on the one hand of Swedish mining and gunfounding with the aid of Dutch capital and technicians – on the other hand of the Portuguese/Brazilian sugar industry; this was the major development in the Atlantic economy at this time. Both enhanced the United Provinces' position between the complementary Baltic and Atlantic systems.

By the 1590s the merchants of Amsterdam were ready to take the offensive against the other Iberian monopolies; a pioneer voyage was made to the Gold Coast for slaves in 1594, and the same year a Company of Far-off Lands was formed to break into the East Indies trade at source. The following year four ships sailed to the spice islands; despite the usual appalling losses in men, the survivors returned with sufficient pepper to show a profit, and in 1598 no less than twenty-two ships sailed for the East; eight from the Company of Far-off Lands returned a 400 per cent profit. Although the first English expedition to the East Indies had preceded the Dutch by four years, their resources were quite unequal to the competition when the merchants of Amsterdam, Rotterdam, Middelburg, Delft, Hoorn and Enkhuizen sensed the profits to be made; they swamped the English effort with no less than ninety-two ships in eighteen separate expeditions in the first seven years; the English sent out some seven ships in the same period. The English, who had made most of the running in exploration for routes east, were called in as navigational advisers; in 1598 all three Dutch expeditions to the East had Englishmen as chief pilots. One of these, going west-about via the Straits of Magellan under Oliver Noort – Captain Mellis as chief pilot – made the first Dutch circumnavigation of the world. As important as the English expertise were the detailed reports of Jan Huyghen van Linschoten, who spent twelve years travelling in the Portuguese East and returned in 1593 with descriptions of trade, routes, harbours, anchorages, even tolls, taxes, administration and the shortcomings of the Portuguese and Spanish domains. This important information contributed to the rapidity of the Dutch advance in the East, but it was their wealth which determined the scale of the effort.

The different competing companies were merged in 1602 into the Dutch East India Company with monopoly rights east of Good Hope and west of the Straits of Magellan – a move that went against the grain of the free-trading merchants, but in view of the capital needed, the long-established Portuguese and Spanish presence which had to be dislodged with armed force, and the local rulers who had to be won over, coerced or overthrown, they allowed themselves to be persuaded into co-operative effort; however no less than six Boards of Directors were set up in the ports which had pioneered the enterprise, each with its own employees, ships and crews! The English had formed a joint-stock company for the East Indies two years earlier, and the French formed one two years afterwards; neither could match the Dutch effort, and while the Dutch drove the Portuguese from the Moluccas, chief source of the most valuable spices, and took the smaller islands of Tidore and Ternate, the French concentrated on colonising the far less promising shores of Madagascar in the Indian Ocean, and the English, while not altogether giving up the spice islands, established factories at Surat on the coast of mainland India.

The relationship of the English and Dutch in the spice islands in those early years was a strange mixture of mutual support and bitter trade rivalry. The Dutch on the spot felt that their efforts against the Spanish Empire entitled them to a monopoly in the area conquered. The English, who established a factory at Bantam, were not prepared to concede this; the Factor there wrote of the Dutch, 'though we were mortal enemies in our trade, yet in all other matters we were friends and would have lived and died one for the other.'[4] There are accounts of English and Dutch ships sailing together on the long voyage home for protection and aid against the natural hazards of the sea.

It was, nevertheless, the far stronger Dutch company which prevailed against the Portuguese protecting their long-established position and monopoly; here Dutch success rested on superior ships and guns. It was the story of the race-built English galleons against the lofty ships of the armada repeated in countless small actions. While the Portuguese employed light craft in local trades their ships of force in the annual fleets were huge and cumbersome; a later observer reported:

> the deck is so spacious that the sailors often play ball. The rooms are numerous, spacious and with plenty of headroom so that the galleons resemble comfortable houses rather than vessels . . . the planking is thick enough to resist gunshots. In short, these vessels would be unequalled if they were not such sluggish movers. . . . The Dutch vessels which are handier to manœuvre by the wind overcome the Portuguese galleons very easily. To the Dutch any small wind is enough while for the Portuguese vessels half a gale is necessary.[5]

For a view of these Dutch ships here is a seventeenth-century Arab historian, Al-Djarmūzi; significantly he uses the same metaphor as so many observers in the Spanish armada describing the English galleons; of a Dutchman mounting sixty guns, thirty each side, he writes:

when the guns of the first half have been discharged they swing the galleon over so as to fire the other half, for they have the ability of manœuvring it for the purpose of fighting just as a horseman can wheel his horse on dry land.[6]

The account goes on to describe the powder pots which the Dutch prepared, sealed and with fuses protruding, 'and when anyone closes in, whom therefore on account of the close quarters the guns cannot touch, they throw [them] in such manner that the people on board the opposing vessel perish.' Although it is impossible to gain a detailed picture from the scant accounts of actions, the Dutch tactics seem to have been similar to the English group attack from the windward position, discharging the broadside, tacking and coming back with the other side. In some fleets, pairs of vessels were instructed to support each other, an order well adapted to the boarding tactics with which the Dutch concluded their preliminary stand-off bombardment.

The Portuguese had established gun foundries at Macao and Goa, which produced good quality ordnance; nevertheless in the early seventeenth century their ships seem to have lacked sufficient heavy guns, and the Dutch had undoubted superiority. With the help of their capital and enterprise, Sweden, with its extensive deposits of first quality iron ore and copper and abundant timber to fuel the smelting furnaces, had been raised to a predominant position in gun manufacture; during the 1620s the country took over as unquestionably the world's leading armaments manufacturer; practically all its production of bronze and iron guns – by then probably as good as the English iron guns which had provided the model – went to Holland. Dutch entrepreneurs had also spread iron gun manufacture to Westphalia and the Rhineland around Koblenz; as these cheaper weapons began to make an impact on naval warfare by their quantity the Dutch were in control of all significant areas of production except for England. As they were also in control of Baltic timber and timber-based preservatives on which Spain and Portugal were becoming increasingly dependent due to the exhaustion of the most convenient Mediterranean sources over the centuries, the Dutch had every naval advantage – except perhaps longer routes and the dangerous shoal water off their coasts. They sold guns and naval stores to their enemies, legally in the periods when trade was sanctioned, illegally when it was prohibited, thus profiting indirectly from their enemies Atlantic and Eastern systems as they were profiting directly from the assault on their monopolies. The fact that they were at the same time aiding their enemies did not discourage the self-seeking merchants, and as they pulled all the levers of power it was condoned by the state on the payment of certain dues. Figures are not available, but it is probable that trade was a surer way of relieving Spain of its American silver than the privateering war which was carried on at the same time.

Spain meanwhile was becoming exhausted by the military efforts in the

Netherlands and in France, her various armadas against England and the constant attrition of the war at sea. In 1596, after an Anglo-Dutch force had destroyed or captured four of the new Spanish warships in Cadiz and sacked the town and burnt a fleet of merchantmen into the bargain (the most notable English success in the post Hawkins/Drake period), the Treasure fleet was held in the Indies, and Philip II was forced to declare himself bankrupt for the second time and convert his short-term loans to long-term. By the end of his reign interest on the borrowings accounted for two-thirds of his enormous revenues, and he was resorting to a debased currency – this despite the flow of silver from America which he enjoyed in normal years and which peaked in the early 1590s, and despite ever-increasing taxes on the Spanish people. It is significant that nobles were exempt from these taxes which fell, therefore, on peasants, artisans and merchants – the very areas in fact in which Spain was failing: she was often unable to feed all her people in bad years, and her industry was unable to compete with the Dutch in her own colonial markets. In short, she was locked in to a declining cycle of increased expenditure on defence of the empire, consequently increased borrowings and higher taxation which bit into the already weak industrial and agricultural base. The Dutch, by contrast, were rising on a spiral of ever-increasing sea-borne trade and industry, feeding their population despite their small agricultural base and supplying the workshops despite the almost total lack of raw materials within the country by sea-borne imports. The other two northern enemies of Spain had dropped out of the struggle exhausted, France in 1598, England in 1604 after the accession of James I. When a truce was signed between Spain and the United Provinces in 1609, it was Spain that was dropping from exhaustion, the United Provinces that forced peace negotiations by threatening to create a West Indies Company that would attack the Caribbean with the same purpose as the East India Company had attacked the Portuguese Moluccas.

During the twelve years of the compromise truce that emerged, but which never extended 'beyond the line' to the East or West Indies or the west African coast, the Dutch increased their gains in all three areas. Expeditions raided the Portuguese west African coast for slaves – establishing a Dutch settlement in the Gold Coast (1612) – and crossing the Atlantic easily undersold the official Spanish slave contractors in the Americas, capturing a predominant share of the market just as they had already captured the market in manufactures. The largely uncoordinated efforts did not gain any territory though and they failed to turn the Portuguese out of their forts on the African coast.

In the East meanwhile a more effective route to the spice islands was pioneered in 1611 when Hendrik Brouwer, instead of sailing north-easterly after rounding the Cape of Good Hope, continued easterly in the belt of the 'roaring forties' until in the eastern quarter of the ocean he was able to strike up into the trades, making the spice islands by way of the Sunda Strait.

Besides being a faster route independent of the monsoons which always hampered the Portuguese, it brought the Dutch to windward of the Portuguese eastern base at Malacca. When the Dutch Governor-General Jan Coen – who has been called the Dutch Albuquerque – established the East India Company's main base at the little settlement of Djakarta just inside the Sunda Strait – naming it Batavia – he gave the Dutch the advantage of a permanent windward position.

Although the first Dutch attacks on Malacca itself failed, they were able to maintain patrols to divert native shipping to Batavia, cutting out Malacca, and soon gained a more complete control of the most lucrative spices, cloves, ginger, nutmeg, mace, than the Portuguese had ever managed, turning Batavia meanwhile into a thriving *entrepôt* for all Eastern wares. This policy of tying up both suppliers and consumers by force contrasted oddly with the merchants' protestations on behalf of free trade and freedom of the seas whenever anyone else claimed a monopoly! It was effective though, and the men on the spot claimed it was essential. Gradually the flow of spices through the Red Sea and Persian Gulf faded away; the balance shifted further from the Mediterranean towards the oceanic economies.

By the 1620s Amsterdam was the unquestioned capital of the Western oceanic system. The population had grown from some 30,000 in the early years of the revolt to over 100,000, making it larger than all but Venice and a handful of capital cities. It had long been the leading commodity and insurance market. Since the foundation of the Bank of Amsterdam in 1609, to facilitate the exchange of different currencies, it had become the leading money market as well; following the Exchange Bank, a lending bank had been established in 1614 and the capital and small savings attracted to Amsterdam and banks established later in Middelburg, Delft, Rotterdam, kept interest rates in the United Provinces incomparably low and increased the competitive edge of Dutch merchants, shipowners and industrialists. Neither banking nor central government banking were Dutch inventions; like all the other book-keeping and insurance tools of commerce they had come direct from the Italian city states. Nevertheless they effected a financial revolution in Holland; as one envious Englishman wrote half a century later when proposing to 'Outdo the Dutch without Fighting', the Bank of Amsterdam was 'the great sinews of Trade, the Credit thereof making Paper go in Trade equal with Ready Money, yea better in many parts of the World than Money.'[7]

As in Renaissance Venice, the emergence of the sophisticated machinery of capitalism triumphant went hand-in-hand with an artistic and intellectual flowering; the well-fed burghers were caught and preserved on brilliant canvasses, together with their wives and bonneted children, the scrubbed interiors of their houses and the elegant façades of the merchant quarter. Above all, the ships and the sea were celebrated as they had never been before: *jaghts* still lean to the wind; the sun brightens patches of opaque, sand-stirred water; great ensigns with horizontal red, white and blue strain out stiffly above folds of backed maintopsails; the warships and the India-men sit the water sweetly, all solid timbers and easy curves from the round beakheads up to the carved and gilded poops; the sun strikes diagonals from rows of raised gun port lids and the stubby barrels that poke out beneath. Surely there was more to the Dutch empire of the seas than profit. So there was. It was caught in these moving sea- and harbour-scapes, a spirit of bustle and liveliness and hope and freedom; the ships themselves are a symbol of freedom and a promise of profit, variety, the stimulation of different scenes and cultures. The essential differences between the United Provinces and the mighty Spanish Empire shine out with extraordinary clarity. While the equally talented Court painters patronised by Charles V and Philip II concerned themselves with the spirit and abstractions of the True Faith, Van de Velde, Rembrandt and all the others celebrated material things and humanity itself in all its diversity, grossness and pathos. Can it be doubted on the evidence of the canvas that sea power and territorial power are basically different?

The second and final phase of the Dutch assault on Spain began in 1621 when the Twelve Years' Truce ended, as it was bound to end: Spain had not conceded any of the monopolies she claimed, East or West, and the mer-chants of the United Provinces, flushed with the success of their assault in the East, were ready to repeat it in the West. Spanish-American treasure and the triangular African slave/colonial planting trades were the magnets. Brazilian sugar was now worth more to Portugal than all her spices and exotic ware from the Indies; as a contemporary put it there was more vanity to be found in Pernambuco than in Lisbon.

Unlike the individual initiatives which had established Dutch merchants as the leading illicit traders and carriers in the Atlantic system, but which had failed to take any bases or break the colonial power of Spain or Portugal, this second assault was as carefully planned as the earlier Portuguese assault on the Indian Ocean. The vehicle was a West Indies Company, formed in 1621 on the usual joint-stock basis, to have its own warships and rights to conquer, settle and administer overseas possessions. At first it was conceived on a privateering basis to pay for itself and help pay for a simul-taneous land offensive in the Spanish Netherlands with loot from Spanish America, but funds were slow to come in and the disappointing capital raised forced a change of target to the less well-defended Portuguese colonies in Brazil; this actually coincided with the views of the driving force behind the Company, Willem Usselinc; he realised that permanent results would come only from settlement and planting.

In December 1623 a fleet of twenty-seven sail with 1,700 troops, Dutch, German and English, set out for Brazil under Jacob Willekens; his Vice-Admiral was Pieter Pieterszoon Hein, who came to occupy the same position in Dutch legend accorded Drake in English. By the following May they had taken the Portuguese colonial capital of Bahia. By this date the Spanish navy had been put on a more permanent basis and Philip IV was able to collect a fleet of fifty-two sail and send them out with 12,000 men in October that same year, with the result that Bahia was back in his hands by the following April. Despite the setback, the Dutch Company had won a great deal of booty from the capture, and they now switched their attack, arming powerful fleets with the intention of taking San Juan de Puerto Rico as a permanent base for operations in the Caribbean. They succeeded in occupying the city itself and ravaged the coast, but the Spanish castle held out and finally, crippled by disease, the Dutch were forced to abandon the island. They did not abandon their ambitions; over the following years a succession of powerful Dutch fleets cruised the West Indies practically sweeping local craft off the sea.

At this stage in the mid-1620s, the overall position in the Atlantic system seemed little changed from the Elizabethan age; the United Provinces had taken over from England in sending joint-stock fleets to ravage the Americas and west Africa, but despite the financial strength of Amsterdam they were still only singeing the King of Spain's beard; they had effected no change in the system of fortified bases which allowed the annual Spanish fleets and the treasure to get through; in west Africa they had failed to take the fortress of el Mina from the Portuguese, whose slave baracoons still stretched from the Gold Coast south to Angola, supplying the flourishing Brazilian colonies – which successfully resisted a second assault from Piet Hein in 1627. Meanwhile the other breakaway Atlantic provinces, coastal France and England were locked in struggle with their territorial centres, and were consequently of little account.

In England, Charles I had succeeded in 1625; desperately short of cash, he had sent his naval chief, the Duke of Buckingham to The Hague to propose a Protestant League against Spain, and afterwards despatched a great expedition with the idea, unchanged from Elizabethan times, of 'possessing some place of importance in Spain' from which to 'intercept the Plate fleet'.[8] But the Royal Navy had sunk, both in terms of material and leadership, from the heady days of Elizabeth: the majority of the vessels making up the expedition were small merchantmen, their sailors and so-called soldiers an ill-disciplined rabble, and the results were chaos, disease, drunkenness, total failure and an increase in Charles's debts; those who returned were not paid.

In France, Cardinal Richelieu had become Chief Minister of Louis XIII in 1624; he had been confronted immediately by the need to take action against the Huguenots of the Biscay area. The Huguenots were a state within a state, garrisoning their own fortresses, practising their own religion and possessing a privateer fleet stronger than the French Royal Navy. So low had the navy sunk in the previous half-century of civil strife that Richelieu had to hire ships from the Dutch and the English to mount a blockade of the chief Huguenot stronghold, La Rochelle. The following year Charles, anxious to placate the Protestants who controlled the English Parliament (and much of his finances), changed sides and sent an expedition against Richelieu's forces on the Île de Ré, off La Rochelle. It was a desperate throw for a king already sunk in debt, and it failed disastrously, as did another expedition the following year, 1628. La Rochelle surrendered to Paris; peace was signed between England and France.

One subsidiary reason for the war had been the question of prizes and England's claim to the right of search for contraband going to her enemy, Spain; she had felt able to take a high hand because of France's almost total lack of a navy! But even here Charles's gamble had rebounded disastrously, for while there are no firm figures, it seems certain that during the time England was pitted against both France and Spain she lost nearly 400 ships, many of them sizeable vessels employed in long sea trades, meanwhile taking with her own privateers a motley collection of mostly small French or Spanish fishermen and coasters.[9]

It is apparent that neither England nor France were of much help to the Dutch in their assault on the Spanish Empire at this time. Probably more helpful were pirates and privateers. Pirates came in all nationalities, chiefly Moorish, English, French and Dutch, the most significant of whom operated from the north African cities, chiefly Tunis, Tripoli, Algiers and Sallee, a newcomer among the leading strongholds outside the Straits of Gibraltar on the Atlantic coast of Morocco. Some of the most redoubtable pirates were European renegades like the ex-Sea Beggar, Simon Danser of Dordrecht and the disgruntled English thug, Captain John Warde, one-time Royal Navy. These two settled in Algiers and Tunis and operated pirate squadrons, the largest of whose vessels were the equal of most northern warships; in alliance they became a minor naval power like the early Barbarossas, and they grew as wealthy, building palaces in their adopted cities 'more fit for a prince than a pirate'. Under their tuition, and that of scores of others like them, the native pirates adopted northern sailing ships and tactics alongside their traditional methods. Pirates of all nationalities also haunted the Caribbean cays and wooded fringes of Hispaniola. However, these operated in the main from small, lightly armed vessels on hit-and-run raids against ill-defended settlements, small traders and stragglers from convoys; they had little effect on Spanish power until much later in the century.

The Spanish, for their part, had the most highly organised and successful privateer squadrons operating from the Flanders coast against Dutch and English shipping; these were the famous Dunkirk frigates; long, low, fine-lined and faster than conventional warships. The coves and inlets of the rock-bound coasts of Cornwall, Devon, southern Ireland and Brittany sheltered other violent wreckers and rovers who made no distinction about which nationalities they robbed. In short, lawlessness and plundering under the guise of privateering or 'letters of reprisal' (for real or trumped-up charges) were endemic in every sea. The Dutch as the traders and carriers to the world, who had to run the gauntlet of Flanders and the western approaches to the Channel probably lost far more than they gained from the anarchy; much of the naval effort that might have been devoted to the assault on Spanish America was diverted to convoy escort and anti-pirate patrols around Europe.

The one area in which the Dutch undoubtedly triumphed during the 1620s was the East. At the beginning of the decade they were still acting in concert with the English company when it suited them; their first blockade of Goa in 1621 was undertaken with the aid of an English squadron. Besides cutting off the life-blood of commerce from the Portuguese eastern capital, this kept Portuguese warships inside, and the English Commander, John Weddell, acting entirely on his own initiative, afterwards sailed up to the Persian Gulf, drove off a small Portuguese squadron from before Ormuz and allowed a Persian force to cross from the mainland to take the island. Thus, just over a century after Albuquerque's death in these waters, the fortress which stood as a symbol of his most remarkable triumph fell, never to be recovered. In the spice islands themselves where the Dutch were established in strength, matters were different. A series of incidents arising out of the English company's obstinate retention of its toehold in Bantam and other minor settlements in the southern Moluccas culminated in 1623 with the trial of English residents at Amboina; they were accused of conspiracy to massacre the Dutch and after being tortured, ten were executed. The 'massacre' at Amboina signalled the end of the uneasy toleration of the English presence in the spice islands; they were forced back on their bases on the west coast of India, and the Dutch who followed up with a ruthless drive against the island natives who had sided with the English – removing and enslaving those whom they failed to slaughter – were left in total control of the archipelago, hence of suppliers and consumers in the most valuable spices.

In 1630 they began a commercial blockade of Malacca, which they had failed to take by assault on two previous occasions, and resumed similar blockades of Goa and the Malabar and Ceylon coasts, aimed at removing the Portuguese completely from the Eastern Board. They were aided by the monsoons which effectively cut their task to half the year; otherwise it must have been beyond their resources. The English by this time recognised the Dutch as their most dangerous rivals in the area and came to an agreement with the Portuguese whereby differences between them were to be settled peaceably. And while Portuguese commerce was slowly strangled by the Dutch they concentrated their efforts on breaking into the inter-ocean trades, especially to the Red Sea and Persian Gulf, operating from small, unfortified warehouses, one of many trading communities sanctioned by the great Mogul Emperor.

Other English and French companies were taking similar advantage of the Dutch naval assault in the West. While Dutch fleets ravaged the Caribbean in wave after wave, engaging all Spanish attention, English and French companies settled the St Lawrence, the eastern seaboard of North America, and those uncolonised small islands of the Caribbean remote from the large Spanish islands; these were the Leeward and Windward groups, so called because of the prevailing easterly and south-easterly winds of the area. They were all dead to windward of the Spanish islands, another reason for their comparative immunity, and in some cases a reason for their original settlement as bases from which to attack Spanish trade. By the mid-1630s a chain of settlements and plantations had been established in the unoccupied areas which the Spanish still regarded as theirs by right of discovery – from the St Lawrence in the north down to a few miles off the South American coast. The English had the lion's share in Nova Scotia, Newfoundland, Massachusetts, Rhode Island, Connecticut, Maryland, Virginia and the West Indian islands of Bermuda, Barbados, St Christopher, Nevis, Antigua. The French were confined to Quebec and the St Lawrence area and the West Indian islands of Martinique, Guadeloupe and half of St Christopher. The Dutch themselves had only settled the Hudson River area and Manhattan Island until they realised that plunder was a diminishing return; in 1634 they took the Caribbean island of St Eustatius for use as an *entrepôt* for trade, soon followed by the neighbouring small islands.

In the long run it was the English and French colonisation which was to prove the most significant event of the era – a nice paradox since the Royal Navies of both were at their lowest ebb, incapable even of policing their home waters for much of this time. As Paul Kennedy puts it, 'these facts present the historian with a major problem concerning the relationship between naval strength on the one hand, and commercial and colonial expansion on the other.'[10] The answer must be that the North American continent and the lesser Antilles were wide open to anyone with a few flintlocks and a ship capable of a transatlantic voyage, and the settlements were made from the loose alliance of the breakaway fringe under the umbrella of its most potent force, Dutch sea power.

To contemporaries, the most impressive event of the time was Piet Hein's fulfilment of the dream of all West Indian interlopers for three-quarters of a century. In September 1628, off Matanzas Bay on the north coast of Cuba some fifty miles east of Havana, he surprised and took the whole of the annual flota carrying the produce and treasure of New Spain and Peru. His plans had been carefully laid; his fleet was thirty-one sail strong against nine merchantmen and four treasure galleons, which succumbed with scarcely a fight. The decisive factor, however, was that local Spanish craft had been driven from the seas by a previous Dutch fleet and local pirates, and the treasure fleet, deprived of warning, sailed straight into the ambush he had laid. Besides rich colonial produce, nearly 200,000 lb of silver and

135 lb of gold were taken; all was brought home safely and fetched the enormous sum of 15 million guilders – twice the original capital subscribed for the West Indies Company. Perhaps more surprising than the apparent ease with which the coup had been brought off was the fact that it was the first time; the regular treasure fleets had been the focus of every violent ambition for nearly one hundred years and were to remain so for many more, yet Hein's feat was unique. The significance of the triumph also has to be set against the fact that the Dutch West Indies Company efforts had not paid their way; the assault had been foiled in South America; in the Caribbean and central America it had taken no major bases or territory, nor had it really affected the Spanish colonial system based on vast but loosely connected territorial holdings: ranches, plantations and silver mines. In short, up to that fortunate never-to-be-repeated stroke the ferocious campaign into which so much treasure and human capital had been sunk appeared to have failed.

Whether it failed, or how much it weakened the Spanish Empire is impossible to determine. Spain was in decline in any case. The population of Castille and New Spain was falling, a pointer not simply to food shortages afflicting the whole Mediterranean world but to absolute industrial/commercial decline. This is apparent when contrasted with the rising populations of coastal, north-west Europe, particularly Amsterdam, Leiden, Rotterdam and the other thriving ports and industrial towns of the Netherlands; prosperity attracts growth: the reverse must be equally true. Meanwhile the Spanish-Italian possessions, like the whole Mediterranean system were declining in relative terms against the flourishing Oceanic/Baltic system controlled from Amsterdam. As for the bullion which sustained her great period, the gold flow from Portuguese west Africa had dried up by the end of the sixteenth century, and the treasure from Spanish colonies in the New World was falling drastically as the easiest silver seams became worked out. Her shipbuilding industry was also in decline due to Dutch competition and shortage of timber, hence dependence on Baltic supplies via the Dutch; about one-third of her vessels were Dutch-built, another one-third colonial-built, chiefly in Havana; some of her ships seem to have been old with worn-out gear. Again, she relied on her main enemy for a large proportion of her ordnance and powder. A Royal gun foundry had been established at Seville in 1611, but produced under forty average-calibre guns a year – against some English and Swedish factories turning out up to 200 a year – not to mention foundries in Amsterdam, Rotterdam, The Hague, Utrecht, Maastricht, and numerous German establishments in Dutch control. Even in the most basic supply of grain to feed the homeland, Spain relied on her enemy's shipping from the Baltic. It is apparent that the Spanish decline had its roots in the failure to retain control of the Netherlands in the previous century; this was accentuated by the exhaustion of New World silver ores, but how much the attrition of the sea war in the Caribbean and on the west African coast contributed is an open question.

To contemporaries, the Spanish empire seemed as fixed as ever, her navy far stronger than in the Elizabethan period, her New World treasure inexhaustible and abundant beyond accounting.

The climax of the Dutch assault coincided with the rise of the French navy and French influence under Cardinal Richelieu in the late 1630s. This was no coincidence; it was the recovery of France from her internal struggles – as it turned out only temporarily – and her increasing weight in the scales against Spain that finally toppled the colossus.

Richelieu was a centraliser whose policy was to rebuild a united France and extend its borders; those borders as in the past abutted one or other of the Austrian or Spanish Habsburg territories, hence France's policy was quite simply anti-Spain, anti-Austria/Holy Roman Empire. From the first Richelieu saw the importance of naval strength: the stature and wealth that Portugal, Spain and above all the United Provinces derived from their overseas trade and possessions had not gone unnoticed, especially among the merchant classes in France – although courtiers and landed nobles were less enthusiastic! Richelieu himself considered that Providence, by giving France coastlines and harbours facing both the Mediterranean and the Atlantic, had handed her the 'empire of the seas' if she would only bestir herself.[11] Specifically he recognised the need for a powerful navy to act against Spain's communications with her Italian possessions and with her army in Flanders, and to support French operations against Spain's coastal provinces. 'He who is master of the sea is master of the land'[12] was a maxim of his that was particularly appropriate to the Franco-Spanish struggle.

In 1626 Richelieu created a new post for himself, *Grand maître* of the commerce and navigation of France, and over the next few years he bought out the Admiral of France and the officials of the decayed provincial admiralties, putting in their place a central Marine Cabinet under a Secretary-General of Marine who reported to him. He chose four ports, Le Havre, Brest, Brouage (south of Rochefort, which was later preferred) and Toulon. These were to be turned into main fleet bases and dockyards, and he appointed a finance and supply director and an executive chief to each; these reported to the central Marine Cabinet. Large warships were ordered, principally from the United Provinces, and smaller vessels were built at French yards under the guidance of Dutch experts. To aid manning, he had annual lists compiled of all sailors, masters and gunners in the coastal provinces, which were divided into eight districts under civilian 'lieutenants general' reporting to him. From this splendid administrative conception and the injection of over four million *livres* annually there grew in very short time a splendid fleet. It was short of experienced officers since in theory these had to be nobles who were traditionally inclined to the army, or if they had to go to sea, to an apprenticeship in the galleys of the Knights of St John. Privateer captains were employed to fill the gaps, and they provided a core of hard experience.

The first test of the new force came in 1635 when Richelieu took France into the Thirty Years War. This confused, separatist, nationalist struggle inflamed with religious passion had been ravaging the German states of the 'Empire' since 1618 and had drawn in or been used by practically every other country in Europe. The Dutch were involved because the rival Baltic nations were involved and because their German borders were threatened; France was involved long before her formal entry with aid to the Dutch against the Spanish army in Flanders and since 1629 with aid to Sweden, whom she wanted to keep in the field against Austrian Imperial forces.

Sweden was by that time a major factor in the European balance. With the wealth from her expanding industries she had built up formidable armed services; the gun decks of the *Wasa* with their uniform batteries of 24-pounder bronze cannon, which can be seen in Stockholm today, indicate the naval strength she derived from the combination of timber and armament industries with Dutch tuition and capital; this particular example was too extreme in weight of upper battery and overturned on the maiden voyage. The army had moved the other way with the development of a revolutionary, light field gun which could be drawn by one horse instead of the teams needed for other contemporary pieces; equally novel tactics of movement, high discipline, the leadership of an undoubted martial genius, the King Gustavus Adolphus, had brought the country into the first rank of European military power. She had spent the early years of the war fighting Poland and had gained valuable coastline, hence customs dues, in the southern Baltic. Meanwhile the imperial forces had pressed northwards, conceiving a scheme of linking with Danzig and other Hansa ports to build a fleet and with Spanish help take control of the Baltic. Gustavus Adolphus naturally turned against them and Richelieu, recognising a most powerful ally against Austria, helped with subsidies. After a remarkable trail of Swedish successes deep into the heart of Germany, Gustavus Adolphus was killed and the tide turned back in Austria's favour to such an extent that in 1635 Richelieu entered the war openly on the Swedish/Dutch – or so-called Protestant side.

At first the naval war went against France: Spain seized and occupied the Lerin Islands off Cannes on the Provençal coast, and in the Atlantic she successfully convoyed armadas to Dunkirk to reinforce her Flanders army, taking a number of valuable Dutch and French prizes in the process. Richelieu's fleet, hampered by lack of experienced commanders, made a fumbling start. However in 1637 it succeeded in retaking the Lerins, and the following year achieved two successes. One of these was a galley battle in the old style fought off Genoa; a French squadron of fifteen galleys learned of a Spanish force landing troops near Genoa, chased, and on 1 September cut off nine

Spanish and six Sicilian galleys; with the forces exactly equal and the sea calm, both sides formed line abreast and pulled towards each other, holding their fire until the last moment, then clashed in the smoke of the bow batteries and engaged in desperate musketry and armoured hand-to-hand combat. After a confused and terrible slaughter, three French galleys were in Spanish hands, six Spanish in French hands; these included the Sicilian flagship, and although the French lost three prizes to the weather or slave revolt, they claimed a victory. The action is regarded as the last of the great galley battles.

More important was a victory won by the French western fleet under the Archbishop of Bordeaux, Henri de Sourdis. The fighting prelate was ordered to support a French invasion of the Spanish Basque provinces abutting France in the south-east corner of Biscay; he had with him forty-one vessels, many of considerable force, together with fireships and transports. A Spanish squadron of fourteen galleons ordered to relieve his blockade of the coast was forced by its inferiority in numbers to put in to anchor at Guétaria, short of the French army, and de Sourdis, after bombarding, sent in fireships which destroyed the whole squadron; this was one of the most notable victories ever achieved by fireships, and it gave a stimulus to the use of these craft in all navies, particularly the Dutch.

Those first successes of Richelieu's fleet were in the summer of 1638; the following year de Sourdis was again out in strength to attack a Spanish force gathering in Corunna for a third expedition to Flanders; this time there was a boom across the harbour entrance and he was dissuaded from attempting to break through and send in fireships; instead he landed troops at Ferrol nearby. A Spanish counter-attack forced him back to the ships, and finally a southerly gale drove him off the coast. He came out again in August, but by that time the Corunna force had been joined by other powerful divisions and was too strong for him to tackle; he contented himself by burning a galleon on the stocks at Santoña, taking another as a prize, and after a short cruise returned to base; the focus shifted back to the Spanish and Dutch.

By this time the Dutch had succeeded in tilting the overseas balance decisively in their favour: the West Indies Company, renewing the attack on Brazil with the loot from Piet Hein's coup, had taken the rich north-east sugar-producing area around Pernambuco. Simultaneously their continued assault on the Caribbean – aided by increasing numbers of Huguenot privateers, French colonists patronised by Richelieu, English Puritans and privateers disappointed by Charles's policy of neutrality, and freebooters of all nationalities who were establishing themselves on Providence Island and Tortuga close off the coast of Hispaniola – had paralysed local traffic; Dutch traders had seized the lion's share of commerce and carrying with all the colonists. On the west African coast the Portuguese stronghold of el Mina had fallen at last to the Dutch Company, who had carried the assault south into Angola, taking every Portuguese base, and coming close to establishing a monopoly in slaves. In the East, the garrisons at Goa and Malacca still held out, but the Dutch commercial blockades and diversion of shipping to their own ports, had ruined both as *entrepôts*; the commercial quarters were ghost communities and officials recognised that it was only a matter of time before both bases, and with them the whole Portuguese position in the East collapsed – indeed Malacca dropped into Dutch hands two years later in 1641.

Meanwhile in the Spanish Netherlands, Dutch and French troops pressed in. Dutch squadrons maintained a blockade of the coast – with varying success against the Dunkirkers – and French troops marching across the Rhine cut the overland route for reinforcements from Italy; French galleys from Toulon also threatened the sea route from Spain to Italy. In this crisis for the empire Philip IV prepared two great expeditions to break out of the ring; the first and largest was despatched to Brazil through 1638 and January 1639; the second, gathering the same year in Corunna, Cadiz, Cartagena and Naples, was designed to sail north, destroy the Dutch and French fleets in Biscay and the English Channel, and afterwards land troop reinforcements in the Netherlands; it was the Corunna division of this force that de Sourdis had failed to destroy in June.

In supreme command of the Spanish armada was the Admiral-General of the Ocean Sea, Don Antonio de Oquendo, son of one of Medina Sidonia's commanders; his flagship was the 1,000-ton *Santiago*, mounting sixty guns, with a complement of 800; as Flag Captain, and what would later be called Chief-of-Staff, he had a veteran Dunkirk squadron-commander, Miguel de Orna, well known to the Dutch as the redoubtable privateer, Michiel Doorn. There were altogether seventy sail in the fleet, fifty of them warships of varying strength from a light and handy Dunkirk squadron up to flagships of over 1,000 tons, exceptionally heavily constructed, armed with sixty bronze guns and numerous musketeers. They represented the whole of Spain's remaining oceanic naval strength – since the despatch of the Brazilian armada – and many were hired and fitted out as warships under contract in the usual Spanish fashion. Packed into them and twenty hired transports – some nine of which were English vessels – were 10,000 soldiers, so-called. In fact most of these were untrained men, obtained by the Crown on a contract basis at twenty-one ducats per head; they had been seized by a commercially motivated 'press', which had left whole areas of Spain even more depopulated than they were already. Herded together in and around Corunna while the armada was preparing, they had dropped away by disease and desertion; in order to bring their numbers up again before sailing, a press was sent out into the surrounding country with orders to exempt no one. Many are the harrowing scenes throughout history of men ripped from their occupations and families to feed the insatiable gods of war, but the scene around Corunna in that summer of 1639 beggars description; the officers of the armada shut themselves inside their houses to avoid being implicated in the miserable procession of chained men followed by their frenzied womenfolk. A foreign invasion could scarcely have created more misery.

The armada departed Corunna towards the end of August; Oquendo's instructions were to sail direct to Flanders, a change from the earlier intention of seeking out and destroying the enemy fleets, but he was ordered to attack them at all hazard if met on the way. He missed de Sourdis, but in the Channel the Dutch blockading squadron under Maarten Tromp was patrolling the narrows on the lookout for him. The two forces came in sight of one another on 15 September, off the Sussex coast between Selsey Bill and Beachy Head. The Dutch force was only twelve sail strong as Tromp had left a squadron of ten sail, under de With, blockading Dunkirk whilst another detachment under Banckert was cruising the North Sea on fishery protection. Oquendo, seeing the light force opposing him was confident of triumph – not surprisingly – so confident that when his squadron commanders came aboard for battle orders, he merely enjoined them to do their best; they had an easy task; '*La Real dara buenos exemplos!*' 'The flagship will set a good example!'[13]

Tromp was typical of the Dutch fighting sailors of the era, who literally grew up in ships; in contrast to the grandees who commanded the Spanish forces, he was totally unpretentious, simple in the best sense, fiercely independent, stubborn to the point of bloody-mindedness, and with a complete mastery of every aspect of his ships, their navigation and fighting. Born at den Briel near Rotterdam in 1597, he had served in his father's ship from an early age and taken part in the engagements with Spaniards, privateers and pirates that were a normal accompaniment to sea life; at one time he had been held as a slave in north Africa. He had taken service with the Rotterdam Admiralty in 1622, but had been dismissed later for pungent and too-accurate criticisms of the administration. However his exceptional qualities as a commander, revered by officers and men alike, could not be overlooked and in 1637 he was brought back as Lieutenant-Admiral of the United Provinces. In September 1639 he was flying his flag in the *Amelia*, a race-built galleon of fifty-six guns on two battery decks; the rest of his force was composed of smaller ships of forty guns or less.

When Oquendo's sails appeared, he sent one of these eastwards to fire guns every half hour and attract de With and Banckert back to the flag, and, with the rest, beat towards the armada. By nightfall, when both sides lay-to under easy sail the opposing forces were just outside extreme gunshot one from another, the massed hulls of the Spaniards to the west (windward) somewhere off where Littlehampton now stands.

The following morning, with the wind still in the north-west quarter, Tromp led his eleven ships south-westerly in an attempt to weather the Spaniards, who emerged from the night in considerable disorder; soon realising the task impossible as the armada was dead to windward he bore away with the wind towards de With, who had appeared in the meantime with five of his division in the east; they joined at about nine o'clock off Beachy Head. Tromp immediately called a council, and announced his intention of attacking; his reasoning or inspiration bears a striking resemblance to Nelson's before Copenhagen: he pointed out that the ships of the enemy milling about in disorder were strong in numbers, not in force, and since they served only to increase the confusion 'the more of them you find, the surer you will be of victory.'[14] His specific instructions and the reasons he gave for them have an important place in tactical history; they were to form the ships into a line so that together they acted as a single ship. 'If they attack us they will be the rash ones, for who in their senses would try and attack an unbreakable rock defended by the 500 cannon we have amongst us?'[15] And he told the captains to unite the ships so closely that the enemy could not force a way between them. This is held as the first example of fleet line of battle; it is probably more helpful to regard it as a typical example of defensive line of battle as practised for over a century, perhaps longer, by groups and squadrons of sailing warships or armed merchantmen confronted by a numerically superior enemy – the outstanding recorded examples being Vasco da Gama and Vicente Sodre off the Malabar coast in 1501. It is even possible to interpret Tromp's instructions as meaning squadronal line defence with the fleet divided into his eleven and de With's five ships. In any case, since sailing warships had their batteries ranged along the sides the line was an entirely natural, not to say obvious formation for an inferior force to adopt to beat off an enemy who, because of superior numbers would inevitably attempt to close and board. Tromp's tactics in more equal situations were very different. His explanation of the 'line' as a device for enabling each ship to support its consort – in fact for the whole line to act as one – is interesting as it is precisely the explanation given by the most influential French tactician of the eighteenth century when the line reigned supreme, the Viscount de Morogues, and followed by all French fleet commanders.

Having formed close line, some of their ships with their jib-booms almost touching the taffrails of the next ahead, Tromp waited the onslaught close-hauled on the starboard tack, thus sailing south-westerly. Oquendo, who had been following in supreme confidence, not bothering to form his fleet, bore straight down towards the *Amelia* with his towering flagship, determined to grapple her and enter his men. Tromp bore away slightly causing Oquendo to fall astern of the *Amelia*, whereupon the Spanish Commander-in-Chief tried to grapple de With's flagship; the same tactics were repeated and he was left astern of the whole Dutch force. He hauled to the wind, then filled his sails again in pursuit. Behind him came the Dunkirk squadron more-or-less in line, but the rest of his ships were in no kind of formation, only trying to follow as best they could without running into consorts. As the Spanish flagship and the Dunkirkers drew ahead of the main body, Tromp hauled his wind again, shortened sail and received the group with broadsides, then tacked and gave the other broadsides in succession, easing the sheets and bearing away again whenever the Spaniards looked like pressing in too close. There was a fresh wind and a running sea, and most of the shot went high, carrying away the enemy spars and rigging and tearing holes in the canvas, while an unfortunate accident in one of the Spanish vessels caused it to blow up; a similar accident to a powder cask in de With's flagship blew the side of his sterncastle away. So the running, often fierce clashes continued into mid-Channel and thence towards the shoal water off the estuary of the Somme south of Boulogne. Some time after two o'clock Oquendo, his rigging hanging loose and some 150 casualties aboard the flagship alone, tacked and lay-to, repairing damages and allowing his straggling force to catch up. Tromp also lay-to, heads to the northwards, and allowed his squadron to drive northerly as the wind backed into the south-west quarter.

So the two forces rode with tide and wind towards Dungeness until sunset, just outside long gunshot of each other as they refitted. During the night Tromp lost sight of the Spanish lights, and thinking perhaps that Oquendo might be trying to make past him up-Channel, he set a little sail and steered easterly. The following morning he was some four miles from the French coast off Gris Nez; it was hazy and there was no sight of the enemy until about nine o'clock, when the mist cleared and he saw them still against the English coast in the north-west. The wind was light in the south-south-west, and he steered towards them but failed to reach them as the breeze died away altogether. In the late afternoon, as the tide started to ebb, both sides came to anchor, the Spaniards off Folkestone, Tromp one mile to the southward of them. He was firing guns every half hour to direct Banckert towards him, and Banckert, making westwards on the ebb, was answering. An hour before midnight, the tide turned again; a light breeze had sprung up from the south, and Tromp having the weather gage, weighed and bore down on the Spanish fleet, all his ships carrying a light on their poop for recognition. As the action opened again, Oquendo also weighed.

> The night, though calm, was dark; but the flame of the discharges of cannon and musketry was so continuous, as it blazed up first in one then another part, that it lit up the sea; and as it never died down it maintained a certain brightness before the eyes which atoned for the absence of daylight. The discharges of ordnance pealed out ceaselessly so that it appeared to be a continuous thunder, as if the world were dissolving in disorder.[16]

The fighting drifted easterly through the early hours, when Banckert's squadron of nine ships joined, and continued after sunrise, by which time the fleets were off Dover. It seems from a Spanish description that, whether or not Tromp and de With had been formed in a single line before, they were now working as two divisions, 'which in the manner of dextrous cavaliers on a civic festival, wended in and out, vomitting their broadsides'.[17] The Spanish ships still lacked order, massed four or five deep so that only the starboard line took the full force of the Dutch attack; those behind did little, some firing into their own consorts, others trying to break away and run. Oquendo himself was always to windward, attempting to close, but actually forcing the smaller Dutch vessels to keep a respectful distance from the powerful batteries and massed musketeers of the flagship; a cartridge count afterwards showed that 1,520 shot had been fired from the starboard guns alone – more than fifty per gun. Her stout timbers seem to have resisted all that the Dutch hurled at her, as did those of the flagship of the Portuguese squadron, *Santa Tereza*, the largest – and most sluggish – vessel on either side, also armed with sixty bronze pieces and carrying 600 musketeers.

From Dover, Oquendo shaped an easterly course for the Flemish coast. Tromp, de With and Banckert continued harassing him from the windward (southern) flank exactly as Howard, Drake, Hawkins and Frobisher had harassed Medina Sidonia, and with the same tactics of group attack in succession. About nine o'clock they were rewarded with two disabled vessels dropping astern of the armada; they surrounded and took them, but Oquendo tacked back to the rescue and the swift Dunkirkers re-took one, the flagship of a hired squadron of Mediterranean ships whose mainyard had been carried away. The Dutch retained the other, a hired transport, as their sole prize. After this incident Tromp, whose ship was practically out of ammunition, broke off the engagement and steered for Calais to replenish. Many of Oquendo's galleons were too damaged aloft by this time to continue athwart the southerly wind and flood tide running strongly northwards, and he bore away, eventually coming to anchor off Dover at the southern end of the sheltered water known as the Downs between the east Kent coast and the Goodwin Sands. (See map, p. 202.)

Tromp worked hastily to replenish powder and shot from his French allies at Calais, then sailed back across the Channel the following morning with twenty-four of his least-damaged ships. The Spaniards seeing him approach, cut their cables and ran north into the Downs, anchoring close by a small English Royal squadron under Sir John Pennington. Tromp came to anchor to the south of them, and Pennington shortly brought his ships between the belligerents, sending officers to both Commanders-in-Chief, warning them not to fight in English waters and to avoid giving offence by wearing national flags. Pennington's squadron was too weak to give much force to these instructions, but they were obeyed for the moment; Tromp was only too pleased to allow the Spanish force to lie there while he obtained reinforcements from home; as for Oquendo, who had instructions from Philip IV to take no account whatever of English neutrality if it were a matter of attacking and destroying the enemy fleets, it must be concluded that he had taken the measure of the Dutch force and realised that he could not defeat it. He virtually conceded his impotence that night by sending his Dunkirkers and a few of the other small and weatherly ships out of the Downs northabout; by dint of superb navigation they succeeded in escaping with 3,000 soldiers and silver bullion for the payment of the Flanders army. Tromp was furious when he learnt of it, accusing Pennington of telling him that the Spaniards could not escape that way; the English officer acting as liaison agreed that Pennington had said he believed the Spaniards neither could nor would go that way – and he was correct so far as the main body was concerned – but that he had made no objection to Tromp stationing some ships at the mouths of the northern channels. Afterwards Tromp sent fourteen ships to the north of the Spanish fleet to prevent a recurrence.

Despite this weakening of the southern division, Oquendo made no move to escape. Tromp made no move to attack. Every day that passed brought him reinforcements as the Dutch Admiralties exerted themselves to fit out warships, convert merchantmen, re-direct convoy escorts, despatch powder and shot to him as well as musketeers from the garrisons ashore, and combustibles for fireships. He received secret instructions from the States General to attack the Spaniards directly a favourable opportunity presented itself without taking any heed or consideration whatsoever of territorial waters, nor of any French, English, Scots, Swedes, Danes or Baltic ships which might attempt to hinder him. By October his original force of twenty-four ships had grown to sixty-five – against fifty-four Spaniards remaining – and he confided the secret instructions to his captains at a council, telling them to be ready to fight at any time. Another council the next day decided that the time was not yet ripe; the English squadron, with the addition of some hastily converted merchantmen, was now twenty-four sail strong, and Pennington had warned that he would enter battle on the side of whichever force was attacked.

Charles I meanwhile, was trying to raise cash from the situation – specifically a payment from Philip in return for an English guarantee to protect his armada! His guarantee was worthless. He had started to rebuild the English fleet with 'ship money' levies from the counties, but he was still hopelessly short of money to man and maintain them since he had been ruling for a long time without the support of parliament and the money which parliament might have voted him: hence his need for such a desperate expedient, hence the weakness of his own position to guarantee the bargain he proposed! This became increasingly clear to both sides; aboard Oquendo's ships the mood became sombre, disease rampant; aboard the *Amelia*, by contrast, an English visitor noted that the men were 'lusty, healthy and frolicke, encouraged by former good successes and this present fortunate opportunity'.[18]

By 13 October, Tromp was ready to strike, and he gave his divisional commanders their instructions; de With with thirty sail of war and four fireships had already been ordered to watch Pennington's squadron and resist them if they attempted to come in on the Spanish side; now the Zeeland admiral, Evertsen, with fourteen ships and one fireship was given the Portuguese galleons with their huge flagship, *Santa Tereza*, as his target. A Rear-Admiral, van Catz, with eight ships and one fireship was given the remaining Dunkirkers and other small ships, while Tromp himself with eleven warships and three fireships took Oquendo and the galleons about him. Small divisions of eight and seven warships were also assigned to guard the northern and southern flanks of the Spanish force. As the Dutch aim was to drive the Spaniards from the Downs and tackle them in the open sea, it was decided not to attack unless the wind were in a westerly quarter. For the next few days it remained in the east, rising to gale force, which heeled the ships so much under sail as to preclude use of the lower tier of guns. Reinforcements continued to arrive; by the 18th, Tromp had 103 warships and sixteen fireships. The next day dawned with the wind in the north-west and he was about to attack when it went round suddenly to the east again, and blew up into a gale. Pennington, whose liaison officer was constantly aboard the *Amelia*, and had seen her cleared for action and Tromp's own cabin bare, had no doubts about the Dutch intentions – nor indeed had anyone in the Downs – but his request to Charles I for instructions drew only the cryptic reply, 'You must make as handsome a retreat as you can.'[19]

On the 20th, the wind still strong from the east-south-east, Tromp weighed and moved his division up to a position north-east of Oquendo, and de With moved his ships north-east of Pennington's squadron. It was apparent to all that the blow was about to fall. During the night the wind died away; the following early morning was heavy with mist skirling before the lightest northerly airs. At slack water (about 6.30 a.m.) Tromp fired a gun as a signal to make sail, and as the mist began to lift at sunrise, weighed and steered for the Spanish force; the light breeze was backing towards the north-west quarter, but the tide was in full flood, north-north-easterly, holding him up in the windward position. Oquendo was alert; his flagship was already under sail, and Pennington after a rapid council, weighed too and stood north-easterly with the flood in an attempt to weather the Dutch; de With conformed to the movement outside him.

The action began at about 8.30 a.m.; Tromp claimed the first gun was fired by the Spaniards, and it seemed so to many in the English fleet as they watched the Dutch force move slowly down on Oquendo, barely stemming the tide under their lee bows. Whoever opened, Tromp's broadsides were soon rending the calm morning, and the smoke of continuous discharges hanging in the moist air began to obscure the scene; within half an hour the haze was so thick it was impossible to see friend or foe, and the firing died away. Soon, Pennington, judging himself far enough to the northward, stood in on the other tack, while Tromp laid his sails aback, driving southerly against the tide. After a while the visibility cleared, and a confused, running action was joined, during which some of the Spanish vessels steered straight for the shore under Walmer Castle and ran themselves aground in an effort to escape; the Dutch guns drove others after them, and several fireships were set ablaze and rode in amongst them all as the Castle opened fire on the Dutch. Other Spanish ships stretched southwards between Walmer and the South Foreland, making for the open Channel. Tromp followed these and, joined by de With, engaged a compact group of some twenty galleons around Oquendo and the great Portuguese flagship, *Santa Tereza*, as they steered a southerly course past Dover, thence south-westerly towards Dungeness. Pennington meanwhile, who had distanced himself sufficiently to allow de With to join Tromp, opened a long-range ineffective fire from the northwards then anchored, as he explained afterwards, to prevent himself being swept down as the tide turned soon after noon.

At about three o'clock with the ebb pushing strongly under the sterns of the main forces continuing the running battle down-Channel the Dutch sent five fireships down on the two great flagships at the centre of the Spanish group; three went clear, but two became entangled with the *Santa Tereza*, setting her ablaze. Oquendo stood by her until the fire had gained such a hold it was evident that she was lost, then he spread more sail and ran westwards with some seventeen others still in company. Tromp pursued, resuming the artillery action at dusk, but he lost the quarry in the dark – probably running on past them. At sometime before midnight the wind backed more westerly and he stood north, fetching up just east of Beachy Head the following morning, which came in thick and squally.

The Dutch force had become separated during the night, and the day was spent searching among their scattered sails for the enemy main body; some isolated Spanish ships were taken, the *Amelia* herself capturing one which had her mainsail and topsails blown from the boltropes in the squalls, but Oquendo and most of the galleons with him escaped back through the Straits and thence to Dunkirk while Tromp tacked and filled off the Sussex coast. The next day Tromp ran back to the Downs, and found some twenty-two of the Spanish ships aground, burnt out or deserted, and a few others riding at anchor. Pennington was soon aboard to inform him that he had affronted Charles in his own chamber, and to ask what he wanted this time. When Tromp replied that he had come to see if all the Spaniards had been chased ashore, the English admiral, to avoid another humiliation, told a bare-faced lie: all those ships he saw still afloat had been bought by the English. Apparently Tromp was satisfied; he watered his fleet, and on the 26th, sailed back for the Fatherland.

During the battle of the Downs, the Spaniards lost perhaps forty of the fifty-four vessels that had been cornered there; most were driven ashore on the Kent coast, one on the Goodwin Sands, a few lost later on the French or Flemish sands, three were sunk, one burned in action, four taken by the Dutch as prizes; many of those that did escape to Dunkirk were in a shattered condition; Oquendo's flagship, which had borne the brunt of the fighting in all its phases had some 1,700 shot in her hull! It has been estimated that in all about 7,000 Spaniards were lost against about one hundred men and just one ship from the Dutch force – an extraordinary disparity reminiscent of the 1588 actions in the Channel. While far from the total annihilation often claimed, it was an overwhelming victory. The moral effect was perhaps greater even than the physical. It was the last great northern armada ever despatched from the Spanish Empire. Oquendo himself was crushed, and died soon after returning home with the remnants of his fleet.

The following January, 1640, the Spanish/Brazilian armada suffered a similar fate. Sailing from Bahia towards the Dutch at Pernambuco, it was engaged by Dutch forces in another running encounter along the coast. The weather was stormy, and again the Dutch ships' superior powers of manœuvre enabled them to beat down Iberian resistance, shatter their spars and rigging, leaving the sea and the rocks to complete the work. After four days' confused fighting, known as the battle of Itamarca, the beaten survivors straggled back for Bahia.

These two terrible defeats signalled the finish of the great days of Spain. At the end of the year Portugal rebelled, never to be brought back under the Habsburg Crown; Catalonia also broke away; significantly this coastal province with its capital Barcelona, one of the great commercial cities in the Mediterranean system, had been growing in population while rural Spain declined. It had always shown centrifugal tendencies; now it looked to France to support its independence and Richelieu was only too happy to assist.

As what remained of Spain's energies were turned inwards the struggle in England between Charles and his Parliament broke out in open civil war. Towards the end of the decade, France, which had been heavily taxed to pay for the efforts in the Thirty Years War – finally brought to an end in 1648 – also erupted in civil strife. Territorially she had gained a great deal from the European conflict and her colonists in Canada and the West Indies had gained from the oceanic struggle. But of all the powers, the most triumphant was the United Provinces. They were not entirely free from strife since the Portuguese Brazilian colonists, helped by a revitalised independent Portugal, rebelled and drove them from South America soon after mid-century; the Portuguese also recaptured their bases in Angola. But on the European side of the 'line', the United Provinces were at peace from 1648 while England, France and Spain were embroiled in internal struggle. Dutch ships and traders made the most of the opportunity, capturing an even greater share of every market from the Baltic and Mediterranean to the far oceans, Japan and the eastern archipelago, where Malacca had long fallen, India, where the blockade on Goa had been lifted since it had achieved its purpose of ruining the city, Malabar, Ceylon, and most particularly in the Atlantic. Since the Portuguese rebellion, Philip had deprived the Portuguese of their slaving contracts, and the Dutch, supreme on the Guinea coast and temporarily in Angola, had filled the gap, becoming the principal slave suppliers for the whole colonial plantation economy; as they also provided skills and capital to set up the new English and French colonists as sugar planters they increased the total numbers of slaves required at the same time as they engrossed the sugar trade. And while Amsterdam became the foremost importer of colonial produce, cheapening and widening the European market for tobacco and especially sugar, the Dutch *entrepôts* in the Caribbean islands of Curaçao, St Eustatius, St Martin, Aruba, Buen Ayre thrived as emporia for every conceivable European manufacture.

Thus by remorseless concentration on commerce and shipping, by a single-minded war of attrition on the Spanish and Portuguese oceanic monopolies, by wealth inherited from Spanish Antwerp, augmented by an unrivalled three-way middleman position between the oceans and the Baltic and central Europe, by control of the leading sources of armaments and naval supplies, by alliances with other interlopers, finally with the aid of the re-structured territorial power of France, the United Provinces had become the wealthiest and strongest trading nation there had ever been. They dominated world commerce and carrying to a greater extent even than Venice had dominated the Mediterranean world in her prime, and for a brief period in mid-century they had no serious rivals.

CHAPTER 6

THE RISE OF ENGLAND

The success of the United Provinces naturally inspired the envy of its oceanic rivals, England and France; the first of these to emerge from internal struggle was England, hence England was first to strike. That this happened despite England's new leaders, notably Oliver Cromwell, who wished union, not war, between the two Protestant nations is striking testimony to the power of commerce to shape events. Here, very clearly, commercial wealth and envy can be seen as the irresistible groundswell of history. Whatever storms blew above, in whatever direction surface currents flowed, the struggling individuals and groups in the path of the swell were lifted from beneath, enjoying a dazzling ride before the commercial peaks passed and let them down, threshing in the wake. This is so evident in the case of the Anglo-Dutch wars that conventional history, obsessed as it is by religions and dynasties, has recognised them as the first trade wars. If the previous chapters have been near the truth they were far from the first; the whole hideous, piteous tale of slaughter and massacre known as the wars of religion was sparked off and carried to success on trading strength. The Anglo-Dutch wars were no different. England, in the course of Scottish, Irish and Royalist/Parliamentarian struggles, had acquired an effective central administration, an effective army and a full-time navy supported by money from the estates of the defeated Royalists and by the merchants of the parliamentary party. By contrast with the United Provinces, however, she was still economically undeveloped, and much of her overseas trade had been taken over by Dutch ships. She had reached that dangerous period when the compulsions of the underdog combine with inklings of real power.

The object of envy was the United Provinces; the real power was the English Royal Navy. For the Dutch, in building their remarkable empire of the oceans had created an intensely vulnerable structure: a large proportion of the food for their industrial towns, the raw materials for their industries, and the exports which paid for both – in short not only their prosperity but their very existence – depended on the uninterrupted passage of ships to the ports of Holland and Zeeland. Both England and France lay on the flank of these oceanic routes; England had the better position of the two since she had more numerous deep-water harbours and was placed to interrupt the alternative to the English Channel route, northabout round Scotland. Directly she acquired naval strength the temptation to cut the Dutch life-lines and seize a share of the enormous wealth that flowed along them became irresistible.

The situation was clear to contemporaries on both sides. Those misled by the religious bonds were soon corrected by a press of publicists, from crude pamphleteers to the most luminous intellectuals. One word epitomised the Dutch defence of their position – freedom. On the high seas, 'free ships, free goods', meaning that neutrals were entitled to trade with whomsoever they wished because freight was covered by the flag of the carrying ship irrespective of the ports of origin or destination – except for contraband of war which they sought to define within the narrowest possible limits. And they maintained that the sea itself was free for the use of all nations, denying the legality of Spanish or Portuguese claims to exclusive rights in their own 'spheres'. They argued the case first with guns, but just as the Spanish and Portuguese use of force had been accompanied by high theological arguments about the conversion of souls, so the Dutch onslaught developed its own high theoretical arguments; these were transcribed in legal form by Hugo Grotius in *Mare Liberum* – 'The Free Sea' – in 1609, and expanded in later works. They contained reasonable ideals; they were the obvious line for a free-trading world carrier to take.

They would have been more convincing, perhaps, if the Dutch overseas had practised what the Dutch at home preached. Englishmen were not slow to point to the Dutch West and East Indies Companies' seizure of trading areas; their spice islands monopoly and the 'massacre' at Amboina were issues which rankled on a deeper level than theoretical argument. But the real difference between the two nations was that, whether the Dutch defended their trading activities by force or by greater commercial efficiency, they had an enormously larger share than the English even in English waters and English trades. Everywhere they looked the English saw their interests invaded. Huge Dutch fleets of specialised, sea-going herring 'busses' swept the east coast from the Shetlands to the Thames estuary each year, while English fishermen put out in small, locally based boats. Attempts had been made to promote large-scale fishing to compete with the Dutch, but they had failed. The Baltic trades had also been taken over to such an extent that English merchants imported iron, timber, hemp, naval stores of all descriptions from Dutch re-export houses, or direct from the Baltic in Dutch hulls. In the East, the English East India Company had been forced out of the spice islands, in the West, their colonists relied on Dutch traders for their slave-labour force and European manufactures, Dutch ships for the carriage of their produce. Meanwhile England's own principal export of unfinished woollens went chiefly to Dutch merchants who finished and marketed it, reaping the enhanced value for themselves, even selling it back to England! Quite naturally in the circumstances, Englishmen saw themselves everywhere exploited by Dutch middlemen.

The English theoretical arguments developed from this overwhelming commercial inferiority; in reply to *Mare Liberum* came *Mare Clausum* – 'The Closed Sea' – by John Selden at the request of Charles I in 1631. While not refuting all Grotius's claims for free navigation it upheld the old concept of territorial waters, a band of unspecified width around a state subject to the sovereignty of that state; ancient precedents were disinterred to prove English sovereignty of the Channel and North Sea, the outward and visible sign of which was the salute by lowered topsails and ensign due to all English king's ships in these waters. The English attitude to prize was also significantly different, and more in line with ancient custom; goods to or from an enemy were *not* covered by the flag of the carrying ship; they could be seized from neutrals and allies. And while the Dutch tried to limit contraband of war to actual armaments, the English predilection was to widen the list to naval stores and anything which might help an enemy prolong the struggle. The lines of argument were as basic to an aspiring power poised over the jugular of a successful sea power as the Dutch arguments were basic to the successful sea power itself. As Charles Wilson puts it:

> Behind the loud clamour and palpable humbug of the arguments about international law, ancient custom and the like was the fact that the Dutch Republic had taken a lead in trade, shipping and technology which not only aroused the jealousy of her neighbours – England and France in particular – but gave them a plausible excuse to argue that they were economically exploited. . . Much of what later ages came to regard as almost abstract theory was in reality rooted in fictions that arose from the economic relationship between England and Holland in the seventeenth century.[1]

This applied equally to economic theory. Englishmen recognised that their failure to compete stemmed from lack of finance as much as from the reputed price-cutting policies and hard graft of the Dutch. Theologians of the old school could still maintain that money produced nothing, that it was 'a metal rich but sterile', but practical men throughout Europe had seen too many arguments to the contrary; the Italian city states, Spain, now the United Provinces were living demonstrations of the supreme value of money. Whether it were dug from the ground, seized from enemies or gained by trade it could be seen as the sinews of power, war and trade itself. And from these practical demonstrations, a belief had spread throughout Europe that the object of trade was to secure a favourable 'balance' – in short to export a greater value of goods than was imported, retaining a surplus to add to the national wealth. As trade was conducted in coin, or bills which were exchanged for coin, the surplus and the wealth were reckoned in terms of precious metals; all over western Europe the value of a trade to a nation was judged by whether it resulted in an inflow or an outflow of precious metal. Those which resulted in an outflow were regarded as bad and increasingly discouraged by tariffs and prohibitions, those which resulted in an inflow were regarded as good, to be encouraged by state aid, preferential treatment, often by prohibitions and monopolies – everywhere that is except in the United Provinces. For the tariffs and protectionist policies of others were against the interests of the universal traders and carriers. While the rest of Europe was in the grip of what has become known as 'bullionist' thinking, the Dutch espoused freedom from inter-ference of any kind – securing it with their guns, ensuring it where necessary by illicit trading – and working it up into an intellectual doctrine that per-vaded all aspects of life; Dutch thinkers argued for religious and ethnic freedoms, workers' freedom from guilds as well as manufacturers' freedoms from tariffs, unrestricted trade and universal freedom of navigation; in their philosophy freedom was indivisible, central control anathema.

To the English, Dutch 'freedoms' of trade and navigation seemed little different to Spanish claims of overseas sovereignty; the result in both cases appeared to be the exclusion of English trade! To advance their own interests the English moved towards a practical position somewhere between the two theoretical extremes. A policy of protection for their own industries against the Dutch by prohibition of exports of raw materials and unfinished cloths for the woollen industry and a ban on colonial trade with the Dutch were combined with a move away from monopolies towards freedom of trade between English merchant houses. This culminated in the famous Naviga-tion Act of 1651. The Act banned the import of goods except in English ships or ships of the place of origin or port of final shipment, banned the import of fish, and restricted the coasting trade to English vessels; thus in one blow it struck at the Dutch as carriers and middlemen and protected English merchants and shipping. It can be seen both as a strategic move against Dutch shipping in favour of English shipping as the nursery of naval power, and an economic move against Dutch middlemen in favour of English middlemen who would be able to buy raw materials in the cheapest markets, work them up and obtain the enhanced value for themselves. At bottom the idea was to secure a more favourable balance of trade for England at the expense of the Dutch. It was a significant development of English economic nationalism, marking a shift from Elizabethan and Stuart policies of joint state/private ventures enjoying monopoly rights to what Paul Kennedy has defined as 'a general alliance between government and business, with the former ensuring that the latter could flourish, and gaining in return increased customs and excise receipts, and Parliamentary votes of supply to finance its policies of trade protection.'[2] To use an economic analogy, it represented a more efficient division of labour: merchants and merchant

shipping were to pursue their tasks unrestricted by government or by war-
like necessities, while the government represented their interests and the
Royal Navy protected them against foreign interference.

It is interesting, therefore, that the movement culminating in the First
Navigation Act went side by side with a remarkable increase in English
naval strength. This had its beginnings in a reaction to the low state the
service reached under James I in the second decade of the century; it had
become incapable of protecting the coasts of the kingdom or even of keeping
the Thames estuary free from blockade by the Turk! So low had English
power sunk so soon after the legendary glories of Elizabeth's sailors! The
merchants who suffered most had been prominent in rooting out corruption
from the navy and making a start on rebuilding. The growth of Richelieu's
navy provoked further ship construction under Charles I, notably the great
Sovereign of the Seas (1637), whose three continuous gun decks mounting
one hundred pieces of ordnance, and huge size and tall rig anticipated the
first-rate battleships of the following century. She was the most splendid,
and splendidly decorated, warship of the time, carved and gilded from beak-
head, along the upper tier of gunports to a sunburst of golden reliefs
spreading around her aftercastle and intricate stern galleries. She cost over
£65,000, ten times the cost of an average two-decked warship! To pay for
her and man her and the rest of his fleet, Charles had introduced the 'ship'
money' levy on the coastal ports in place of their ancient duty to provide
ships for defence; it was an attempt to impose similar duties on inland
counties that brought his troubles with parliament to a head. During the
civil war that followed, the greater part of the fleet declared for the parliamentary side, and played a vital part in their subsequent victory by supplying parliamentary forces, safeguarding the merchants' trade – hence their
money – and preventing foreign aid from reaching Charles.

Under parliament, naval administration was remodelled; and an Admiralty Council of State decided policy while a Committee of Navy Commissioners attended to everyday business with a minute care for detail that
had not been seen since John Hawkins's time.[3] In 1649, after the execution
of Charles I the fleet itself was remodelled under three of Cromwell's
colonels, Alexander Popham, Robert Blake and Richard Deane. These
military leaders – one of whom, Blake, is accorded a position close to Nelson
in the British naval pantheon – gave the service an entirely new conception
of discipline and morale, and themselves set an example of duty to the state
of a different order from that of the more renowned Elizabethans; it is in
this period that the moral and operational ascendancy of the Royal Navy
had its real beginnings. At the same time the Admiralty Committee commenced shipbuilding and buying on a scale that added forty-one new vessels
within three years, and in 1652 persuaded parliament to approve the construction of no less than thirty warships; this unprecedented programme was
beyond their resources and seems not to have been completed, nevertheless

at the time of the First Navigation Act, the navy was stronger than it had ever been.

Had this not been so the Act would have been a desperate measure. As it was, the Act and the navy were two facets of an English determination to alter the oceanic balance in their own favour. The navy had been developed and seasoned against quite different enemies, but it was ready (hence the Act) and there was a connecting thread; underlying its growth and its use against both the old and the new enemy was the power of the English merchant community. This is plain without looking far beneath the surface of events: from the positive purging of James I's naval administration by a wealthy merchant, Sir Lionel Cranfield – one-time apprentice who married the master's daughter! – to the negative attitude of parliament in withholding funds for the maintenance and routine duties of Charles I's apparently splendid force, the consequent defection of much of that force to the parliamentary side, the composition of the Admiralty committees of parliament, the administration of the customs duties which provided much of the money for the naval building programmes, in all there are clear glimpses of merchant power. Just how strong this was can be gauged from the fact that the 1651 Navigation Act followed hard on the heels of an English delegation to the States General proposing union between the two Protestant nations for the defence of their common interests! The scheme had been defeated by the Dutch merchant community who had no wish to share their hard-won commercial 'freedoms' with the English; they suspected all political ties as a restriction on freedom, specifically their freedom to trade in peace, and they had no wish to become embroiled in religious, territorial or dynastic wars in Europe.

The need for peace, at least with their European trading partners in European waters, was quite as distinctive a feature of Dutch policy as free trade, indeed peace was the freedom on which free trade and navigation rested; war, especially with a strong naval power, was the ultimate negation of both. Hence their reaction to the Navigation Act was not to fight but to try for its repeal by negotiation; a delegation from the States General travelled to England with instructions to this effect before the end of the year.

The two nations, meanwhile, were entangled in naval broils arising out of the English Civil War. French privateering interests had seized the opportunity to plunder English merchantmen by declaring support for the English Royalist cause; parliament had replied by issuing English privateers with 'Letters of Reprisal' against the French. As the English did not recognise neutral flags as a protection for enemy or 'reprisal' goods, Dutch ships were searched for French cargoes and some were seized and sent into English ports. Here, at the physical level, the violence of English seamen, and their feeling against the Dutch rivals, whipped up by pamphleteers, combined to produce a series of incidents which might easily have been used by the Dutch as an excuse for war. Dutch skippers were kept in solitary confinement while their vessels were awaiting adjudication, Dutch sailors tortured for information about their cargoes. The incidents grew so widespread that the Judges of the English Admiralty Court issued a warning, 'touching the cruel and barbarous acts of punishment and torture done and committed by the captains, officers and companies of several private men of war upon the persons of the masters and companies of several Dutch ships'[4] that the offending parties would be proceeded against in the Court. Still the Dutch delegation sought to smooth the issue by negotiation, the States General instructed its admiral in the western approaches – who had also been subject to indignities from rude English fellows – to do nothing provocative.

Then in February 1652 news reached the States General of a number of ships captured by an English squadron under Sir George Ayscue at the Caribbean island of Barbados. Ayscue had been sent out to enforce the law prohibiting colonials from trading with the Dutch; among his bag were nineteen Holland and five Zeeland ships. It was this incident that set in motion a train of events culminating in the Dutch war that the English merchants – although it must be repeated not their military masters – wanted.

For the States General realised at last that it would come to a fight; at the end of February they prohibited Dutch sailors from serving in foreign vessels, warships or merchantmen, and banned the export of ships, guns, gunpowder and its constituents, and naval stores;[5] in March they resolved to fit out an extra 150 warships, raising a levy of two million guilders and imposing duties on imports and exports to pay for the programme.[6] It is interesting that while they also laid an embargo on merchant shipping until the required number of men had been found for the warships, they exempted the herring fishers and the Baltic traders lest foreigners take advantage of their absence. The standing naval force of forty Dutch warships on routine patrols, convoy duties and fishery protection, had already been raised by thirty-six vessels in 1651, so the new programme anticipated a total of no less than 226 warships, an indication of the seriousness with which the States General regarded their position. The English, in the manner of all belligerents before and since, affected to see this huge defensive increase as an aggressive gesture! They speeded their own preparations; a spate of instructions issued from the Council of State:

To General Blake [Commander-in-Chief, home waters] 21 March.
Sir – It is not unknown unto yourself that there is extraordinary occasion for the hastening forth of the summer fleet . . . therefore we desire you to repair to Deptford, Woolwich and Chatham and examine the cause of the backwardness of the fleet and certify us in whom the fault lies and we shall endeavour to remedy the same by removing the officers whom you shall find negligent.[7]

While the Dutch had the apparently overwhelming advantage of wealth and sophisticated financial machinery to raise the funds for fleet expansion at a remarkably low rate of interest, between 4 per cent and 5 per cent, the division of responsibility between the five different Admiralties and groups of merchants known as 'Directors', who also fitted out warships on a local basis for the national fleets, went a long way to reducing it. By comparison, the centralised English system was a marvel of administrative efficiency. The Dutch were also hampered by the shallowness of the approaches to their harbours which resulted in generally smaller, shallower-draft ships than the English built. The average Dutch warship mounted no more than thirty comparatively light guns – 12-pounders on the lower tier augmented by four 24-pounders, with 6-pounders above. Of these only the 24-pounders were real ship-damaging weapons by the standards of later centuries. They carried an average of 110 men, twenty-five of whom were trained soldiers. Many of the flagships were not a great deal larger, and were generally inferior in weight of metal to the English flagships. Their only advantage was in numbers, by May 1652 there were 112 to 59 in the main fleets; this determined their subsequent tactics of group attack for boarding mêlées.

The Dutch Commander-in-Chief was Maarten Tromp, hero of the victory of the Downs – not a man inclined to take the high-handed English activities lightly. He was ordered by the States General to concentrate his main fleet in the region of Scheveningen – about one-third of the way from the western end of the Dutch coastline – to guard against an English invasion, while detached squadrons protected the fisheries, Baltic traders and the Channel shipping route. His orders to his captains and squadron commanders were to:

> maintain and defend the ships of these Provinces from all visit or search, excluding necessary questions at sea [to] defend them against all and everyone that would injure them, and to deliver them from the hands of any that may have captured them.[8]

The English interpretation of their rights of search and prize being what it was, a conflict was bound to develop at some time. In the event it arose from the English claim to the salute due to their men of war by virtue of English 'sovereignty' of the Narrow Seas – a conceit quite as intolerable to any Dutch sailor as their claimed rights of search.

The opening incident occurred off Start Point, Devon, on 24 May 1652. An English naval captain, Anthony Young, in the thirty-six-gun *Great President* met a Dutch convoy from the Mediterranean escorted by three men-of-war; he bore down on the flagship, compelling her to strike her flag, but another Dutch escort shortly passed him to windward with her flag still flying defiantly; when Young filled in chase, the Dutch captain yelled out an invitation for him to come aboard and strike the flag himself. The upshot was an exchange of broadsides and musketry until the Dutchman rendered the salute. In the course of the action Young lost one killed and four wounded, but he allowed the convoy to proceed as the ships were not from the colonies and, as he explained, he did not wish to exacerbate the already tense situation between the two nations.

To the eastward, meanwhile, Tromp with the main Dutch fleet of some forty-two sail was forced off station by bad weather and took refuge under the Kent coast. He weighed again on the 29th with a north-easterly wind, and set course back across the Channel for Calais. On the way he met the Dutch warship that had been fired on by Young; the captain told him of the skirmish and reported that he had left the merchantmen off Fairlight on the Sussex coast in the midst of an English squadron whose boats were visiting the Dutch ships – presumably to search. It takes little imagination to conceive Tromp's mood on hearing all this. He immediately wore round for the English coast with the intention of taking the merchantmen under the protection of his fleet, or if they had been captured by the English, of releasing them. Unfortunately a portion of the English fleet, some fifteen ships under Blake, was making up-Channel at the time; knowledge of this had been one reason for Tromp standing over towards the French coast for he had no wish to become involved in a dispute over the salute. Now he could not avoid one.

As he approached the English flagship off Dover he brailed up his courses, lowered both fore and main topsails halfway down the masts in salute, and sent a man up into the maintop to attend the flag halyards. He did not give the order to strike the flag, however, and Blake sent a shot over his masts to remind him – shortly followed by another. No doubt these confirmed the old sailor in his determination not to humble himself before English arrogance; instead of ordering the flag to be lowered he ordered a gun fired in reply to miss the English ship, and had his launch brought alongside, intending to send his captain across to speak with Blake. Before the boat could get away, the English flagship fired again – whether from one gun as in the English account, or from several as in the Dutch account is now impossible to determine, but a ball carried away the arm of a Dutch sailor and flying splinters wounded others. It was all that was needed to spark an action. Both sides claimed the other fired the first broadside; it is impossible to reconcile the stories without assuming that what the English referred to as their final warning shot was actually fired from enough guns to justify the Dutch claim of a broadside. The details are not important; the attitudes made a conflict inevitable, and the preliminary manœuvres would have been sufficient indication of intent to such seasoned sailors as both admirals were. The Dutch ships around Tromp were soon passing to windward of Blake firing their broadsides in succession as the English ships bore down to support their Commander, and the engagement became general, running down-Channel, with another English squadron of nine sail from the Downs shortly joining in to attack the Dutch rear. About six o'clock in the evening Tromp, whose ships had the worst of the encounter, bore away towards the

French coast; Blake followed for a while, but when he broke off to repair damages to his spars and rigging the fleets became separated. Two Dutch thirty-gun ships were left disabled in the wake of the Dutch fleet and were taken, one so holed that she soon sank. As Tromp was balked of his intention to take the Dutch convoy under his wing, the encounter was an undoubted victory to the fewer but heavier English ships. Blake's flagship had only six killed, despite having borne the brunt of the action, an indication of the small effect of the light Dutch broadsides.

For the English, the encounter was proof of Dutch warlike intent; the commander of the Downs squadron, Bourne, saw it as revealing that the Dutch had 'war in their hearts whilst peace in their lips, which wickedness the Lord will judge.'[9] Blake himself wrote to Tromp greatly astonished at his account of the start of the action and accusing him of committing an act of hostility without receiving the slightest provocation, ending in the expectation that Parliament 'will keenly resent this great insult and the spilling of the blood of their unoffending subjects'.[10] Both men were perfectly sincere; to them 'the honour of the flag' was no legal fiction, but an ancient right due to English men of war. In their perception it was the Dutch who not only started the quarrel but whose usurpation of English waters and English trades was the root cause of the bitterness. Certainly the English parliament took this line when it came to examine the cause of the fight. They were predisposed to do so; it was just the kind of incident the 'war party' needed to justify an assault on Dutch shipping. Despite the utmost efforts of the Dutch delegates, still negotiating in England, parliament took the darkest possible view of Dutch motives:

> The extraordinary preparations of 150 sail of men of war without any
> visible occasion . . . the Instructions themselves given by your said
> superiors to their commanders at sea, do find too much cause to
> believe that the Lords the States General of the United Provinces have
> an intention by force to usurp the known rights of England in the seas,
> to destroy the fleets that are, under God, their walls and bulwarks,
> and thereby expose this Commonwealth to invasion at their pleasure,
> as by their late action they have attempted to do.[11]

Even before this finding was delivered to the delegates, the Dutch ambassador had reported,

> we can clearly see preparations and arrangements are being made as
> though an open rupture had taken place, and as though with the
> foreknowledge and by the orders of their High Mightinesses [the
> States General] which, indeed they [the English] do not hesitate to
> assert openly and publicly.[12]

The implication was correct; the activities of the Navy Commissioners were now directed to a very specific purpose; by mid-June they had assembled in the Downs under Blake a fleet of thirty-eight sizeable warships, eighteen converted merchantmen and some fireships.[13]

> Whereas the Parliament upon consideration of the late acts of hostility committed by the fleet of the United Provinces upon the fleet of this Commonwealth in the very roads of England, and of their intention by force to usurp the known rights of this Commonwealth in the seas and destroy their fleets . . . you are therefore authorised and directed to take and seize upon the Dutch East India Fleet homeward bound, and secure the same or so many as shall be taken.[14]

So ran Blake's instructions from the Admiralty Council. As the East Indies fleet was expected northabout round Scotland, Blake was instructed to disturb the Dutch fishery on his way up the east coast and take their 'busses', also to disturb and interrupt their Baltic trade, seizing and taking their ships, and he was required to 'take and surprise, or otherwise to burn, sink or destroy, all such ships or vessels that shall withstand or resist you in the execution of the foregoing instructions.'[15]

These orders are confirmation, if any is needed, of the whole drift of the English assault. While the preamble excused the attack on the ground that it was the Dutch intention to destroy the Commonwealth war fleet and invade England, the instructions were to destroy the Dutch *merchant* fleet and fishery. On the strategic level this has been misinterpreted by naval historians as an English failure to realise that the enemy battle fleet was the correct target. It was not. The aim was to cut Dutch seaborne trade and fishing – with the acquisition of ships and cargoes as an important bonus – hence ruin Dutch commerce and threaten the very existence of the Dutch state; the attack was well-calculated for this purpose; time enough to tackle the Dutch fleet when it came to the defence of its merchantmen. It was only later, when merchant shipping was as important to England as it was to the Dutch in mid-century, that the enemy battle fleet became the prime target. At the start England was a predator, Dutch trade, in the words of the Dutch ambassador, the 'mountain of gold' they had determined to attack.

At the beginning of July the States General issued instructions to Tromp, now over one hundred sail strong:

> You should allow no serious opportunity which you can seize as a soldier or sailor to attack the English fleet, either united or separated, without any distinction of place, and to do all imaginable damage to it. You are also to capture or destroy all other English ships of war, and to capture all other merchantmen taking care however that these merchantmen be not plundered, mis-handled or injured.[16]

This disposes of the naval historical myth that the Dutch did not realise that their prime target was the English battle fleet. The two sets of instructions, so different in aim, were perfectly suited to the positions and purposes of the belligerents – for so without any formal declaration they had now become.

The weather thwarted the purposes of both sides in the opening moves. While Blake succeeded in taking or sinking one entire fishery protection squadron of twelve warships, and dispersing the Dutch fishing fleet on his way north, a violent gale prevented him from meeting the returning East Indiamen. Tromp for his part, was delayed in chase by northerly winds, and when he attempted to enter the Downs instead to attack an English squadron under Sir George Ayscue sheltering under Deal Castle, he was prevented by calms and more head winds, so he resumed his original course after Blake. Reaching Fair Isle between the Orkneys and Shetlands, his fleet was caught on a lee shore and dispersed by the same gales that caused Blake to miss the Indiamen. Afterwards he cruised for some days to collect his force, but only met with some forty from more than one hundred, and on 9 August, 'finding ourselves so extraordinarily punished by the mighty hand of God and being exhausted'[17] it was resolved at a council to return home. In fact Tromp was desperately short of provisions, and many of his crews who had been out during the period of tension preceding the outbreak, were going down with scurvy. Most of the rest of his scattered fleet made their own way home later.

Meanwhile the merchants of Amsterdam had become anxious about the English Channel route. They had intelligence of the Spanish silver fleet off Cape St Vincent on 29 June, and anticipated their own merchant ships returning from Spain before long with silver to the value of fifteen to sixteen million guilders, and also ships from Portugal and the Mediterranean with valuable cargoes. They had petitioned the Amsterdam Admiralty for men-of-war to meet the fleet at the entrance to the Channel; 'having regard to the magnitude of the interests at stake the prosperity of the country itself is concerned to a great extent in the preservation of these ships'.[18] The Amsterdam Admiralty whose revenues were already declining because of the curtailment of trade, sent the petition to the States General, asking for a national force to be made available to 'open up and secure the Channel between England and France'.[19] The States General set about collecting such a fleet, appointing as its commander, Michiel de Ruyter.

Like Tromp and the majority of Dutch admirals, Ruyter was a man of humble origins. He had gone to sea as a boy of eleven from Flushing in his native Zeeland, and by his early twenties had experienced a boarding action, been wounded and taken prisoner, escaped, re-joined the merchant service, and worked his way up to boatswain. During his twenties he took time off to study navigation, qualifying himself for command, and becoming a privateer captain before the age of thirty. It was about this time that he had adopted what had been a nickname, 'Ruyter', meaning cavalryman, as his surname; the reasons for this change from his family name are not clear.[20]

Although his first cruises in command were so unsuccessful that on one occasion his crew mutinied and forced him home – not an unusual event among the notoriously unmanageable privateersmen – he was soon successful enough to start buying stock in a moderate way, and he gained sufficient reputation to be appointed, at the age of thirty-four, Rear-Admiral of a force hired out to the Portuguese after their secession from Spain. With them he had, so far as is known, his first experience of fleet action – the battle of St Vincent in November 1641. Both the allied and the Spanish fleets suffered heavily in this inconclusive encounter during which Dutch tactics were to act in pairs of ships to board and enter. They failed as the Spanish gunfire kept them off; Ruyter's own ship was so badly holed that he had to induce a list by shifting the guns to one side until the leaks had been stopped.

At the end of the commission Ruyter returned to the merchant service, capturing sufficient prizes to enable him to retire. He was living ashore with his third wife – the daughter of a modest sailor like himself – when the English war broke out. His reputation stood so high that the Zeeland Admiralty offered him fleet command, and despite his wish to remain ashore, they prevailed on him to accept. As flag officers for national fleets were decided by politics between the rival provincial Admiralties, it came about that while a Holland admiral, Witte de With, was appointed to succeed Tromp – out of favour because of his northern failure – the Zeelander, Ruyter, was appointed his Vice to command the fleet for the Channel. It is doubtful if the States General could have made a better choice however they had come to it; nevertheless it can be seen that the Dutch fleet, with its many converted merchantmen and ex-merchant captains and officers was far from the modern image of a regular fighting service; few of its commanders had experience of fleet action, let alone any theoretical appreciation of fleet strategy or tactics.

There is no doubt that Ruyter, like Tromp, had a thoroughly practical grasp of strategic essentials – as indeed had the Admiralty Boards. These advised the States General to leave fleet movements and dispositions to the entire direction of the Commanders-in-Chief 'to inflict the utmost damage to the enemy on all occasions'.[21] Ruyter, while waiting impatiently in the Scheldt through August for reinforcements and merchantmen from the Zuider Zee which he was to convoy down Channel, wrote to his Admiralty Board, 'If we had the said ships with us we should be in a position to attack the enemy.'[22] In short, English battle fleets were the Dutch targets in the campaign for the protection of trade, and although Dutch fleets were frequently drawn off on other objects, principally to meet and convoy their own merchantmen, they never lost sight of the prime requirement to destroy or in more practical terms cripple the hostile fleets.

Dutch tactics were equally practical. Commanders-in-Chief divided their fleets into three, or sometimes four or even five squadrons, each of which was further divided into three divisions under three squadronal flag officers, and the ships sailed into battle grouped around their respective flags; thus Tromp instructed each Captain 'on penalty of 300 guilders' fine [rather over two months' salary] to gather around the flag officer under whom he serves'.[23] In battle, when in equal or superior numbers, Dutch tactics were generally to surround and overwhelm individual ships by boarding and entering, usually after they had been crippled by gunfire and so isolated. Each captain meanwhile, had a duty to look out and support any of his own consorts in distress; Tromp's battle orders contained the death penalty for captains or officers who failed to free one of their consorts from the enemy when they could have done so. The same duty was enjoined on Flag Officers: 'each squadron when another is vigorously attacked, shall second and free the other.'[24] Dutch fleets, in fact, had no system of tactics, only guiding principles of mutual support, ship for ship and squadron for squadron. The results were furious mêlées without order or central control – ships tacking to fire their other broadsides quicker than the engaged sides could be reloaded, or trying to gain the weather gage, or simply trying to avoid collision. There are few descriptions of individual ships' evolutions in fleet engagements, but it is clear from several accounts that Elizabethan group concentration tactics were still in vogue at the beginning of the war. Here is the Dutch Mediterranean Commander-in-Chief, van Galen, describing his action with a smaller English force in the summer of 1652:

> Then every captain bore up from leeward close to us to get into range, and so all gave their broadsides first on the one side and then again on the other, and then bore away with their ships before the wind till they were ready again; and then as before with the guns of the whole broadside they fired into my flagship, one after the other, meaning to shoot my masts overboard.[25]

And for an idea of the leisurely nature of these artillery duels with which battle was opened, here is an account by an Englishman, Richard Gibson, describing an action between the English *Sapphire* of thirty-six guns, and two Frenchmen of twenty-six and thirty-six guns commanded by brothers-in-law, Captains Colaert and Spragge:

> When the *Sapphire* could weather Coleart she hauled her mainsail up the brails, and with two topsails, foresail and mizen, bore down on Colaert stem for stem, and in two ships' lengths, clapt upon a wind and fired all his lower tier with round shot and bar shot, and his upper tier with round shot and partridge [bags of old iron], and all his muskets at Colaert, and presently tacked, and stood away, keeping firing at one another while in shot. In less than two glasses [one hour!] all their great guns and muskets being loaded, and backstays shot-walnutted, then about ship, and served Spragge as his brother was served before.

[194]

This was repeated three or four times to each with this advantage, that the *Sapphire* always coming up to windward of them, gave each dangerous shot under water, and received none.[26]

This last point was an important additional reason why the weather gage was always sought; the guns of the weather vessel, with her engaged side heeled downward would point low, while the guns of the lee vessel pointed up above the opponent's hull.

The Dutch tended to set great store on fireships, Ruyter had five of these in the fleet that was eventually gathered; he divided them among his three squadrons and instructed their captains to hold themselves in readiness at all times, and in action to do their utmost to get alongside one of the enemy's largest ships and set her on fire.[27] This was yet another reason for seeking the weather gage; fireships were generally small, worn-out craft which could not be expected to work to windwards to grapple their targets, but which could in favourable conditions run down before the wind, and at the least create some confusion among the enemy. The slowness of loading drill made this form of attack a good deal less hazardous than it became in the following century when great guns could be discharged at intervals of two minutes or less; nevertheless fireships needed commanders of the utmost nerve and resolution, who would stay and grapple an enemy before taking to the boats.

While Ruyter was champing at the bit in and off the Scheldt, the English Admiralty Committee was urging Sir George Ayscue westwards for the defence of English shipping in the Channel. He was given leave to make his own dispositions to 'secure the English trade from the southward' (the West Indies, Mediterranean and Atlantic coast), meantime he was to 'endeavour to take and seize upon all ships as well men-of-war as merchants men and other vessels belonging to the United Provinces'[28] – also any French vessels – and authorised to sink or destroy all vessels that withstood him. He moved from the Downs and had reached Plymouth with a total of some forty-five vessels by the beginning of August when Ruyter had only twenty ill-found converted merchantmen and some fireships under his flag. It was not until the middle of August that Ruyter's reinforcements reached him, bringing his total force up to some thirty ships fitted for war, most mounting between twenty-four and thirty guns with 100 or so men; Ruyter's flagship, *Neptunus* mounted only twenty-eight guns, as did his Vice-Admiral's. There were two rather larger converted Indiamen mounting forty guns and carrying 200 men each, more than the flagships.

On the afternoon of 21 August the fleet of sixty sail that he was to convoy down Channel hove in sight, and he immediately set course westerly, not even calling a council to distribute signals and instructions until the following morning when they were drifting in a calm off Dover. The calm continued most of the next day, but in the late afternoon they picked up a light north-easterly which they held for the next three days, steering west-south-westerly down the French side of the Channel passing Guernsey six miles off on the 25th. The following afternoon at two o'clock when they had reached a position some twenty miles off the coast of Brittany due south of Plymouth, a fleet was sighted to the northwards. This was Sir George Ayscue. He had been cruising about Plymouth picking up prizes since his move from the Downs, and that morning – apparently fortuitously – had determined at a council to steer south to look for the Dutch fleet on the French coast.

His own fleet numbered some forty-five sail still, including five fireships, thus he was stronger than Ruyter by about ten warships – or so Dutch fleet lists suggest. However it seems probable that Ruyter had a dozen or so warships additional to those listed – merchant escorts perhaps, or powerful Indiamen – for a week later, after he had sent the merchantmen on their way, he records his fleet as forty-four sail; five were fireships. This journal entry, together with a later piece of evidence suggests that he had approximately the same number of warships as Ayscue, indeed it is difficult to explain the result of the encounter without assuming an approximate numerical equality between the forces, for if earlier Dutch reports are to be believed, the English had a decided advantage in size and weight of broadside. All Dutch prior intelligence suggested that both Ayscue's flagship and that of his Vice-Admiral, Captain Haddock, mounted between fifty and sixty guns and that seven or eight of the others were sizeable vessels described as 'capital' ships mounting between thirty-six and forty guns. It seems probable therefore that the core of the English force was a great deal stronger than the Dutch. English reports of the action credit Ruyter with fifty-five to sixty men of war, but this is probably because the English mistook those of the Dutch merchantmen who kept with Ruyter as warships, for only about half of the merchant fleet made off southwards before the action commenced.

Both commanders were eager for action; Ruyter hauled round to point as close as he could towards the enemy, thus close-hauled north-north-westerly, while Ayscue crowded sail and bore down on him with a strong quartering wind, and the two fleets, probably strung out by inequalities in sailing performance of individual ships, met at about four o'clock. The Dutch force was grouped in three squadrons, Ruyter leading the centre squadron, his Vice-Admiral to his right and his Rear-Admiral to his left; probably the merchant ships still with him were strung out astern. How the English fleet was ordered, if at all, is impossible to determine. It seems that Ayscue was in the lead with his Vice-Admiral and Rear-Admiral with him and three or four other ships of force acting in a group with the flag officers. English accounts agree that Ayscue 'charged through the whole body of the enemy fleet',[29] tacked and weathered them and 'charged' through them again. Ruyter's account implies much the same – 'we ran into the midst of their fleet and we attacked one another furiously, we having twice fought our way through their fleet' – without however being able to gain the weather gage.

> If we had been able to get the wind of them with our ships as they did of ours, we should with God's help have utterly routed the foremost of them, for I with six or seven of our ships, was in the midst of their fleet between the Admiral and the Vice-Admiral, and our Rear-Admiral was close under the lee with the rest of the ships.[30]

The phrase 'charged through', although used time and again in accounts of battles in the Dutch wars, is almost certainly misleading since if Ayscue had done this he would inevitably have ended up to leeward of the Dutch. What he must surely have done to preserve the weather gage was haul to the wind on the same tack as the Dutch, probably still north-north-westerly, and then closed them, no doubt aiming for Ruyter's flagship, which he succeeded in engaging. A subsequent tacking duel for the weather gage would have taken the fleets past and through each other on opposite courses – fitting the descriptions from both sides of 'charging through the enemy' twice. However the question is open. All that seems certain is that Ayscue retained his initial advantage of the weather gage, which probably explains the view, implicit in all English accounts that:

> we shot altogether low at them and they received many shot in their hulls. They shot high at us, aiming thereby to spoil our masts, sails and tackles, in which most of our ships received their greatest loss.[31]

Despite this, Ayscue's flagship, which all accounts agree was fought gallantly in the thick of the action, had some sixty shot in her hull, another English ship, the *Bonaventure* was seriously damaged and almost taken by surrounding Dutchmen, and an English fireship which went to her rescue was so holed that she began to sink; she was abandoned after being set alight; the diversion did, however, save the *Bonaventure* from capture. The Dutch fireships, from which Ruyter had hoped much were left way to leeward, unable to get into the action.

The mêlée continued until about an hour after sunset, when the two fleets separated and lay to repairing damages through the night. It is not clear which side suffered most; the Dutch had up to 60 killed and 50 wounded, against suggested English totals of some 31 killed (12 in Ayscue's flagship) and 60 wounded, many by the accidental explosion of a powder barrel.[32] Although the English had lost a fireship and nearly lost the *Bonaventure* one Dutch ship, *Eendraght,* was in such a battered condition Ruyter thought he would have to send her in to a French port for repairs, and others were according to Ruyter's journal 'much damaged'. If the English advantage in gunweight was as great as Dutch reports suggest, and if it was augmented by lack of skill or courage among some of the Dutch captains (as Ruyter's correspondence suggests) as well as the advantage of the weather gage, it is difficult to imagine how the result could have been anything but an advantage to the English in terms of ship damage. Nevertheless Ayscue did not press the attack the following morning, despite a council of war at which it was agreed to engage again, and Ruyter was allowed to sail away south-easterly while Ayscue repaired damages and then sailed back for Plymouth. The answer may lie in the considerable mast and rigging damage the English had received; according to one account this would have put many ships in danger had they met with 'any ordinary blowing weather'.[33] Whatever the reasons the action was an undoubted defensive triumph for Ruyter, who had preserved his convoy without the loss of a single ship. Ayscue, having returned to Plymouth and been held up by repairs, then southerly winds, never again put out in chase.

The Dutch, meanwhile, repaired their damages at sea, and on the second day after the action a council of war decided unanimously to make for Plymouth to try and surprise the English:

> care must be taken that they do not suspect our coming, and very likely their commanding officers may be carelessly on shore, so that with God's help we might be able to destroy their fleet before they could get any further assistance to come and seek us out.[34]

This was a remarkably bold stroke, again suggesting that the Dutch sensed they had had the edge in the action of the 26th. They sailed north-north-easterly with a light east wind, and by noon the next day were only five miles from Start Point. All the captains were summoned so that Ruyter could sound out their opinions on the proposed attack, and after they had confirmed the previous decision to go straight in, they shaped course for Plymouth. Then the wind veered sharply south and freshened, obliging them to stand off the land, and afterwards continual southerly gales forced Ruyter to abandon the plan. The fact that he came so near to carrying it out with what appears to have been an inferior force of small, converted merchantmen is testimony to rare tactical genius and strategic appreciation.

For the next few days he cruised off and on between Ushant and the Scillies, meeting returning Dutchmen and shepherding them past the Devon coast, meanwhile receiving a series of reports about a large English fleet under Blake's command destined for the Channel. On 7 September a privateer whom he had despatched four days earlier with letters for the Zeeland Admiralty rejoined him off Start Point with news that Blake's fleet of seventy-two sail was off Beachy Head.

> He informed us that the Admiral was doing all he could to make to the westward, so that we are bound to remain to the westward of him that according to the orders of their H.M. we may await the merchantmen from Spain. We therefore beg your Lordships to send

us all the help you can, as we are not strong enough to make head against so powerful a fleet, or withstand it to advantage, seeing that it is more numerous than ours by 30 men-of-war.[35]

This would be conclusive proof that Ruyter's fighting strength was nearer forty than thirty ships were it not for evidence that he had only twenty-eight warships with him at the end of the month;[36] the answer may be that he included armed merchantmen as fighting ships.

He remained cruising in the western approaches to the Channel for most of September, once when off the Start chasing a squadron of twenty or more English ships under Blake's Vice-Admiral, William Penn, but losing them in thick, gusty weather. Finally at the end of the month, with provisions almost exhausted, some ships out of water and beer, and ten barely sea-worthy after their constant seakeeping, he decided that he was in no con-dition to meet an English force, and worked his way back home – again keeping to the French side of the Channel – determined to come out again with fresh forces to meet the 'silver' ships from Spain. Ayscue, whose inac-tivity during this time may have been due to ill-health after his West Indies cruise and continuous service since, or to political differences with the military leaders of the Commonwealth, retired home and was not re-employed until after the restoration of the Stuart monarchy.

Meanwhile, in the United Provinces a fleet of forty-five warships had been gathered under Tromp's successor, de With. The details of this force provide the severest indictment of divided control; the different Boards of Admiralty were agreed on only one point, that they were in debt; in other respects they were at variance, not only in the time they took to fit out and man the required ships, but in such basics as rates of pay for the crews, dilatoriness in payment and granting shore leave, all of which naturally led to anger when the different Boards' crews were gathered together in one fleet, able to compare notes. Added to this was endemic rivalry between the chief maritime provinces of Zeeland and Holland, heightened by Zee-land's championship of the Orange party – in the person of the two-year-old Prince of Orange – and the general unpopularity of de With, a violent, short-tempered, fiercely intolerant and insensitive fighting sailor. It is scarcely surprising that there were desertions and mutinies. With the return of another group of ships from Tromp's northern voyage things got out of hand: 2,000 sailors with drawn knives, complaining they had not been paid, rampaged through the streets of Flushing vowing to cut the throats of their High Mightinesses of the States General. Troops were called in; three of the ringleaders were hanged, and the crowds were dispersed with musketry which caused numerous deaths and injuries.

When de With finally got away on 20 September, he intended to sail down-Channel to convoy some merchantmen, meet Ruyter and engage Blake with their combined forces, but westerly winds held him near the

Straits – 'God knows with this contrary wind, which cuts into my very soul, we cannot advance'.[37] Eventually he met six of the expected 'silver' ships from Spain, and escorted them back to the Zeeland coast. His reports to the States General contain repeated complaints of the undermanning of his ships, their poor sailing qualities, and above all of the uselessness of his fireships, all eight of which had gone missing from the flag! 'My Lords, I venture to say they were not fit to put to sea with us, both because they were bad sailers and ill-equipped.' He recommended fitting out at least a dozen two-deckers of 260 to 300 tons, excellent sailers and able to keep with the fleet, otherwise 'all the expense incurred for these fireships will be wasted, as has now been the case'.[38] De With comes through these despatches as understandably impatient of the inefficiency of the administrations, also as a progressive thinker. He was, according to his own account, unusual in using parchment to make cartridges (rather than canvas) for his great guns; he advocated their use by the whole fleet to obtain greater accuracy, presumably by virtue of more instantaneous discharge. Had he deployed his practical talents and extraordinary aggression only against the enemy he would have been a fleet commander of the first rank; but his power was turned too often, too intolerantly on his own men and captains.

On 2 October Ruyter made back through the Straits and met him off Nieuport; ten of Ruyter's ships were found unseaworthy and sent home, but the rest were joined to de With's flag, provisions and ammunition shared out and they sailed for the Straits. South-westerly winds forced them north however, and on 5 October they found themselves off the Goodwin Sands across which they saw in the Downs some forty English men-of-war, and twelve more to the southward patrolling the Straits. This was Blake's fleet; he had been ordered back from the west after de With's first sortie. At a council of war aboard the Dutch flagship it was decided to attack at the first opportunity the weather afforded, but as the wind had backed into the south they could do nothing that day, and they continued up past the Goodwins to anchor that evening just north of the Gull Stream Channel into the Downs. De With burned to repeat Tromp's stroke against the Spanish fleet in 1639, and raged at the Admiralty Boards who had failed to provide him with a single seaworthy fireship.

Blake was a very different character, a modest, even-tempered man, who had expressed genuine surprise at his original appointment as a 'General at Sea' as 'extremely beyond my expectations as well as my merits'.[39] The reasons for his appointment are not on record, but as he had proved an able commander of parliamentary forces on land in the defence of the West Country, and he was before that an active partner in his family ship-owning business at Bridgewater, it seems reasonable to suppose that he was chosen because he combined an expert knowledge of ships with proved military ability. He had learned his business as a fleet commander against the Royalist squadron in campaigns which are notable for perseverance in blockade work. Perseverance, simplicity, straightforwardness, above all perhaps faith in God were his abiding characteristics; he was the epitome of the solid Puritan of the minor gentry and merchant classes. As his biographer points out:

> he seems to have conceived of himself as a man called of God for
> great purposes which he must endeavour to carry out; such 'checks'
> as Providence saw fit to lay on him were not due to mistaken purpose,
> but his own unworthiness.[40]

It is impossible to know his exact fleet strength by the time he had con-centrated his ships in the Downs to meet de With's 62 men of war; it may have been a shade more numerous; Ruyter put it at 68 sail, de With at 73, although the only English account to mention numbers puts it between 50 and 60. Where the English were undoubtedly stronger was in a core of seven great ships of 50 guns and upwards, the largest of which, the *Sovereign* – formerly the splendid *Sovereign of the Seas,* now cut down by one deck to reduce her draft and allow the lower gunports to be opened when she heeled, but still mounting 88 guns and carrying 550 men – was equal to a dozen average Dutch ships. In fact the seven great ships, together with some twenty other 'capital' ships of thirty guns and over which Blake had with him could have taken on the whole undermanned Dutch fleet without the smaller 'frigates' – single gun-deck craft possibly copied from the Dunkirkers, probably with a longer length/breadth ratio than galleons, although the term is somewhat obscure – converted merchantmen and fireships which made up the numbers.

Blake intended to take the fight to the Dutch, but the night was stormy and the next day blew in with south-westerly gales, which continued for the best part of the 7th. The winds moderated that evening, and the following morning both opposing Commanders-in-Chief gave the signal to weigh. The wind was fresh in the south-west quarter, veering westerly, and Blake was soon threading his way out northwards through the Gull Stream Channel, apparently with little regard for order. De With, whose ships had dragged in his more exposed anchorage off the North Foreland, and who was swept north-easterly by a strong ebb tide and the wind as he strove to collect his fleet, was not sighted until noon, when he was some twenty miles off the north Kent coast. He stood close-hauled towards the north-west, and as Blake approached him from straight upwind lay to, under backed foresails to await him, according to one of the English captains 'in a close body'. He had lost some of his ships during the gales, and was probably only fifty-nine strong, arranged in four divisions, Ruyter leading, de With in the centre, de Wildt astern and Cornelius Evertsen with a reserve to succour whichever part needed him – in short an essentially 'galley-warfare' for-mation. The English fleet approached in a column some six miles along, and at about three o'clock Blake, who was leading in the *Resolution* (eighty-

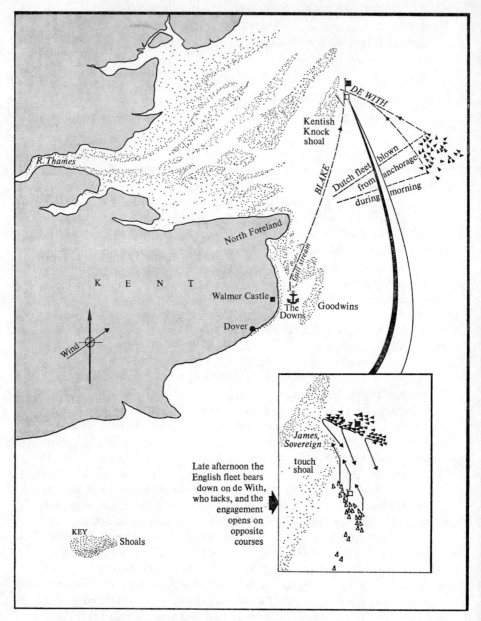

Battle diagram 6: Battle of Kentish Knock, 8 October 1652

eight guns) lay to just outside gunshot to allow the stragglers to get up with him. His Vice-Admiral, William Penn, in the *James* (sixty-six guns) seems to have collected his squadron first, and he sent to ask Blake if he should bear down on the enemy; before the message was delivered the distance between the flagships narrowed and Penn impatiently bore up, passed under Blake's stern and asked the question himself. 'As soon as some more of our fleet come up we shall all bear in amongst them,'[41] was the reply. Penn tacked and ran back 'to give room for my squadron to lie between him and us'.[42] This is an interesting statement suggesting that while 'fleet line of battle was not established in a formal sense, flag officers did attempt an informal line approach, as indeed on this occasion they would need to if the Dutch were awaiting them in an informal close-hauled line with intervals between the flag officers.

After about an hour, Blake considered he had enough of his fleet with him, and bore up towards the enemy; his movement was followed by the other captains and the whole fleet stood downwind for the massed Dutch, who had been firing odd taunting shots. De With, meanwhile, had left his own flagship, intending to hoist his flag in the recently joined *Brederode*, Tromp's former ship; the crew there, loyal to their former chief and particularly disliking de With, refused to let him aboard. He was forced to move instead into a forty-four-gun Indiaman, the *Prins Willem*, which he averred later was the worst sailer in the fleet. As Blake's ships neared him, hauling to the northwards to give their broadsides from the windward position, he filled and tacked, so that the two fleets closed suddenly and engaged on opposite tacks, Blake sailing north, the Dutch southwards. Neither Penn's flagship nor the huge *Sovereign* took part in this initial clash as both vessels touched the sand spit known as the Kentish Knock – which gave its name to the battle. Fortunately the water had calmed, and they were able to tack and get off, then tack again and sail southwards as the southernmost Dutch began to clear the main body of the English fleet – 'indeed it fell out better for doing execution upon the enemy than we could have cast it ourselves; for as the Dutch fleet cleared themselves of the General, we fell pat to receive them.'[43] Astern of them, Blake and the rest of his fleet tacked and followed. The action drew slowly southwards, the sound of the guns reverberating like distant thunder in Essex and Kent. Soon the English superiority in weight of metal and probably in gun discipline – firing only when very close and, according to other contemporary accounts by signal from the captain on the ship's bell – began to tell. Many of the Dutch captains, lacking the discipline of a regular service, seem to have held off, firing wildly over and through their consorts. De With, whose Indiaman was at the front of the battle despite her poor sailing qualities to windward, vented his rage and frustration afterwards in his Log. 'Never have I seen in all my life, I must declare, such cowardice among sea captains as these have shown.'[44] Both his flagship and Ruyter's were crippled aloft by about seven o'clock and unable to tack; at least two other Dutch ships had lost masts. One of these was under tow by a consort when an English frigate captain, John Mildmay, bore down on them and boarded and entered both, one after the other with little resistance. They had been so shattered by the English shot earlier that the prize crew had to abandon one in a sinking condition the following day.

As dusk fell the fleets separated, the Dutch straggling to leeward a beaten force; Penn wrote, 'they did flag very much in the latter part; and I do really believe, through the mercy of God, they could not have stood it one hour longer.'[45] His opinion is confirmed by subsequent events in the Dutch fleet. As for the English, only one ship was seriously battered; she was commanded by a Captain Badiley, whose brother was in command of the English Mediterranean squadron; apparently he charged in amongst the enemy so recklessly that he was closed and surrounded by a number of Dutch vessels before the 54-gun *Speaker* and two other ships worked down to his rescue. He had to sail downwind and put in to Yarmouth for repairs. For the rest, the English sustained a great deal of mast and rigging damage, as to be expected, but remarkably few casualties, some forty killed in the whole fleet, among whom were three in Blake's flagship and two in Penn's. The Dutch figures are not known, but an English report from The Hague afterwards stated that they landed 2,000 wounded. This may have been an exaggeration and no doubt it included scurvy cases and diseased men who had been out for months in Ruyter's fleet. Nevertheless, there can be little doubt that the Dutch suffered heavily.

The next day the fleets were only some two miles apart, but ten more Dutch ships had gone missing during the night, two or three taken or sunk, the rest either so damaged or disaffected they had run for home. De With called the remaining captains aboard his flagship and expressed his dissatisfaction with the conduct of many in the action. 'I charged and implored them again to take better heed for the service of our Fatherland.'[46] Later the breeze went around to the north-east giving him the windward position; he stood towards Blake, but despite the homily he was so badly supported he could not press the attack and his ships were still widely separated when the breeze dropped away altogether. He hoisted a flag for a council; only Ruyter and Evertsen attended, apparently because they were the two nearest, and Ruyter succeeded in persuading him that to throw their weakened, scurvy-ridden force of forty-nine ships against the far more powerful and numerous English would be to hazard the safety of the Fatherland. When the breeze got up again de With reluctantly headed easterly. Blake followed, but only the light English frigates and the *Sovereign* managed to get up with the Dutch rearguard and exchange an ineffective fire before darkness closed in.

The following morning the fleets were only visible to each other from the topmasts. De With again summoned his captains and charged them to fight, perhaps hoping to lure the deeper draught English ships to destruction on the shoals off the Flemish coast, but they gave him a unanimous refusal, and he continued his course for home. Blake also summoned his captains, and learning that many were not victualled for more than three days had to give up any ideas he may have had about following and blockading; he too set course for home.

So the battle ended; de With had failed to break the English grip on the Straits, and the Dutch position, only six months after the start of the war, was parlous. The majority of their 'silver' ships and others from Spain and the Mediterranean were waiting in Atlantic ports for an escort; hundreds more were waiting in Dutch ports for the outward passage down-Channel, and already the interruption to trade was causing bankruptcies in Amsterdam.

Elsewhere the picture was brighter: in the Baltic the Dutch had the whip-hand. A policy of support for Denmark against its rival Sweden, combined with commercial pressure, resulted in the Danes seizing English ships and shutting the Sound to all English trade. This was a blow which struck at the heart of English naval strength since practically all the masts, spars, cordage, pitch, and tar vital for making good wear and tear and the considerable spar and rigging damage that always occurred in action, came from Scandinavia and the Baltic. A squadron of eighteen men-of-war despatched to convoy the English Baltic traders home, failed to persuade the King of Denmark to release them. Parliament, which had insufficient strength to open another offensive in another theatre, retaliated by placing an embargo on Danish ships in English ports and robbing them of naval stores, meanwhile hastening a search already begun for alternative sources of supply from Scotland and the forests of New England.

In the West Indies, Dutch trading instincts were in the ascendant and the colonials of both sides had a tacit agreement not to become involved in the European conflict; in the Mediterranean, however, the Dutch had the upper hand. Two small, separated English squadrons of three and four ships and the Levant traders they were protecting were blockaded by a concentrated Dutch force of double their combined size. The one general action, fought on 28 August between fourteen Dutch warships under Van Galen and four English convoy escorts under Badiley, had been as fierce as anything seen in home waters, the English escorts putting up such a stout defence that they lost only one vessel by boarding and entering, and meanwhile punished the Dutchmen so severely that the other three warships and the whole of the convoy escaped to port in the island of Elba. There is little doubt that this remarkable defence was made possible by the broadside weight and fire discipline of the English flagship, the 52-gun *Paragon*. Nevertheless the English Mediterranean merchantmen were as immobile as the Dutchmen waiting for escorts through the Channel, and after de With's defeat the Admiralty Council – probably under some pressure from Levantine merchants – acquainted Blake with their resolve to send twenty ships from his fleet to the Mediterranean; 'it is not the intention of the Council to disable him [Blake] by the taking of these ships, which the Council doubt not, but will be supplied by the coming out of others appointed for the winter guard.'[47] Whatever was intended by way of replacements, the idea of weakening the main battlefleet was a mark of over-confidence. Reports were coming in every week of preparations being made by the United Provinces to equip a huge fleet of over one hundred warships under Tromp – back in favour again – to reverse the decision off the Kentish Knock and free the Channel. It seems that the spirit of over-confidence was shared by Blake for there is no record of any remonstrance by him, and the ships were duly taken to be fitted out for the Mediterranean.

This decision is rendered more inexplicable in view of a severe shortage of seamen for the fleet. The shortage was affecting both sides, and the accounts of mass desertions and mutinies over non-payment of wages are quite as frequent from the Dutch ports as from the Downs and English ports; nevertheless by early December, when the decision to take the twenty ships from Blake was confirmed, the Dutch had managed to concentrate and man a fleet of eighty warships under Tromp off Helvoetsluys in the Goeree channel off South Holland, and others were gathering in the Zuider Zee and the Scheldt, together with over 300 sail of merchantmen – facts very well known to the English authorities. Neither they nor Blake appear to have been alarmed and no effort was made until too late to concentrate the English ships from Portsmouth and the West with Blake's force at Dover. The explanation can only be that Blake and the English generally considered their great ships more than a match for almost any number of light Dutch warships.

When the States General received intelligence that Blake's force was only some forty to fifty strong, and that shortage of hemp and naval stores was crippling English yards, Tromp was ordered to avail himself of the first favourable wind to put to sea and convoy as many of the merchant ships as were ready

> to and through the Channel, with this modification . . . that if the said
> Lieutenant Admiral receives information that the English fleet is
> lying in or near the Downs, or anywhere in the Channel, he shall
> attack the said fleet with all his force and might, and if possible
> destroy it.[48]

Much attention has been focused on Tromp's comments on instructions given to him the previous month; these were that his principal object was 'to do all possible harm to the English fleet', and also to convoy merchantmen down Channel, and detach escorts with different groups.[49] He had replied that it would be necessary to keep his whole fleet together if he were to meet, pursue and blockade the English fleet in harbour, and he had asked which he was to do, protect the merchantmen, or neutralise the enemy fleet.[50] Both the instructions and Tromp's reply, once again dispose of the myth that the Dutch were not aware that the enemy battlefleet was the proper target for their fleet. But they had the practical necessity of getting trade flowing again and their strategy, as revealed by Tromp's final instructions, was to combine escort in full fleet strength with attack on the enemy fleet as opportunity offered. This was a practical, commonsense response to their dilemma, allowing the Commander-in-Chief the utmost freedom to interpret his orders as he thought best in the circumstances as they developed, and employing the utmost economy of force. The strategy cannot be faulted.

Tromp put to sea on 2 December with a southerly wind; he had seventy-eight warships divided more or less equally into four squadrons under himself, Evertsen, de With and a former merchant captain, Pieter Florissen. Ruyter, who had come under a cloud for his opposition to de With in the violent accusations and counter accusations following the defeat off the Kentish Knock, was only a Vice-Admiral in Evertsen's squadron. Nearly 300 merchantmen also came out, and the next day their sails were spread over a wide area. The following day, as the wind shifted into the west, they beat north-north-westerly towards the English coast.

Blake was waiting in the Downs with a fleet of forty-two; if he was anxious about the great force massing against him, no sign of it has passed through the filter of the years: 'I hourly expect and hope to be in readiness to attend the Dutch fleet at sea,'[51] he wrote as Tromp approached the Goodwins. And later,

> Soon after I had despatched away my letter to Your Honours, there
> was descried this afternoon from our topmast head to be off the
> North Foreland above 80 sail of ships plying to windward, conceived
> to be the Dutch fleet, or part thereof so long spoken of. Since evening,
> intelligence is brought me that from the steeple of Margate there was
> observed above 400 sail.[52]

He called a council at which it was decided in view of the threatening weather to remain at anchor for the night, and take council again in the morning. The next day blew in with a south-westerly gale and rain, and they stayed at anchor. Tromp who had not seen the English fleet in the thick weather, set course south-east, returning all the merchantmen to the Goeree channel or the Scheldt, after which the warships lay-to under small sail, head to the west, letting themselves drive. For the next three days the south-westerly gales continued while Tromp beat on and off the coast, his ships colliding, often seriously damaging themselves in the thick weather; during this period de With went sick and left the fleet; Tromp moved Ruyter up to command his squadron. In England meanwhile, the Admiralty Committee had at last sent instructions to the ships in Portsmouth to join Blake; it could not send similar instructions to those fitting for the Mediterranean since their crews had refused to sail until paid!

On 9 December, Tromp managed to beat far enough west to catch his

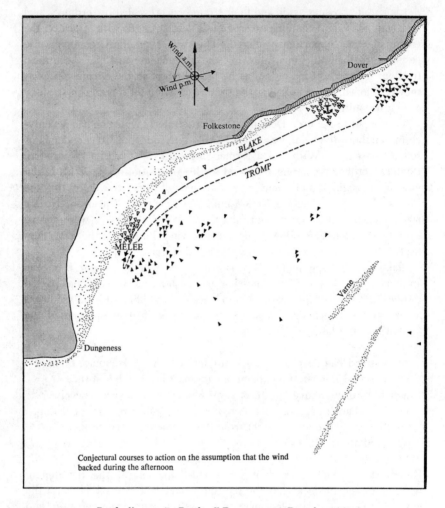

Battle diagram 7: Battle off Dungeness, 10 December 1652

first glimpse of the English fleet. At sight of his sails Blake called another council, and after prayers, weighed and stood out of the Downs southwards to meet him; by evening when both fleets came to anchor in strong north-west winds, they were a bare two miles spart, Blake close under the cliffs west of Dover, Tromp just south of Dover, his fleet extending eastward. Next morning the wind was still strong from the north-west raising a steep swell as both fleets weighed with difficulty. Blake, dead to windward of the Dutch, who drove south-westerly as their anchors came up, set a course down-channel close to the land to keep clear of the mid-Channel shoals before engaging. Tromp hauled up as close to the wind as he could in pursuit, and at about one o'clock in the afternoon his leading ships were exchanging fire with Blake's rear. By this time the fleets must have been extended over a considerable distance by the different performances of individual ships – some of the Dutch had even been driven right across to the French coast, and Tromp's fireships had either gone missing the night before or were trailing some miles to leeward. As Blake approached Dungeness, the wind may have backed into the west or south of west heading him, for Ruyter's journal states that they ran westward to off Dungeness, which the English could not make against the wind;[53] the entry bears other interpretations however; all that seems certain is that Tromp, in the van of the Dutch fleet with his weatherly flagship, *Brederode*, stretched far enough to tack on the English and bring Blake to a close fight; it seems probable that he was able to do this because Blake was embayed between Folkestone and Dungeness, and forced to steer more southerly to clear the point. Tromp made for the English flagship, passing her on the opposite tack, exchanging broadsides, and then steering for one of the poorer sailing Englishmen which had sagged to leeward; this was the 44-gun *Garland*. Tromp was able to run her aboard, carrying away the *Brederode*'s bowsprit and beak in the collision; grappling hooks were thrown and musketry cleared the way for boarders when the *Garland*'s consort, the 36-gun *Anthony Bonaventure* (Captain Hoxton) bore up and laid the *Brederode* aboard on the other side. For a while the fighting was sharp across the three ships, rolling locked together. Then the Dutch Vice-Admiral, John Evertsen, brought his flagship aboard the *Anthony Bonaventure* and turned the tables decisively. Between them the two Dutch flagships had an overwhelming superiority in numbers of men, and they soon carried both English ships by storm; in the course of the struggle for the *Garland*, a barrel of powder exploded in her stern, blowing her quarterdeck and poop into the air. It was sunset by this time:

> we saw a ship blown up, as we conceived with powder, for a great smoke arose up of a sudden and continued in one place for a good while. At last when it grew a little dark we saw it flame out and another great blast and much smoke arose; but in the end it was quite extinguished.[54]

It was perhaps this explosion which drew Blake's attention to the fight for the *Garland*; he was in the thick of another mêlée, perhaps with Ruyter, whose flagship was as usual to the fore, and he gave orders to bear away to the rescue of the two English ships, 'but immediately our fore-topmast was shot away, our mainstay being shot before and our rigging much torn so that we could not work our ship to their relief.'[55] Darkness saved him from falling into the midst of the leading Dutch ships, and during the night he ran back towards Dover, followed by the rest of the English ships; Tromp lay to repairing damages.

In this decisive defeat for the English only a small portion of the ships on either side took part. While the Dutch flagships – with the exception of Pieter Florissen's *Monnikendam* – and the better sailers of the fleet were engaged in the mêlées around the *Garland* and Blake's *Triumph* and another great ship, *Victory*, most were well to leeward, struggling to work up into the wind; as for Blake's fleet, which probably had seven great ships of 54 guns and upwards, and another seven 40- to 44-gun ships, more than half were more concerned to preserve their windward position than to come to close action; this applied chiefly to the smaller vessels, but four of the largest class and two 40-gun ships scarcely fired their guns. One English account states that only eight ships stood to the action with any effect. Blake wrote afterwards, 'I am bound to let Your Honours know that there was much baseness of spirit, not among the merchant ships only, but many of the State's ships.'[56] The reason offered by many captains in the subsequent examination into their conduct was such shortage of men that they scarcely had sufficient to work their sails. One of the offending captains who was dismissed the service, never to be employed again, was Blake's own brother, Benjamin. The Dutch lost one ship during the action to a fire whose cause was never discovered; it had nothing to do with English gunnery, and was probably another accident of powder. Otherwise their casualties do not seem to have been heavy: Tromp's ship lost nine killed, twenty-one wounded, Evertsen's only three killed and eight wounded. Blake's flagship also had few casualties, six killed, ten wounded despite being in the thick of a fierce mêlée: it is probable that the high winds and steep seas threw the guns' elevation out. Tromp wrote of extensive spar and rigging damage, 'not a round spar whole, hardly a shroud did not need splicing'.[57]

The next morning Blake and his ships were back at anchor in Dover Roads. Tromp remained off Dungeness, chasing three of the English men-of-war from Portsmouth bound east to join Blake, driving one ashore and afterwards taking her; she was the 36-gun *Hercules*. During the next few days the Dutch beat about the Straits, complete masters of the Channel, taking English merchantmen who sailed up unsuspecting, landing on the Kent and Sussex coasts, driving cattle and sheep away, while Blake made an ignominious retreat into the Downs, then northward into the Thames: 'neither indeed do we dare so far to tempt God as to expose the interests of the Commonwealth, so much concerned in the safety of the fleet, to the attempts of so potent and experienced an enemy by continuing in this road [the Downs].'[58] The loss of the two ships was as nothing to the moral defeat the English had suffered. Blake himself was so downcast he asked that he be given a 'discharge from this employment, so far too great for me, that I shall spend the remainder of my days in private retirement and in prayers for a blessing upon you and the nation.'[59]

It was as well that Blake did retreat, for his men were deserting in droves for lack of pay and the greater opportunities for prize to be had in privateers, and Tromp, directly he was able to collect his fleet and beat up against north-easterlies, sought him out in the Downs. Not finding him there, he sailed north to anchor off Margate, and sent scouts to run up the East Anglian coast as far as Orfordness to try and discover his whereabouts. Directly he learned that he had retreated up the Thames, he called a council at which it was resolved unanimously to follow him and bring him to action; a reward of £50 Flemish was offered to whoever would enter the *Triumph* and bring her out of the river. As so often in coastal actions throughout history, the bold scheme fell through for lack of nerve among the pilots of the fleet. Despite the fact that many had sailed up the London river, all offered excuses for not doing so with a fleet, and the probability of the English removing all navigation marks behind them. So instead Tromp hovered on and off the Thames estuary and the Dover Straits as wind and weather permitted 'so as to keep them hemmed in, or defy them if they come out; but we have seen no English'.[60] Finally at the end of the month, still with no sign of the English, he sailed with another fleet of merchantmen down the Channel, reaching Ushant in the evening of 31 December. Westerly gales held him up for the next fortnight, scattering the ships over a wide area of the western approaches, but the greater part of the fleet reached the convoy rendezvous at Saint Martin (Île de Ré) on 15 January.

For the Dutch it had been a triumphant end to a year begun with the English assault, and the moral effect of turning the tables so completely and gaining total mastery in the English Channel and Thames estuary was extraordinary. Tromp himself wore a broom at his masthead, and when asked what it signified, replied that he was going to sweep the narrow seas of all Englishmen.[61] In Holland, black depression and talk of settling the dispute on any terms the English might choose was replaced by talk of bringing the English to their knees! It is doubtful if such a trifling affair as Dungeness had been in terms of ship losses and casualties has ever had such huge results – at least temporarily. 'It is incredible how drunkish they are with their success at present', a correspondent reported from Amsterdam. 'How high these men are in a moment, not minding what turn may be next.'[62] Another wrote, 'They are so elevated with their late unexpected success that they spurn the thought of any accommodation unless it be on their own terms.'[63]

In addition to their mastery of English waters, the Dutch were heartened by reports of the desertion of sailors from Blake's fleet, his extreme diffi-culties in finding men to replace them, and above all by the English shortage of masts, spars, rigging, pitch and tar. They determined to press the advan-tage by an extreme (thoroughly English) form of commercial blockade, which went directly against their principles of free trade, the sanctity of the neutral flag, and their own practice in former wars. They forbade all trade with the English on pain of death, and seized numbers of neutral ships carrying naval stores not even bound for England on the pretence that the

H

cargoes might afterwards find their way to London. Among these were thirteen Baltic ships bound for the Spanish Netherlands. 'How the Spaniard takes this, time will try', wrote the Amsterdam correspondent,

> but this bout hath made them so frolic here that they dare not only tempt his patience, but resolve likewise to impose terms on other nations [so mighty are they made on a sudden] . . . to forbid other nations likewise with supplying the English with ammunition or victuals upon pain of forfeiture of all if taken, which is no other than to give law and lord it at sea, supposing this good day will never have an end. [64]

This immediate result of naval mastery is interesting not only for the way in which profound principles were suddenly cast overboard, but because it is precisely the attitude the English adopted when they won naval mastery later – and it brought precisely the same trouble with neutrals. By the end of January the Amsterdam Admiralty was seriously concerned about the effects and wrote to the States General asking that the captured neutrals be restored 'to prevent the displeasure and estrangement of allies and neighbours'. [65] They thought the policy of seizing all Baltic traders 'on the mere suspicion of their being smugglers' would have 'disastrous consequences, the more especially as trade with England in such goods as are not contraband is not forbidden to neutral nations', and advised a far more circumspect policy.

For the moment however, the Dutch could not contemplate failure. They planned a great fleet of 118 warships to continue the blockade of the Thames estuary and Dover Straits in the coming spring, and sought subscriptions for another West Indies Company to drive the English from the Caribbean; 'they are so puffed up with Tromp's sovereignty', an Amsterdam correspondent wrote:

> [they are] resolved to set up a West India Company, for taking of the Carib islands, which is so forward that officers are appointed and divers have underwrote great sums near to the value of twenty tons of gold. [66]

It is often remarked that the salutary effects of defeat are more important in the long run than a victory; so it was with Dungeness – and indeed the Kentish Knock. Both sides in turn took similar steps; both realised that the smaller ships of the fleet, especially the converted merchantmen whose commanders were often part-owners of their vessels and naturally disliked hazarding them without compensation, were a hindrance rather than an addition to the strength of the regular State's ships. Tromp wrote, 'undoubtedly we shall accomplish more with 60 ships properly built for war than with 100 such as we have now, for the greater the number the greater the confusion.'[67] Blake and some of his captains wrote after Dungeness,

> Supposing the enemy to consist of 90 sail of ships of war at present, we humbly offer it will be required to have a fleet of 60 sail to engage them, all of which we humbly desire to be State's ships and none of them under 26 guns, 40 sail of them to carry 36 guns upwards, but if there must be some merchant ships we would willingly have them not above one fifth the above-mentioned number and none to carry less than 28 guns.[68]

The lesson of the greater English broadside weight and effectiveness had been driven home to the Dutch in all the actions of the war, but especially by the Kentish Knock. After that the States General prepared designs for a class of thirty heavy ships to carry 18-pounders on the upper deck and heavier guns below – a far cry from the position only six months' earlier when 12-pounders had been considered suitable for the lower tier. Tromp was so impressed with English gunnery that he conferred with the master carpenter at Rotterdam to prepare bilge pieces, presumably to prevent his ship rolling, 'to make her able to use her guns as well as the English ships'.[69]

As important as ship design and gun weight and discipline was the discipline of the captains themselves. Complaints of faint-heartedness, downright cowardice, bad station-keeping were a theme in the reports of Commanders-in-Chief on both sides in all the actions, more particularly after losing actions. The Dutch after the Kentish Knock and the English after Dungeness imprisoned and tried numerous commanders for shirking close action and failing to support consorts. Much of this was the natural result of employing so many merchant captains unused to the disciplines of a fighting service and commanding ships of such differing performance that many could not keep up however diligently they might try; however Tromp demanded a Fiscal, or disciplinary officer for his fleet and made a point of bringing captains to a court martial for infringements such as tacking instead of wearing, not keeping their squadronal flag flying, outsailing their consorts, as well as serious misdemeanours, like holding back in chase or action. The English, after Dungeness, drafted a set of Laws of War in thirty-nine articles – most prescribing the death penalty – which formed the basis of the disciplinary code known as the Articles of War used in all subsequent fleets of the Royal Navy. This first set gives an indication of the chief weaknesses the Commonwealth leaders recognised in their fleet: after two articles enjoining sober and reverent worship, forbidding oaths, profanities and uncleanliness, no less than five were directed against aiding the enemy or rebels – for Royalist sympathies were still strong in sections of the fleet. There followed three articles against embezzlement and one against beating or pillaging the crews of enemy vessels taken; with the eleventh and subsequent articles come the regulations about discipline in action and prohibitions on cowardice, negligence, disaffection, backwardness and the like.[70]

The most obvious defect in the English fleet, however, was shortage of men, and the most important reform after Dungeness was to raise the rates of pay and shares of prize money to make service in the State ships as attractive as in privateers; the pay of able seamen 'fit for helm, lead, top and yard' was raised from 19s. to 24s., an additional month's pay was granted in lieu of prize money to all men who had served six months, and for the future prize was to be granted at the rate of 10s. a ton, and £6 13s. 4d. for every piece of ordnance of a captured ship; in addition, captains, officers and crews were granted rights of pillage for all goods found on or above the gundeck of the prize. Along with increased pay went an increased awareness of the plight of men wounded in the State service, and a proportion of hospital places in all the seaports was made available for wounded sailors. Allied with these reforms went a division of ships of the fleet into 'ranks' by their scale of manning; thus a first rank ship was one with a complement of 400 or more, a second rank ship, 300 or more and so on down to the sixth rank. Commanders and officers of the higher ranking ships were paid more than those of the lower ranks.

The reforms decreased the rate of desertion and brought in many sailors – not enough however to man the fleet which was being fitted with all possible speed to contest the supremacy of the narrow seas in the coming year, and instructions went out to all the coastal counties to impress seafaring men between the ages of fifteen and fifty, similarly to London and Westminster to impress Thames watermen. Meanwhile 1,200 foot soldiers were drafted to the fleet 'to perform as far as they are able all services as seamen and to be ordered in the like capacity to the rest'.[71]

So on both sides the seeds of a regular disciplined service were sown among the somewhat haphazard, individualist traditions of the north Atlantic sea powers; it was only a matter of time and resources before merchant ships and merchant captains disappeared entirely from war fleets.

The Navy commissioners made extraordinary exertions to fit out and man a fleet to intercept Tromp on his way back from St Martin, and Blake was able to move down to Dover with a substantial force by 22 February. Tromp had sailed on his return voyage nearly a fortnight before; his fleet consisted of 75 men of war, a fireship and five storeships with a convoy of about 145 merchantmen. Blake had almost as many warships, probably seventy, but as usual there was a core of substantially heavier ships than the Dutch had; most were fresh from the yards and this time well manned, hence more than a match for Tromp's force which had suffered the usual wastage from disease and was running short of provisions. One of the disciplinary reforms the English Admiralty had brought in was the division of the fleet into three squadrons, red, white and blue, each with three flag officers flying distinguishing coloured flags. Two of the Generals-at-Sea, Blake and Deane, commanded the fleet from the *Triumph* as Admirals of the Red Squadron, which had a Vice- and a Rear-Admiral; William Penn was second-in-command, hence Vice-Admiral of the fleet, but Admiral of the Blue Squadron with his own Vice- and Rear-Admirals, and the third General-at-Sea, George Monck, was Admiral of the White Squadron, again with his own Vice- and Rear-Admirals.

On 24 February, as Tromp reached the Scilly Isles at the entrance to the Channel, the English fleet, making down-Channel in search, reached Beachy Head; there the wind came round to the west and north-west, and they beat across to the French coast, speaking several ships who told them that Tromp was some ninety miles to the west. They continued beating down Channel against the wind for the next two days, passing the longitude of the Isle of Wight as Tromp, hampered by the need to keep his merchantmen together, reached Start Point, Devon; as Blake took another tack to the southwards towards the Channel Islands, the Dutch fleet, hugging the English shore, steered east-north-east for Portland. Blake's scouting arrangements are not clear, but that day, 27 February, he spoke a Spanish ship whose commander 'confidently' informed him that the Dutch were sixty miles to windward, and during the night he stretched back again from Alderney towards Portland, a dead beat against the wind which had veered into the north-west. The next morning, the 28th, the first grey light revealed the sails of the Dutch fleet dead to windward, the nearest only some five miles from the *Triumph*, then on the westerly leg of her beat. Beyond the Dutch lay the long spur of Portland.

Not surprisingly by this time the English fleet was scattered over a wide area; the *Triumph*, one of the most weatherly ships, was nearest to the enemy with a group of perhaps half a dozen others; some way ahead was Penn with part of the Blue squadron and a mile or so astern was the Vice-Admiral of the Red Squadron, Lawson. The White Squadron under Monck was some four miles to leeward, and the poorer sailers from all the squadrons were either with him or scattered about. According to Blake, Tromp could have held his course up-Channel and the English fleet would have been quite unable to work up to him; this was correct for that morning and that wind direction, but Tromp must have known that he would not be able to shepherd the slow unwieldy mass of merchantmen all the way home without a shift in the wind or the superior sailing of the more weatherly English ships making a fight inevitable at some time; in any case, after the poor showing of the English at Dungeness, he was very confident; he had the advantage of the wind, and Blake's scattered force positively invited attack. After gathering his warships together and sending the merchantmen ahead with orders to keep up to windward, he bore away directly for the *Triumph* and the handful of ships about her. Blake brailed up his mainsail,

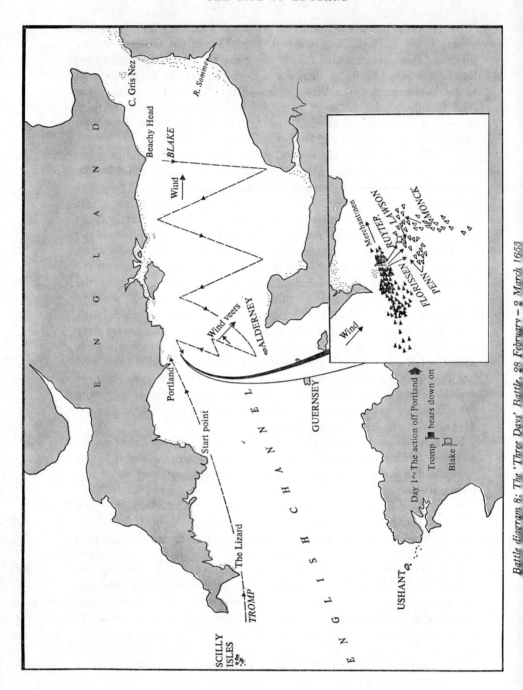

Battle diagram 8: The 'Three Days' Battle, 28 February – 2 March 1653

lay to and prepared to receive the assault. It was a bold decision, committing him to fighting the entire Dutch force for a long time with only half his fleet – for it would take Monck most of the day to work directly upwind to join him. It has been assumed that he stayed as a decoy to tempt Tromp into an attack. In this case it is difficult to understand why, when the ruse succeeded, he could not have borne away and at least fought a running action drawing Tromp towards Monck. Perhaps he and Deane felt that to be seen running from the Dutch would be to hazard all chance of the other English captains doing their duty. The General's reasoning will never be known. They waited, no doubt with the few ships with them formed in a close line, rolling easily to the swell, their broadsides across Tromp's line of advance. Meanwhile ahead, Penn tacked back to join them, and astern Lawson crowded on all sail. So three separate groups converged on the English flagship.

First to arrive at some time after eight o'clock were the Dutch, their principal flagships to the fore. The details of the resulting mêlée are impossible to disentangle. Tromp and his second bore down on the *Triumph*, while the Admiral commanding his rear squadron, Pieter Florissen, according to Florissen's own account 'ran across in front of our Admiral at the English Vice-Admiral so as to separate the English ships one from another'.[72] Perhaps this means that he bore off to starboard to attack Penn who was sailing north-easterly to close Blake. In that case they would have passed on opposite tacks and exchanged broadsides. Again according to Florissen he was not supported by many of his squadron and had to bear the brunt of 'a fearful fire from five or six ships all at once'. However, Tromp afterwards accused him of hanging back and firing at random. Tromp himself closed the *Triumph* and supported by six or seven consorts assaulted the English flagship with a succession of broadsides, tacking and coming back with the other side in the usual fashion. An English account says 'if God had suffered them, they might have spoiled our fleet if they had fallen in upon us, whereas they did but come up and fire and bear off.'[73] The fire practically wrecked the *Triumph* aloft and caused heavy casualties. Evertsen, in command of the centre squadron, also attacked the ships about Blake while Ruyter, on the Dutch left, fell – it seems – on Lawson's squadron which was joining Blake from the rear. In any case Ruyter and his ships were soon clapping themselves aboard the English vessels, four or more to one, Ruyter himself alongside the 44-gun *Prosperous* which his men entered, and after being thrown out once, came back and captured. Several other English ships were also taken after desperate hand-to-hand encounters on board, but a few Dutch warships were so holed about the waterline by the English broadsides at point blank that they filled and sank. It was the closest and most furious action so far. Those Dutch ships which did not board, tacked and filled, firing as they saw a target through the dense clouds of gunsmoke. Here is one account:

I fought with all the ships as I went along and did my best to fire
upon them from to windward; but they [English] aimed always at
our round timbers [bilges] and never shot in a hurry. Then I made
fast with a hawser and was just going to board an Englishman who
was to leeward of me, but he got loose and I gave him a broadside
. . . then I turned again and sailed in among the English, striking as
often as I could and they continued to fire only at my round timbers. [74]

His repeated statements about the English firing low, despite their
position to leeward which usually resulted in high shots, and also their very
deliberate fire is striking testimony, thus early, to the feature which was
to distinguish the Royal Navy in its triumphant period, that is hulling
gunnery at point-blank range, and a refusal to waste shots 'at random'.
How many Dutch ships were sunk in these mêlées as a result of the English
guns is not certain but it was at least four. And despite the English inferiority in numbers they lost only one ship to the same cause, the small
20-gun *Samson*; this probably had as much to do with the heavier build of
English ships as to their generally heavier guns and more deliberate low
gunnery.

Later in the morning the tables were turned on Ruyter by the arrival of
Penn's squadron from to windward; all the English ships which had been
captured were re-taken from their small prize crews, and several Dutch
vessels isolated as a result of rigging damage were taken by the English;
other Dutchmen, running short of ammunition, retired.

The mêlées continued throughout the morning and early afternoon, not
always as furiously as the first onset; on both sides there was much tacking
away to re-load and repair damage before coming back into the fray, but
during the early afternoon it became clear that Tromp's attack had failed;
the thirty or so English ships with Blake, Penn and Lawson had not only
survived, but had inflicted heavy losses, and Monck's fresh ships which had
been working up from the leeward were beginning to join the action. When
Tromp saw that a division of fast English frigates had worked around to
gain the wind of his fleet, he drew off to protect his merchantmen, leaving
Blake master of the day.

The English claimed seven or eight Dutch men-of-war taken or destroyed;
the Dutch accounts bear this out – four sunk, one blown up, two taken and
another – a great converted Indiaman of 46 guns, called the *Vogelstruis* –
so wrecked aloft and her officers and crew so decimated that she fell prey
to the English during the night. According to Dutch accounts, a rope was
put aboard by a consort, but her surviving crew were so drunk that they
were incapable of managing a tow. Both Dutch and English sailors were
given strong drink to encourage them before a fight, and it seems that
English accounts of drunkenness aboard Dutch ships in battle were not
always partisan exaggerations; de With had found the officers drunk

aboard the Indiaman to which he transferred his flag at the Kentish Knock!

On the English side casualties were heavier than in any battle before; the *Triumph*, which had taken the full fury of the onslaught had some fifty killed, fifty wounded; Blake himself was wounded by a bar shot just above the knee. Lawson's *Fairfax* had 100 killed and wounded out of a total complement of 350; three of the English ships which had taken Ruyter's close boarding tactics, been captured and then repossessed were so shattered that they had to leave the fleet that night and sail for Portsmouth to refit. However, it is significant that the *Triumph*, though torn and splintered aloft, was 'so tight in the hull she never so much as pumped for it'.[75]

The wind dropped during the night as both sides drifted, repairing their extensive damages, and 1 March dawned calm. Later in the morning light westerly and north-westerly airs lifted the canvas and Blake stood after the Dutch, his best sailers coming up with them shortly before noon, south of the Isle of Wight. Tromp, who had decided at a council of war with Evertsen and Ruyter that another attack on the enemy was not advisable, directed his merchantmen to press on up-Channel, and formed his warships astern, in a half-moon enclosing them; his flagships and seconds were at the rear in the convex of the arc so that any English ships had to pass them to attack the others. In this formation, he conducted a masterly retreat. For all his skill and spirit he could not prevent the English, pressing hard on the wings, from disabling and cutting off at least five warships. By the time night ended the action, his force was in a critical situation, several of the surviving men of war so crippled they were under tow, and many out of powder and shot. During the night the wind freshened, still in the north-west quarter. Blake followed close astern of Tromp's lights.

The next morning, Sunday, 2 March, the English heavy ships caught up by nine o'clock and renewed the attack on Tromp's rearguard. Blake had given instructions that no ships of force should meddle with the enemy merchantmen, but should concentrate on the fighting ships; meanwhile he sent the lighter, faster frigates ahead on the flanks to get in amongst the convoy. Before long, numbers of Dutch merchantmen and several warships which had run out of ammunition were breaking formation and flying south-easterly towards the French coast. Tromp fired after them, and ordered those that returned to keep with the main body steering east-north-easterly; those warships which were either too crippled or had no ammunition, he ordered into the centre of the convoy. So the running action continued all day, from Beachy Head along the Sussex coast and thence across the Channel, the English sailing through bobbing hogsheads of brandy and other cargo which the merchantmen threw overboard to lighten ship, and despite Tromp's heroic efforts to keep his force together, picking up numerous prizes, including several more warships. By late afternoon, when Tromp was approaching the French coast, his effective warships had been reduced to less than thirty, few of which had ammunition for more

H*

than half an hour's fighting. The wind had veered from the north-west towards north-north-west; ahead was the northerly trend of the French coast terminating in the promontory of Gris Nez, which he had to round; on his weather quarter was Blake, threatening to reach Gris Nez first and cut his whole force from the route home. It was a desperate situation.

Tromp was saved by the English pilots – helped probably by the extensive mast and rigging damage he had inflicted on the English ships – now only some forty, as many had turned for home with prizes under their wing.

Blake explained the situation:

We were some three leagues and a half [about ten miles] off Blackness [Gris Nez] in France, the wind at NW, we steering directly for that point of land, having the wind of the Dutch fleet, so that if it had pleased the Lord in his wise providence, who sets bounds to the sea and overrules the ways and actions of men, that it had been but three hours longer to night we had probably made an interposition between them and home, whereby they must have been forced to have made their way through us with their men of war, which at this time were not above thirty-five. . . . The merchantmen must also have been necessitated to have run ashore or fallen into our hands, which as we conceived the Dutch Admiral being sensible of it just as it was dark bore directly upon the shore where it is supposed he anchored, the tide of ebb being come, which was a leewardly tide. We consulted with our pilots and men knowing those coasts and parts what it was possible for them to do, whose opinions were that he [Tromp] could not weather the French shore as the tide and wind then was, to get home, and that we must likewise anchor, or we could not be able to to carry it about the Flats of Somme.[76]

At the critical moment, therefore, when by the Dutch accounts they could not have borne the action for more than half an hour, the coming night and the English pilots' fear of shoal water off the French coast saved the remainder of the Dutch fleet. While Blake held off and came to anchor some ten miles from Gris Nez, Tromp hung out lights and steered north-north-easterly under shortened sail, Gris Nez being then north-east, four miles from him. He and all the Dutch masters knew this part of the coast intimately; it was their normal landfall on the route up-Channel. They knew that there were no shoals under Gris Nez, which drops sheer into seven or eight fathoms – more than enough water for the largest of them – and the ebb tide, while opposing their north-north-easterly course did not sweep into the coast. The only dangers they faced were the possibilities of the wind veering further into the north, or their wounded masts falling. Neither occurred; they sailed on with a strong, cold wind, passing Gris Nez before midnight, and soon losing sight of the English lights as the tide, now flooding, swept them easterly towards the Flemish coast. At dawn on 3 March, they came to anchor off Dunkirk and Gravelines. They counted less than seventy ships together, but not an Englishman in sight. Their good fortune was brought home to them during the following days as the wind rose with hail and snow storms, and the masts of the warships, wounded in the fighting, began to crash overside. So, with many under tow, they struggled for their home ports.

Total Dutch losses in the 'Three Days' Battle' are not known but were probably not less than sixty merchantmen and twenty warships, taken, burnt or destroyed, and perhaps 3,000 men killed, wounded or made prisoner. The English lost only one ship, although there is no doubt that a number were as shattered and disabled as the Dutch, and estimated their casualties as 600. The strategic result was more important; English command of the narrow seas was reasserted, English privateers haunted the Channel, and Dutch outward and homeward convoys were forced to use the northern route around Scotland; moreover the Dutch plans for a blockade of the Thames by Tromp's fleet reinforced by another forty ships prepared under the command of de With, had to be abandoned. The magnitude of the English victory is made more significant by the fact that a number of great ships, including the greatest of all, the *Sovereign*, were not in Blake's fleet. Tromp for his part – like all the fleet commanders of the war   reported that 'divers of our captains are not as staunch as they ought to be; they did not second myself and their other honest comrades as the English did'.[77] Pieter Florissen's account of indiscipline from one of his seconds bears this out. The United Province's fleet was still very far from a regular navy.

One of the momentous results of the battle for the future was the introduction on the English side of tactical instructions inaugurating fleet line of battle. The *Instructions* were drawn up by the three generals, Blake, Deane and Monck. It is thought they may have been suggested in the first place by Monck, a most professional and accomplished soldier who had never been in a fleet action before, who had almost been prevented from joining this one on the first day because of his leeward position, and who may well have been appalled at the lack of order he had witnessed. Blake and Deane, who had suffered the consequences of the loose formation, and been in some danger of losing the flagship, were probably just as appalled, and Pepys – much later it is true – leaves an impression of Monck as an opponent of formal tactics and a lusty adherent of the mêlée school. It is probably more useful to see fleet line of battle as a logical development of English naval building and fighting techniques than as the idea of any particular man or group. The English built heavier ships, no doubt because of their deeper harbours, mounted more guns in them, held their fire until very close, aimed at the enemy's hulls to decide the action by gunfire, and had long held that to clap ships together for boarding as the Dutch did 'belonged rather to madmen than men of war'. Extending this to fleet action was bound to result in fleet line; then no broadsides would be masked by consorts, and all guns would oppose the enemy's pell-mell approach. It was a defensive posture, indeed a line or crescent had long been the classic formation for an outnumbered or defending force, but England's position across all the Dutch routes to the oceans made defensive tactics appropriate to an offensive strategy. It was up to the Dutch to break through. Whether it was the soldiers' penchant for order and precision, or whether simply formalisation of an order that the English had long been moving towards – witness Penn's movement away from Blake at the Kentish Knock to allow room for his whole squadron to come up between the flagships – the *Instructions for the Better Ordering of the Fleet in Fighting*[78] issued over the signatures of the three generals on 8 April 1653 marks the beginning of a long era of formal naval warfare in which fleet line was the cardinal principle of tactics.

The relevant articles were, number two, instructing the Vice-Admiral of the fleet to come up on the right wing of the Commander-in-Chief and the Rear-Admiral to come up on the left 'giving a competent distance for the Admiral's squadron', number three, enjoining the ships of each squadron to 'endeavour to keep in a line with their chief', unless he was disabled 'which God forbid . . . then every ship of the said squadron shall endeavour to get in a line with the admiral, or he that commands in chief next to him and nearest the enemy', and number seven, which was even more conclusive, that fleet, not simply squadronal line was envisaged:

> In case the Admiral should have the wind of the enemy, and that other
> ships of the fleet are in the wind of the Admiral, then upon hoisting
> up of a blue flag at the mizen yard or mizen topmast, every such ship
> is then to bear up into his wake or grayne [in line ahead of him] upon
> pain of the severest punishment.

A similar duty was laid on all captains if the fleet were to leeward of the enemy.

As important as fleet line in these instructions was the duty of aiding consorts in distress, and of squadrons aiding other squadrons which were hard-pressed. And simultaneously with the *Fighting Instructions* a set of *Instructions for the better ordering of the fleet in sailing* was brought out. In neither set are there more than a few flag signals ordering the most basic 'follow-my-leader' moves, and it was still necessary for flag officers and captains to be given verbal instructions for specific tasks; nevertheless they marked a large step forward in the Commander-in-Chief's tactical control of a fleet.

The question of fleet line leads directly to methods of loading the great guns, for if outboard loading were still in vogue at this date, it could not be expected that the original line could long survive the tackings and returnings with the other side that were necessary with that system to keep the loading numbers from being exposed on the engaged side. 'Fleet line' and 'group line attack' would have been impossible to maintain together and unless fleet line was designed only for the opening phase to ensure that all ships came into action more or less simultaneously – something it could not do unless the enemy also attacked in a parallel line! – it suggests a change to inboard loading, whereby the pieces were allowed to run back in recoil and loaded without anyone having to climb out through the gun ports. That such a change had come in the English service at least is suggested by an earlier set of *Fighting Instructions* issued by Lord Wimbledon in 1625. These contain the only stipulations in any *Fighting Instructions* before or since that date about the numbers of men to be employed in the guns' crews, thus: 'Ten, eight, six or four men to attend every piece of ordnance as the Master Gunner should choose out and assign them.'[79] There would have been no need to assign ten men to the heavy guns and only four to light pieces unless it were necessary to haul the pieces out in action, and the inference from this unique instruction must surely be that the English service was moving towards inboard loading in the 1620s and Lord Wimbledon intended all ships to use the method; it involved passing a stout rope called a breeching around the breech end of each piece, and making it fast either side of the gunport, leaving sufficient slack to allow the piece to recoil, but not enough to allow the gun to run further back than necessary to allow loading from the deck. After sponging to douse burning embers and re-loading with cartridge and ball rammed home, the piece was hauled out again by means of tackles and pointed and laid using metal-shod staves known as handspikes to exert leverage on the carriage.

If inboard loading were general in the 1650s fleet line of battle may be regarded as the logical extension of this new method as well as a natural development of the English preference for heavier ships and decision by artillery action. However there is no doubt from contemporary accounts that the old technique of firing, then tacking and giving the other side was practised in 1652, so there can be little certainty.

The first year of the first Anglo-Dutch war has been described in some detail as it is a vital year for the development of sailing ship warfare. By the time of the English *Fighting Instructions* of 1653 the necessity for professional navies, specialised fighting ships, and formal tactics – in short all the features long since developed in Mediterranean galley warfare – had been recognised by the two foremost Atlantic naval powers. Strategy too had crystallised, with the enemy battlefleet recognised as the target for attack or containment by blockade.

In terms of the war itself, the turning point had been reached: England had regained the control which had always been hers for the taking by virtue of her strategic position and her larger ships. Tromp and the other

Dutch commanders, when asked their opinion about the resumption of trade, advised 'our merchantmen should do best to lie still and not stir outward or homeward while the English are strong at sea, but expect till our ships first go to encounter the English, and either beat them, or drive them into their harbours, which being done our merchantmen may then securely come and go with small convoys.'[80]

Both sides strained every resource to fit out a powerful fleet for the decisive encounter; in both cases shortage of money and lack of men were the chief obstacles. Although the Dutch had lost more in the fighting in the Channel, disease was ravaging the triumphant English fleet, and to make up numbers men were forcibly pressed from merchantmen, privateers and all the southern ports; many fled into the country, some armed themselves with staves and cudgels and with the connivance of merchant shipowners, resisted; many more were caught in the net.

> The watermen and seamen we pulled out of bed from their wives and sent them to the Tower, and from thence to the fleet in barges, two whereof being laden and the wind high, were cast away below Gravesend and all the men lost, which was a sad omen to the rest, who went as unwillingly as they would have done to the gallows.[81]

The Dutch offered higher wages in an effort to attract recruits, thereby provoking riots and mutinies among the long-service men who were receiving less!

While both sides' trading communities were suffering from the delays and hazards their shipping was subject to, the Dutch, having more to lose, were probably in far worse case; legend has it that grass grew in the commercial quarters of Amsterdam. And although the English still suffered the extreme shortage and the correspondingly exorbitant prices of masts, spars, cordage and all the Baltic naval necessities, the Dutch still lacked ships of size to compare with the English great ships; their lists of this time show pitifully few vessels mounting even as many as forty guns. To make up for the inferiority Tromp again begged for fireships: 'we have little chance of success unless at least twenty-four well-equipped fire ships are actually added to the fleet.'[82] He was not given a quarter this number.

It was not until early May that the opposing fleets were ready to do battle, and such was the necessity for the Dutch to get their trade moving again, that Tromp's first task was to convoy merchantmen through the North Sea for the route around Scotland. After he had returned at the end of the month another five weeks was spent by both fleets, who were equally determined on action, chasing and missing each other in the small area of sea bounded by Holland and the Thames estuary. At last on 11 June, when the English fleet under Generals Monck and Deane was at anchor in South-wold Bay, two of Tromp's scouting galleots were discovered, and frigates putting out after them sighted the Dutch fleet to the southward. The English immediately stood towards them, but dusk and the northward-setting tide obliged them to anchor in the late afternoon off the southern end of the Gabbard shoal some forty miles east of Harwich.

12 June dawned with the wind in the north or north by east, and the Dutch in sight dead to leeward. Monck weighed and bore down on them in three distinct squadrons, the Generals in the centre (Red), Penn as Vice-Admiral of England with his White Squadron to starboard, and Lawson as Rear-Admiral with his Blue Squadron to port. In all there were ninety-eight sizeable ships, the same number as Tromp had, but as usual very much heavier. Of the nine flagships five mounted 56 to 58 guns, three 60 or over, and Monck and Deane's *Resolution* 88. In addition there were twenty-five vessels mounting between 40 and 50 guns; all the rest carried 30 or more. By contrast only the principal Dutch flagships mounted as many as 56 guns, most were 40s, and there were numerous ships with fewer than 30 guns of small calibre.

It seemed to Tromp that the English came down in a half moon with the wings forward as if to envelop his force; he lay to in a defensive posture, almost certainly a line in five divisions under himself, Evertsen, de With, Ruyter and Florissen, probably heading easterly. The wind dropped away during the English approach so that it was eleven o'clock by the time they were within long gunshot, when more time was taken deploying from the irregular columns of approach into line as enjoined by the new *Fighting Instructions*. Then sometime before noon the Generals bore down to open the action.

It was for the most part with the great ordnance, the ships of either side coming seldom within musket shot of each other, for the English, having the wind and more and greater guns, made use of their advantages, playing on the Dutch only with their great ordnance.[83]

Once again it is impossible to determine the manœuvres. The English by all accounts kept 'excellent order in file at half cannon shot' (perhaps 500 yards) to windward of the Dutch, 'battering the Hollanders furiously'. The wind meanwhile veered towards the east, heading Lawson, forcing his Blue Squadron down towards the Dutch, and allowing Ruyter at about three o'clock to tack and bear in amongst them for the kind of boarding mêlée that he and Tromp always chose. The shift of wind combined with a period of calm also separated Lawson from the Red and White Squadrons (now to leeward of him) and Tromp tacked between to support Ruyter and keep the English separated. The Red Squadron – now under Monck alone as Deane had been taken off by a round shot from the first broadside directed at the *Resolution* – worked up towards the mêlée, continuing the stand-off gunnery, according to one account from The Hague,

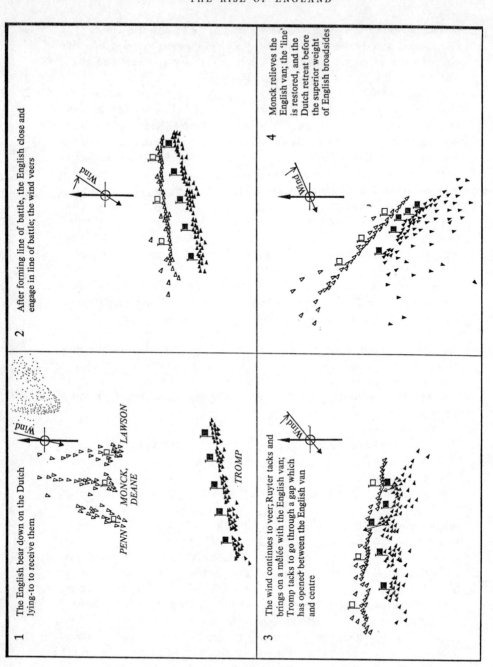

1 The English bear down on the Dutch lying-to to receive them

PENN ∇∇ MONCK, DEANE LAWSON

TROMP

2 After forming line of battle, the English close and engage in line of battle; the wind veers

Wind

3 The wind continues to veer; Ruyter tacks and brings on a mêlée with the English van; Tromp tacks to go through a gap which has opened between the English van and centre

Wind

4 Monck relieves the English van; the 'line' is restored, and the Dutch retreat before the superior weight of English broadsides

Wind

Battle diagram 9: Battle off the Gabbard, 12 June 1653. A possible interpretation of the first action using the English 'line' Fighting Instructions

always battering them [the Dutch] with their great ordnance which was so great a terror to most of the States' fleet as few of their ships durst bear up to abide them. It's certain that the Dutch in this fight showed very great fear and were in very great confusion, and the English fought in excellent order.[84]

Monck succeeded in relieving Lawson, and by dusk the English had the weather gage once more; Tromp bore away before them under a freshening breeze towards Dunkirk.

There was no doubt that the day went to the English although the only ship losses were one Dutchman blown up by an accident of powder and one or two sunk in the close action with the Blue Squadron. Lawson's Vice, Jordan, claimed that three or four of the enemy had been sunk. What seems certain from all the descriptions is that in this first fleet action under the new *Fighting Instructions* the English maintained at least squadronal line and kept together, their faster ships shortening sail so as not to outdistance the rest. Once again Tromp and the Dutch commanders complained of the cowardice of several captains who kept away from the fight, and even ran from the fleet at night. According to Tromp's own account many of these were the smaller Dutch vessels. These repeated accusations by Dutch commanders are the severest indictment of the lack of central control and lack of any system save squadronal subdivision from which United Provinces' fleets suffered. Tromp and Ruyter, for all their individual skill and dauntless courage had no answer to the English stand-off tactics save more of their old, failed game. This may not be fair, but were their aspersions on the courage of their captains fair? Most were fighting in vessels half the size of their own flagships and against vastly superior weights of broadside.

The second day of the battle saw the English garner the fruits of the first, as one account puts it, they 'had the harvest and gleaning of the vintage, and with less loss than ever before'.[85] Both Commanders-in-Chief held councils at dawn; at Tromp's it was decided, in view of shortage of men and powder and shot – for they had been out several weeks and wasted much in a futile demonstration against forts in Kent – to stand on the defensive. As always before battle, Tromp charged his captains to pay attention to their duty to the Fatherland. At Monck's council it was resolved to 'pursue the enemy as far as the shoals would permit'; the English had the idea that the Dutch strategy would be to lure their great ships to destruction on the sandbanks.

The fleets were then only a mile apart, the Dutch east-south-east of the English, the wind in the south-west quarter, and Tromp in an effort to gain the weather gage, steering south-south-easterly towards the coast at Dunkirk. However the wind veered as the sun rose, giving Monck the advantage and when, at about ten o'clock, the English bore down on him he wore and set course east-north-east for the shelter of the familiar sandbanks of the Scheldt entrance, fighting another heroic rearguard action. His smaller ships bunched and masked one another as they sought to keep out of range of the English ordnance, and he sent his sloop through the fleet to instruct them to open out. But many of his ships had suffered heavily the day before, and as the running fight continued along the Flemish coast, some dropped astern and were taken or sunk by the English, others had to seek a tow to keep with the fleet, and as in the Channel fight, his effective force shrank. The English, meanwhile, were reinforced by Blake and a squadron of perhaps fourteen, perhaps fewer; towards evening what had been a desperate but well-fought Dutch retreat had become a rout. A group of four or five Dutchmen entangled together in confusion fell astern of the main body and were snapped up by the English, and numerous others who became separated at dusk surrendered or sank under English broadsides. By the time Tromp gained the banks off the entrance to the Scheldt he had only seventy-four ships in company, many shattered alow and aloft, the *Brederode* herself with five and a half feet of water in the hold; another group of eight ships were ahead making for Goeree; the rest were either on the bottom (seven or eight), their mastheads showing above the shallow water, or prizes (eleven), while the few fireships of which Tromp had hoped so much had set themselves alight without closing the enemy. Monck and Blake reported:

> We do suppose that we should have destroyed most of them but that it grew dark, and being off Ostend among the sands, we durst not be too bold, especially with the great ships, so it was thought fit we should anchor all night.[86]

An English captain wrote, 'The enemy will go where we cannot follow him, like the highlanders to the mountains.'[87]

The following day Tromp retreated into the Scheldt; Blake and Monck sent a dozen disabled vessels home with the prizes, then after repairing, sailed to the Texel to blockade the exits from the Zuider Zee. Tromp, meanwhile, refused to admit final defeat; he set about refitting his beaten force and urging the States General to greater efforts in providing stores, ammunition and fresh ships,

> so that the said fleet may be made ready again without loss of time, and being effectually reinforced, may be in a position to defy the enemy. For if we are not furnished with these things, the country has nothing to expect, humanly speaking, but disgrace, with the force the enemy has at present at command.[88]

Tromp's astonishing spirit in the wake of his second defeat to the heavier English guns, at a time when the English appeared to have an unbreakable grip on their coast, and when de With could burst out before the States General, 'Why should I keep silence any longer, I can say that the English are at present masters both of us and of the seas,'[89] marks him as one of the great fleet commanders.

Blake and Monck held the coast in siege for a month, picking up unsuspecting merchantmen returning home, and causing further acute distress in the commercial quarters of Holland. 'Our trade is nearly gone, our Banks begin to be blank and lose their credit every day and cannot hold out long.'[90] There was much talk of peace, but it was recognised that a naval victory was necessary first unless the English were to dictate the terms. 'Rather than it [peace] shall be on low, base terms, they will venture all,'[91] a correspondent wrote from The Hague. While Tromp's fleet in the Scheldt was refitted and reinforced another fleet was gathered at the Helder under de With, and efforts were made to complete the large ships on the stocks. Similar efforts were being put forth in England, particularly to supply men. 'On Sunday last they pressed whole Church-fulls at Ratcliff.'[92] Although the fleet was forced by sickness and shortages to put back to Sole Bay in the middle of July, it was back on station by the end of the month.

Neither Tromp nor de With had been ready to take advantage of the brief break, even if aware of it, for the Generals had left a small observation squadron on the coast; their problem remained how to unite in the face of the superior English force between them, for the south-westerly or southerly winds favourable for Tromp's approach to the Texel would make it impossible for de With to get out. At the beginning of August, as his preparations neared completion, Tromp asked that de With be instructed to lie outside the Helder to await his approach, and when the English attacked him (Tromp) to fall upon them from the rear. De With's movements in compliance with these instructions were noticed by the English who interpreted its meaning correctly and stood in to close his exit channels. There they hovered for the next few days until in the morning of 8 August Tromp's sails were sighted to the southward; the wind was westerly and it was evident that Tromp was steering to gain the weather gage. Monck, in sole command of the English fleet, as Blake was ill, steered to meet him, and as the wind veered into the north-west, he gained the advantage; at this Tromp wore around and headed south again 'with a view to bringing them [the English] off from the Texel shallows so that the warships there might have an opportunity of coming out and joining us'.[93] The English chased, and the faster frigates were able to catch up and bring on an engagement in the late afternoon, some of the great ships including Monck's *Resolution* joining in between six and seven and continuing in action until dark. Although brief, the fight was sharp, and the *Resolution* lost seventeen killed, twenty-five wounded. As they parted and repaired damages through the night, Tromp steered northerly while Monck, assuming him to be still to leeward, lay heading southwards. Meanwhile de With worked out from the Texel and was able to join Tromp the next day. So far as tactical movements were concerned, Monck had been completely outclassed by the Dutch.

Strong westerly winds and high seas kept both fleets occupied keeping off the sand throughout the 9th, and there was scarcely a shot fired, but the weather moderated early on the 10th, and battle was joined soon after sunrise. The combined Dutch fleet numbered 107 warships and 9 fireships against some 104 warships and 16 smaller craft under Monck. There is no hint in any account of just how the fleets were formed after a night spent beating westward to keep off the shoals, but the wind was south-south-west, the Dutch had the weather gage and the English were rather to the west of them. Probably both fleets formed in their squadrons in line close-hauled to the westwards until about seven o'clock when Tromp bore down on the English and Monck tacked to meet him, the rest of the English fleet following in line. Monck's account states that his flagship and the frigate *Worcester* 'led the English fleet in a desperate and gallant charge through the whole Dutch fleet'. De With's account states that at the first onslaught 'more than half our ships got to windward of the enemy, whilst we and the remainder of the ships remained to leeward of them.'[94] This suggests a close-hauled tacking duel to gain the weather gage in the manner of battles later in the century, and this impression is reinforced by the most precise account that survives, from the captain of the *Tulip*, one of Monck's seconds.

> In passing through we lamed them several ships and sunk some; as soon as we had passed them we tacked again upon them and they on us, passed by each other very near; we did very good execution on him, some of their ships which had all their masts gone struck their colours and put out a white handkerchief on a staff and hauled in all their guns; my men were very desirous to go to them, but the fight being but then begun I would not suffer it. As soon as we had passed each other, both tacked, the Hollander having still the wind and we keeping close by; we passed each other very near one another and did very great execution upon each other. We cut off this bout some part of his fleet which could not weather us.[95]

Nearly all accounts agree that the fleets passed through each other several times; de Ruyter's journal states that he broke through the English fleet four times, a number agreeing exactly with the account from the *Tulip*. The journal of the English *Vanguard* states that each division followed the General, and describes most of the enemy weathering them on the first tack, 'the rest were scattered. We strove to gain the wind which the enemy kept, though many of their ships masts were shot by the board, others sunk to the number of twenty. At last God gave us the wind'.[96] In view of this evidence and the known evolutions in later battles it is probable that both

Battle diagram 10: The United Provinces and the Battle of Scheveningen, 10 August 1653. Schematic diagram conjecture

fleets fought in line, passing and cutting through each other on opposite tacks as they strove for the windward position.

What is not in doubt is that the fighting each time the fleets came together was close and severe. The captain of the *Tulip* described the last bout as 'most desperately fought by either almost at push of pike', and when Monck was beset to windward by two Dutch flagships 'the very heavens were obscured by smoke, the air rent with the thundering noise, the sea all in a breach with the shot that fell, the ships even trembling and we hearing everywhere messengers of death flying.'[97] It was the bloodiest of all the bloody actions of the war, but once again the superior weight of English shot told, and by early afternoon the Dutch force was disabled and in retreat. Tromp himself had been killed by a musket ball in the chest during one of the earlier passes that morning, although his flag was still flying from the *Brederode* to prevent despondency spreading through the fleet. Now Evertsen, his ship shattered and leaking with fifty dead or wounded, made off westward with the remaining ships of his squadron; Ruyter, his foremast and main topmast down, seventy-eight of his crew dead or wounded, was towed off by one of his seconds in the same direction, while ships of de With's, Florissen's and Tromp's squadron were in flight the other way before the wind towards the Texel, de With himself firing after them to bring them back. They would not stay, and de With and several still with him formed themselves into a rearguard and followed north-easterly. The English fleet spread in chase, picking up and sinking more disabled ships before darkness and the shallows forced them once again to give up the pursuit.

The precise number of ships destroyed is open to question; most English accounts speak of twenty Dutchmen burnt or sunk, the captain of the *Tulip* speaks of fourteen after very careful enquiry to ensure that no two reports of sinkings were duplicated, but with some captains not yet questioned. Dutch casualties and prisoners have been variously estimated, but could scarcely have been less than 3,000 men. The English for their part lost one fireship and one warship burnt by a Dutch fireship during the third clash about noon, and their casualties were perhaps 900 killed and wounded – that at least is the number of fresh men Monck requested after the battle, but as there must have been a number of sick after the long blockade, the action casualties were probably less. On both sides many of the ships that survived were almost as shattered as those that succumbed, and Monck, although left in possession of the coast by de With's withdrawal into the Texel, put back to Southwold Bay to refit and land his wounded. In a sense, therefore, Tromp's last fight had succeeded in breaking the blockade. The most was made of this by Dutch propaganda, which like all wartime propaganda, before or since, played down its own losses, magnified the enemy's losses and labelled the defeat as a victory. Tromp himself was given a hero's funeral – rightly, for he was an outstanding admiral. And while the English Navy Commissioners, lacking money, masts and spars, and above all, men, struggled to refit the many disabled vessels, a fleet was prepared under de With to take advantage of the respite and convoy the huge numbers of merchantmen waiting to sail for the Baltic and northabout round Scotland.

De With put out on 11 September with 340 merchantmen under his wing; by this time Lawson and Monck were back on the coast, and he was fortunate to elude them for he had only forty-three warships against some sixty English. He shepherded his merchantmen out of the danger zone and brought back a large convoy of Baltic traders, missing the English fleet again, but losing one-third of his escort force to gales. The voyage brought relief to the hard-pressed Dutch merchants, but it had been a risky venture, and the Channel was still closed, English privateers still active, snapping up vessels which tried to get through on their own. The fisheries were also closed, food prices and unemployment were high, starvation, riots and mutinies disturbed the once prosperous urban streets, and it was known that the English were bending all efforts to fit out a huge fleet for the spring; by the autumn the battle of the Texel (or Scheveningen) could be seen for what it was, at best a very short-term reprieve. The only long-term solution was peace.

The English also needed peace, not so desperately as they were not so dependent on imports and trade, and their privateers were gleaning a rich haul; nevertheless the expenses and debts incurred in the naval campaign were large. But the decisive factor in the peace negotiations that continued through the winter was that Cromwell, who had ousted parliament the previous spring and come to supreme power as the Lord Protector of the Commonwealth, had never been in favour of the war; he regarded the Dutch as natural allies, and it was his influence more than financial strain which brought the negotiations to a successful conclusion in April 1654. The terms were mild in comparison to the magnitude of the Dutch defeat, and the stranglehold which the English Navy was able to exert, but they left no doubt as to the victor. The salute with which the whole business had started was to be strictly observed, permission sought to pass through the Straits of Dover, £170,000 compensation was to be paid to the English East India Company for their losses in the spice islands, a small amount to the dependants of those killed in the 'massacre' at Amboina, and £97,000 to the English traders who had suffered in the Baltic. Above all the chief underlying cause of the war, the Navigation Act, was accepted by the Dutch.

It is an interesting sidelight on the aggressive spirit of the English merchants whose war this had been, that they criticised Cromwell for his leniency; as Paul Kennedy has pointed out in his recent study, their attitude also provides a comment

upon the influence of 'economic factors', for the Lord Protector was clearly the tool of nobody, not even the influential London merchants. Although he genuinely wished to see England strong and prosperous, his motives [in the peace negotiations] were predominantly religious and patriotic.[98]

In short England was not yet a true sea power dominated by the merchant interest.

She was almost there. She had a strong and for the times exceptionally professional navy which had given a convincing demonstration of its force – a demonstration which impressed Cromwell with its potential for world-wide power policy. She also had through the capture of well over 1,000, perhaps as many as 1,700 Dutch prizes,[99] a balanced merchant fleet at last with enough fluyts and other light and economical craft to compete with the Dutch in the northern trades. She also held a string of developing colonies in North America and the West Indies. She was poised for world naval/commercial expansion. The struggle with the United Provinces had hardly begun.

GLOSSARY

Back	(wind) to change direction anti-clockwise.
Bark	(or *barque*) a sailing vessel with *square sails* on fore and main *masts*, fore-and-aft sails on mizen *mast*.
Bearing	the horizontal angle between an object and a fixed reference point, usually the fore-and-aft line of the ship or compass north.
Board	(noun) a (sailing) *tack*.
Board	(verb) to lay a ship alongside another, in fighting usually with the purpose of entering men.
Bombard	a word borrowed from medieval stone-throwing engines to describe any heavy stone-throwing gun or mortar before the advent of cast *cannon*. They were generally fashioned by smiths out of wrought iron, and had a detachable *breech*.
Bowlines	ropes to the edge of *sails* to pull the leading edge forward so that the canvas attacks the wind at the proper angle.
Bowsprit	short mast projecting forward from the stem.
Braces	ropes to the yardarms used to haul the *yards* around to the proper angle to attack the wind.
Breech	that part of a gun where the *charge* is placed.
Cannon	a heavy cast (bronze or iron) gun with a length/bore ratio of 18 or 22 to 1. The *breech* was cast integral, hence the gun had to be loaded through the muzzle (a muzzle-loader). It eventually superseded the built-up wrought iron types which had separate removable *breeches* (breech-loaders). It threw a ball of 50 lb. or so, sometimes more; demi-cannons threw an average 32-lb. ball.
Capstan	a manually-operated drum for heaving on cables or *warps*.
Carriage	(gun-) the support for a great gun.
Cartridge	the canvas, paper or flannel bag to contain the gunpowder *charge* for a gun.

[235]

Charge	in these early days the gunpowder whose combustion produced the gases which expanded to give motion to the projectile in the gun.
Close-hauled	sailing with the *yards* braced forward to the maximum extent so as to steer as close as possible towards the direction from which the wind is coming.
Course	see *sails*.
Culverin	a long cast (bronze or iron) gun with a length/bore ratio from 25 to over 30 to 1. A muzzle-loader, see *cannon* to which it was similar, throwing an average 18-lb. ball; demi-culverins threw an average 9-lb. ball.
Elevation	(gun-) the angle the bore is inclined above the horizontal.
Falconet	a *culverin*-proportioned cast gun throwing an average 2-lb. ball
Halyards	ropes to hoist sails or yards.
Handspike	length of timber used as a lever in shifting, *laying* or pointing guns.
Haul to the wind	to point a ship closer towards the wind.
Helm	timber bar fixed through the rudder head used for angling the rudder; helm 'up' meant moving it towards the *windward*, therefore high side of the ship, so turning the bows from the wind, and vice versa.
Hulling shot	shot striking an opponent's (or own ship's) hull.
Jibboom	spar extending forward from the *bowsprit*.
Larboard	that side of the ship to the left when looking forward, later known as the *port* side.
Lateen	a triangular or near-triangular sail set on a *yard* lying fore-and-aft.
Lay	to give a gun its proper angle of *elevation* (or depression) for the required *range*.
Lee	or *leeward* the opposite side or direction to that from which the wind is coming.
Leeway	the ship's drift to *leeward* of her course.
Luff	(noun) the leading edge of a sail.
Luff	(verb) to point the ship up closer towards the wind.
Masts	the three masts were named from forward, fore-, main- and mizen-mast; above the lower masts were topmasts taking the same name, thus fore topmast, etc. Larger ships of the period had a fourth mast known as a bona-venture mizen.
Point blank	a gun *laid* horizontally.
Poop	the short, uppermost deck at the stern of a ship.
Port	(side) see *larboard*.
Quarter	that part of a ship between about mid-length and the stern, thus a direction some four points (45°) abaft the beam (behind a line extending outboard at right-angles to the keel line).

Range	(gun-) distance between gun and target.
Sails	the lower and largest sails took their name from their *mast*, thus fore-sail, mainsail, etc.; these were also called *courses*, thus fore- and main-*course*. Above them the fore- and main-topsails were spread. On the larger ships towards the end of the period of this book were topgallant sails, or t'gallants. Besides these square sails there were fore-and-aft *lateen* sails on the mizen and bonaventure mizen; caravels, of course, had all masts rigged with lateen sails, except for caravels redondo, for which see p. 30.
Saker	a small *culverin* throwing a 5-lb. ball.
Sheer	the curve of a ship's decks and bulwarks down from the stem to amidships and up towards the stern.
Ship	technically a sailing vessel square-rigged (with square *sails*) on all masts, but used rather more loosely in this book to distinguish mainly square-sailed vessels from mainly lateen-sailed vessels.
Starboard	that side of the ship to the right when looking forward.
Tack	(noun) the direction a sailing vessel is moving with relation to the wind; thus on the *starboard* tack, with the wind on the *starboard* side.
Tack	(verb) to turn a sailing vessel through the wind (ie to go about so that the wind comes on the other side of the ship) by first turning her bows into the wind.
Train	(gun) to move a gun about its vertical axis to aim it.
Trucks	small wooden wheels for shipboard gun *carriages*.
Veer	(wind) to change direction clockwise.
Warp	(verb) to heave a ship along by means of cables (warps) to the *capstan*.
Wear	(past tense *wore*) the opposite to *tack* (verb); thus to put a sailing ship about by first turning her bows away from the wind.
Weather	the 'weather' side means the same as the *windward* side.
Weather gage	to *windward* of the enemy.
Weatherly	describing a ship good at making way towards the wind.
Windward	that side or direction from which the wind is coming.
Yard	the spar to which a *sail* is bent; the ends of yards for square sails (lying across a ship) are the yardarms.

BIBLIOGRAPHY, REFERENCES & NOTES

ABBREVIATIONS

MM   *Mariner's Mirror*, Journal of the Society for Nautical Research
NRS   Navy Records Society

CHAPTER 1 THE CAMPAIGN OF DISCOVERY

Useful books not specifically cited:

G. A. BALLARD, *Rulers of the Indian Ocean*, Duckworth, 1927.
C. R. BOXER, *The Portuguese Seaborne Empire, 1415–1825*, Hutchinson, 1969.
J. H. PARRY, *The Age of Reconnaisance*, Weidenfeld & Nicolson, 1963.

1 J. H. Parry, *The Discovery of the Sea*, Weidenfeld & Nicolson, 1974, p. 145.
2 J. Needham, *Science and Civilisation in China*, vol. IV, part 3, Cambridge University Press, 1971, p. 499.
3 R. S. Lopez, 'Market expansion, the case of Genoa', *Journal of Economic History*, vol. XXIV, no. 4, 1964, p. 460.
4 Washington Irving, *Christopher Columbus*, Nelson, 1892, p. 31.
5 Lindsay of Pittscottie, 1728. Cited *Catalogue of the Museum of Artillery*, Rotunda, Woolwich, 1934, p. 2.
6 H. E. J. Stanley (ed.), *The Three Voyages of Vasco da Gama* (a translation of Gaspar Correa's *Lendas da India*), Hakluyt Society, 1869.
7 ibid., p. 381.
8 ibid., p. 406.
9 T. Stevens, 'A Letter from Goa', 1579, in I. R. Blacker (ed.), *The Portable Hakluyt's Voyages*, Viking Press, 1965.
10 E. G. Ravenstein (ed.), *A Journal of the First Voyage of Vasco da Gama*, Hakluyt Society, 1898, p. 23.
11 ibid., p. 87.
12 ibid., p. 114.
13 ibid., pp. 128–9, citing letter from Girolama Sernigi.

14 Alan Villiers, *Sons of Sinbad*, Hodder & Stoughton, 1940, p. 219.
15 Ravenstein, op. cit., p. 140.

CHAPTER 2   THE CONQUEST OF THE INDIAN OCEAN

Useful books not specifically cited:

B. LEWIS, *The Arabs in History*, Hutchinson, 1950.
R. B. SERGEANT, *The Portuguese off the South Arabian Coast*, Oxford University Press, 1963.

1 W. B. Greenlee (ed.), *Cabral's Voyage to Brazil and India*, Hakluyt Society, 1938, p. 180.
2 ibid., pp. 189–90. Letter of 1 March 1500.
3 ibid., p. 183.
4 ibid., p. 167. Instructions on navigation attributed to da Gama.
5 ibid., p. 85. From the 'anonymous narrative', probably by an official aboard one of the ships.
6 F. C. Lane, *Venice, a Maritime Republic*, Johns Hopkins University Press, 1976, p. 290.
7 H. E. J. Stanley (ed.), *The Three Voyages of Vasco da Gama*, Hakluyt Society, 1869.
8 ibid., p. 311.
9 ibid., p. 355.
10 ibid., p. 365.
11 C. M. Cipolla, *Guns and Sails*, Collins, 1965.
12 Stanley, op. cit., p. 366.
13 Greenlee, op. cit., p. 105. Priest Joseph's account.
14 Stanley, op. cit., p. 367.
15 ibid., p. 368.
16 ibid., p. 371.
17 ibid.
18 Lopez, op. cit. Citing poem by Francisco Quevedo.
19 F. Braudel, *The Mediterranean and the Mediterranean World in the Age of Phillip II*, Collins, 1972, vol. I, p. 453.
20 W. de Birch (ed.), *The Commentaries of the Great Affonso Dalboquerque*, Hakluyt Society, 1875, vol. III, p. 260. Albuquerque to King Manoel, 1512.
21 ibid.
22 ibid., vol. IV, p. 199.
23 ibid., vol. I, p. 52.
24 ibid., p. 77.
25 ibid., p. 81.
26 ibid., p. 82.
27 ibid., p. 106.
28 ibid.
29 ibid., p. 107.
30 ibid., p 108.
31 ibid., p .117.

32 ibid., p. 126.
33 ibid., p. 133.
34 ibid., vol. II, p. 80.
35 ibid., p. 82
36 ibid., p. 111.
37 ibid., vol. III, p. 11.
38 ibid., p. 38.
39 ibid., p. 118.
40 ibid., p. 260.
41 ibid., vol. IV, p. 195. Albuquerque to King Manoel, November 1515.
42 C. Colomb, *Slave Catching in the Indian Ocean*, Longmans, 1873, p. 142.
43 See Braudel, op. cit., vol. I, p. 551 and Boxer, *The Portuguese Seaborne Empire, 1415–1825*, Hutchinson, 1969, p. 59.
44 H. E. J. Stanley (ed.), *The Three Voyages of Vasco da Gama*, Hakluyt Society, 1869, p. 381.
45 ibid., pp. 386–7.
46 I. Wallerstein, *The Modern World System*, Academic Press, 1974, p. 343, cites Godhino, *L'economie de l'empire portugais*, p. 783: 'The Portuguese encrust themselves into the worlds of the Orient, installing themselves everywhere as *casados*, fit themselves into local or regional interests, give themselves over to local or inter-regional operations.' This book, whose prose is at times a caricature of academic writing, provides a useful survey of the various hypotheses with which historians have sought to explain the remarkable expansion of the West and Western capitalism from the fifteenth century. It has been described as 'one of the most powerful pieces of economic history writing that have appeared this decade.' How much more powerful it might have been if the academic jargon had been translated into English.

CHAPTER 3 THE MEDITERRANEAN CENTRE

Useful books not specifically cited:

R. C. ANDERSON, *Oared Fighting Ships*, Percival Marshall, 1962.
P. GOSSE, *The History of Piracy*, Cassell, 1932.

1 P. A. Means, *The Spanish Main, Focus of Envy, 1492–1700*, Scribners, 1935.
2 F. Braudel, *The Mediterranean and the Mediterranean World in the Age of Philip II*, Collins, 1972, vol. I, p. 387.
3 See F. C. Lane, *Venice, A Maritime Republic*, Johns Hopkins University Press, 1976, p. 242 *et seq.*
4 W. L. Rodgers, *Naval Warfare Under Oars*, US Naval Institute, 1939, p. 231 *et seq.* Assuming each oarsman capable of $\frac{1}{8}$ H.P. in short bursts.

5 J. F. Guilmartin, Jr., *Gunpowder and Galleys*, Cambridge University Press, 1974.

6 E. Bradford, *The Sultan's Admiral, the Life of Barbarossa*, Hodder & Stoughton, 1968, p. 140. Citing H. de Gramont.

7 Guilmartin, op. cit., pp. 25–31.

8 ibid., p. 28.

9 D. B. Wyndham-Lewis, *Emperor of the West: a study of the Emperor, Charles V*, Eyre & Spottiswoode, 1932, p. 66.

10 See Guilmartin, op. cit.

11 Bradford, op. cit., p. 171.

12 G. K. Chesterton, *Collected Poems of G. K. Chesterton*, Methuen, 1933, p. 115, 'Lepanto'.

13 ibid.

14 Rodgers, op. cit., p. 192.

15 ibid.

16 ibid., p. 214, to Don John.

17 Sir G. Hill, *History of Cyprus*, Cambridge University Press, 1948, p. 1036.

CHAPTER 4   ATLANTIC WEALTH

Useful books not specifically cited:

K. R. ANDREWS, *Drake's Voyages*, Weidenfeld & Nicolson, 1967.

W. GRAHAM, *The Spanish Armadas*, Collins, 1972.

M. LEWIS, *The Guns of the Jesus of Lubeck*, MM, 1936.

M. LEWIS, *The Spanish Armada*, Batsford, 1960.

A. P. NEWTON, *The European Nations in the West Indies, 1493–1688*, A. & C. Black, 1933.

M. OPPENHEIM (ed.), *Sir William Monson's Tracts*, NRS, 1902.

J. H. PARRY, *The Spanish Seaborne Empire*, Hutchinson, 1966.

E. M. TENISON, *Elizabethan England*, National Maritime Museum, 1933.

J. A. WILLIAMSON, *Maritime Enterprises, 1485–1588*, OUP, 1913.

1 C. M. Cipolla, *Guns and Sails*, Collins, 1966, p. 42.

2 ibid., p. 87.

3 I. R. Blacker (ed.), *The Portable Hakluyt's Voyages*, Viking Press, 1965.

4 J. A. Williamson, *Hawkins of Plymouth*, A. & C. Black, 1949, p. 48.

5 Blacker, op. cit., p. 114.

6 ibid., pp. 139–40.

7 J. A. Williamson, *Sir John Hawkins*, Oxford University Press, 1927, p. 192. Citing Job Hortop, Gunner, *Jesus of Lubeck*, MS. in Cotton MS.

8 Williamson, *Hawkins of Plymouth*, op. cit., p. 145.

9 Blacker, op. cit., p. 167.

10 M. Lewis, *Armada Guns*, Allen & Unwin, 1961.

11 See Cipolla, op. cit., pp. 33ff, and J. F. Guilmartin, *Gunpowder and Galleys*, Cambridge University Press, 1974.

12 Cipolla, op. cit., p. 36.

13 Cited Williamson, op. cit., p. 251.
14 ibid., p. 273.
15 See Guilmartin, op. cit., p. 158. The density and strength of gunmetal increase as a function of the pressure under which it is cast.
16 See R. Pollitt, *Bureaucracy and the Armada*, MM, vol. 60, no. 2, 1974, pp. 119ff.
17 ibid.
18 T. Glasgow Jr., *Gorga's Seafights*, MM, vol. 59, no. 2, 1973, pp. 180–1.
19 Cited P. Padfield, *Guns at Sea*, Evelyn, 1972.
20 Cited Rodgers, *Naval Warfare under Oars*, US Naval Institute, 1939, p. 253.
21 Cited ibid., p. 255.
22 ibid., p. 256.
23 Cited Williamson, op. cit., p. 317.
24 ibid.
25 Rodgers, op. cit., p. 259.
26 ibid., p. 261.
27 ibid., p. 282. 9 April 1588, to Elizabeth I.
28 ibid., 23 April.
29 Williamson, op. cit., p. 299. Howard to Walsingham, 28 January, 1588.
30 P. O'M. Pierson, *A Commander for the Armada*, MM, vol. 55, no. 4, 1969, p. 397.
31 ibid., p. 396.
32 ibid.
33 I. A. A. Thompson, *Spanish Armada Guns*, MM, vol. 61, no. 4, 1925, pp. 355ff. See M. Lewis, *Armada Guns*, Allen & Unwin, 1961, and W. L. Rodgers, *Naval Warfare under Oars*, US Naval Institute, 1939, pp. 270ff.
34 *The Miraculous Victory achieved by the English Fleete upon the Spanish huge Armada*, Hakluyt Society, cited Blacker, op. cit., p. 415.
35 Cited Rodgers, op. cit., p. 266.
36 G. Mattingly, *The Defeat of the Spanish Armada*, Jonathan Cape, 1959, p. 208. Mattingly speculates that the high and most experienced officer in the Spanish fleet who remarked thus to the Pope's emissary may have been Juan Martinez de Recalde.
37 Rodgers, op. cit., p. 266.
38 J. K. Laughton, *State Papers relating to the Defeat of the Spanish Armada*, NRS, 1906, vol. I, p. 288. Howard to Walsingham, 31 July 1588.
39 ibid., vol. I, p. 71. Henry White to Walsingham.
40 Laughton, op. cit., vol. 2, p. 12. Citing the English *Relation of Proceedings* of unknown authorship, but possibly written under the direction of Howard, or, in the author's opinion, Hawkins.
41 ibid., vol. 1, p. 365.
42 T. Glasgow, *Gorga's Seafights*, MM, vol. 59, no. 2, 1973, p. 184.
43 Laughton, op. cit., vol. II, Appendix E.
44 ibid., 26 July.

45 ibid., vol. I, p. 349. Richard Tomson to Walsingham.
46 ibid., vol. I, p. 360. Hawkins to Walsingham, 31 July 1588.
47 Rodgers, op. cit., p. 313. Citing Wynter to Walsingham.
48 ibid., p. 317. Citing Howard to Walsingham.
49 ibid. Citing Fenner to Walsingham.
50 ibid., p. 318. Citing Howard to Burghley.
51 Pollitt, op. cit., p. 125.
52 G. J. Marcus, *A Naval History of England*, Allen & Unwin, 1961, vol. 1, p. 118.
53 P. Kennedy, *The Rise and Fall of British Naval Mastery*, Allen Lane, 1976, p. 27. Citing Sir Francis Bacon.
54 ibid., p. 27.

CHAPTER 5   THE DUTCH EMPIRE OF THE OCEANS

Useful books not specifically cited:

R. C. ANDERSON, *Naval Wars in the Baltic, 1522–1850*, Edwardes, 1969.
C. R. BOXER, *The Dutch Seaborne Empire*, Hutchinson & Co., 1965.
R. DAVIS, *The Rise of the Atlantic Economies*, Weidenfeld & Nicolson, 1973.
K. H. D. HALEY, *The Dutch in the Seventeenth Century*, Thames & Hudson, 1972.
E. H. JENKINS, *A History of the French Navy*, Macdonald & Janes, 1973.
G. LISK, *The Struggle for Supremacy in the Baltic, 1600–1725*, London University Press, 1967.

1 P. G. M. Dickson, *The Financial Revolution in England*, Macmillan, 1967, p. 4.
2 F. Braudel, *The Mediterranean and the Mediterranean World* in the *Age of Philip II*, Collins, 1972, vol. 1, p. 480.
3 Calendar State Papers, Venetian, p. 161. Pietro Contarini to the Doge and Senate; cited D. W. Waters, *The Art of Navigation in England in Elizabethan and Early Stuart Times*, Hollis & Carter, 1958, p. 255.
4 A. de Booy, *William Keeling and Hendick Jansz. Craen*, MM, vol. 56, no. 4, 1970, p. 445. Citing Edmund Scott of the English factory in Bantam.
5 Fr. V. M. di Santa Catarina, *Ill Viaggio all'India Orientale*, Venice, 1678, p. 458. Cited C. M. Cipolla, *Guns and Sails*, Collins, 1965, p. 88.
6 Al-Djarmūzi,*History*, p. 315. Cited R. B. Sergeant, *The Portuguese of the South Arabian Coast*, Oxford University Press, 1963, p. 122.
7 A. Yarronton, *England's Improvement by Sea and Land*, 1677, p. 7. Cited Dickson, op. cit., p. 5.
8 J. S. Corbett, *England in the Mediterranean, 1603–1713*, Longmans, 1904, vol. 1, p. 155. Instructions to Sir Edward Cecil, Commander-in-Chief, 1625.
9 J. S. Kepler, *The Value of Ships gained and lost by the English Shipping Industry during the Wars with France and Spain, 1624–30*, MM, vol. 59, no. 2, 1973, pp. 218 ff.

10 P. Kennedy, *The Rise and Fall of British Naval Mastery*, Allen Lane, 1976.

11 G. S. Graham, *Empire of the North Atlantic*, University of Toronto, 1950, p. 33.

12 Cited ibid., p. 32.

13 C. R. Boxer, *The Journal of Maarten Harpertszoon Tromp, 1639*, Cambridge University Press, 1930, p. 35.

14 Dom F. M. de Mello, *Epanaphora Bellica IV, Conflito do Canal*, Lisbon, 1676, pp. 502–23. Cited Boxer, op. cit., p. 209.

15 ibid.

16 ibid., p. 213.

17 ibid.

18 Sir R. Temple (ed.), *Travels of Peter Munday*, Hakluyt Society, vol. 55, p. 40.

19 Calendar State Papers, Domestic, 1639–40, no. 47, cited Boxer, op. cit., p. 59.

CHAPTER 6   THE RISE OF ENGLAND

Useful books not specifically cited:

R. G. ALBION, *Forests and Seapower; the timber problem of the Royal Navy, 1652–1862*, Harvard University Press, 1926.

P. L'HOSTE, *Naval Evolutions*, London, 1762.

T. K. RABB, *Enterprise and Empire; merchant and gentry investment in the expansion of England, 1575–1630*, Harvard University Press, 1975.

1 C. Wilson, *Profit and Power: a study of England and the Dutch Wars*, Longmans, 1957, p. 144.

2 P. Kennedy, *The Rise and Fall of British Naval Mastery*, Allen Lane, 1976, p. 47. See also R. Davis, *Rise of the English Shipping Industry*, David & Charles, 1962, p. 306, and C. Wilson, op. cit., pp. 53–7.

3 See M. Oppenheim, *History of the Administration of the Royal Navy*, 1920.

4 S. R. Gardiner, *Letters and Papers relating to the First Dutch War*, NRS, 1899–1930, vol. I, p. 81. Citing Declaration of the Judges of the High Court of Admiralty of England, 26 February 1652.

5 ibid., p. 84.

6 ibid., pp. 85–6.

7 ibid., p. 110.

8 ibid., p. 165. Lt Admiral Tromp's Instructions, 25 May 1652.

9 ibid., p. 256. Rear Admiral Bourne's Relation, 8 June 1652.

10 ibid., p. 258. General Blake to Lt Admiral Tromp, 9 June 1652.

11 ibid., pp. 279–80. The Answer of parliament to papers presented by the ambassadors of the States General, 15 June 1652.

12 ibid., p. 239. The Dutch ambassadors to Lt Admiral Tromp, 2 June 1652.

13 ibid., p. 289.

14 ibid., p. 301. Council of State to General Blake, 20 June 1652.
15 ibid., p. 302.
16 ibid., p. 326. States General to Lt Admiral Tromp, 6 July 1652.
17 ibid., p. 398. Tromp, Evertsen, de With, Florisz to the States General, 9 August 1652.
18 ibid., vol. II, p. 15, Petition to Board of Admiralty, Amsterdam.
19 ibid.
20 See P. Blok, *The Life of Admiral de Ruyter*, Benn, 1933.
21 Gardiner, op. cit., vol. 2, pp. 37–8. Deputies of Board of Admiralty to States General, 1 August 1652.
22 ibid., p. 60. Ruyter to Zeeland Admiralty Board, 11 August 1652.
23 ibid., vol. 1, p. 321. Tromp's instructions to his fleet, 30 June 1652.
24 ibid.
25 Cited C. J. Corbett, *Fighting Instructions, 1530–1816*, NRS, 1904, p. 84.
26 Gardiner, op. cit., vol. 1, p. 22. Reminiscences of R. Gibson.
27 ibid., vol. II, p. 64. Ruyter's Instructions, 12 August 1652.
28 ibid., pp. 29–30. Instructions to Sir G. Ayscue, 30 July 1652.
29 ibid., pp. 105, 121.
30 ibid., p. 142, Ruyter to Zeeland Admiralty Board, 8 September 1652.
31 ibid., p. 116. Letter from Plymouth, 30 August 1652.
32 ibid., pp. 107, 116, 159, Letters from Plymouth.
33 ibid., p. 122. Letter from Plymouth.
34 ibid., pp. 111–12. Proceedings, Commander Ruyter's Council of War, 28 August 1652.
35 ibid., pp. 145–6. Ruyter to Zeeland Admiralty Board, 8 September 1652.
36 ibid., pp. 351–2. de With's Log, 29 September 1652 lists Ruyter's returning warships.
37 ibid., p. 237. de With to States General, 27 September 1652.
38 ibid., p. 246, 28 September 1652.
39 J. R. Powell, *Robert Blake, General at Sea*, Collins, 1972, p. 77.
40 J. R. Powell (ed.), *The Letters of Robert Blake*, NRS, 1937, p. 5.
41 Gardiner, op. cit., vol. II, pp. 276–7. Vice-Admiral Penn to George Bishop, 12 October 1652.
42 ibid.
43 ibid.
44 ibid., vol. II, p. 360. de With's Log, 10 October 1652.
45 ibid., p. 277. Vice-Admiral Penn to George Bishop, 12 October 1652.
46 ibid., p. 358. de With's Log, 9 October 1652.
47 ibid., vol. III, p. 58. Orders of Council of State, 22 November 1652.
48 ibid., pp. 67–9. Resolutions of the States General, 29 November 1652.
49 ibid., pp. 23–4. Resolutions of the States General, 19 October 1652, and Tromp's remarks.
50 ibid.
51 ibid., vol. III, p. 75. General Blake to Council of State, 4 December 1652.
52 ibid.

53 ibid., p. 251. Ruyter's Journal, 10 December 1652.

54 ibid., p. 89. Letter to Council of State.

55 ibid., p. 92. General Blake to Admiralty Commissioners, 11 December 1652.

56 ibid.

57 ibid., p. 137. Lt Admiral Tromp to States General, 17 December 1652.

58 ibid., p. 105. General Blake to Navy Commissioners, 13 December 1652.

59 ibid., p. 91. General Blake to Admiralty Commissioners, 11 December 1652.

60 ibid., p. 161. Lt Admiral Tromp to the States General, 22 December 1652.

61 ibid., vol. IV, p. 174. Letter from aboard the *Nonsuch*, 10 March 1653. There is dispute about whether Tromp did or did not wear the mastheaded broom, but this contemporary letter, although only a report at second hand, seems reasonable proof.

62 ibid., vol. III, pp. 150–1. News from Amsterdam, 20 December 1652.

63 ibid., p. 180. 27 December 1652.

64 ibid., p. 150. 20 December 1652.

65 ibid., p. 389. Board of Admiralty, Amsterdam to the States General, 28 January 1653.

66 ibid., p. 179. Letter from Amsterdam, 27 December 1652.

67 ibid., p. 120. Lt Admiral Tromp to the States General, 14 December 1652.

68 ibid., p. 167. The General and divers commanders, 24 December 1652.

69 ibid., p. 137. Lt Admiral Tromp to the States General, 17 December 1652.

70 ibid., p. 293. Laws of War, 4 January 1653.

71 ibid., p. 423. Orders of Council of State, 11 February 1653.

72 ibid., vol. IV, p. 180. *Monnikendam's* Journal, 28 February 1653.

73 ibid., p. 114. J. Pitson to Colonel Whetham, 4 March 1653.

74 ibid., p. 68. Anonymous Dutch account, 28 February 1653.

75 ibid., p. 79. A Relation of the late engagement, 2 March 1653.

76 ibid., p. 167. Generals Blake, Deane, Monck to the Speaker, 9 March 1653.

77 ibid., p. 121. Lt Admiral Tromp to the States General, 4 March 1653.

78 ibid., pp. 262–6.

79 See P. Padfield, *Guns at Sea*, Evelyn, 1972, chapter 12, for discussion of loading method.

80 Gardiner, op. cit., vol. IV, p. 252. News from The Hague, 3 April 1653.

81 ibid., p. 351. Advertisements from London, 25 April 1653.

82 ibid., p. 362. Lt Admiral Tromp to the States General, 25 April 1653.

83 ibid., p. 100. Letter from The Hague, 19 June 1653.

84 ibid.

85 ibid., p. 86. Lyons to Council of State, 14 June 1653.

86 ibid., p. 82. Generals Blake and Monck to Cromwell, 14 June 1653.

87 ibid., p. 86. Lyons to Council of State, 14 June 1653.

88 ibid., p. 74. Lt Admiral Tromp to the States General, 14 June 1653.

89 ibid., p. 147. Reported verbal outburst.

90 ibid., p. 312. Letter from The Hague, 1 August 1653.

91 ibid.

92 ibid., p. 115. News from London, 20 June 1653.

93 ibid., p. 341. Lt Admiral Tromp to the States General, 8 August 1653.

94 ibid., p. 355. de With's Journal, 10 August 1653.

95 ibid., pp. 367–8. Cubitt to Blackborne, 10 August 1653.

96 ibid., p. 427. *Vanguard's* Journal, 10 August 1653.

97 ibid.

98 P. Kennedy, *The Rise and Fall of British Naval Mastery*, Allen Lane, 1976, p. 55.

99 See R. Davis, op. cit., pp. 12, 51.

SELECT INDEX